THE DESTRUCTION OF
THE CHRISTIAN TRADITION

THE
DESTRUCTION
OF THE
CHRISTIAN TRADITION

Rama P. Coomaraswamy, M.D.

PERENNIAL BOOKS LTD.
LONDON

First published 1981

British Library Cataloguing in Publication Data

Coomeraswamy, Rama P.
    The destruction of the Christian tradition.
    1. Catholic Church
    I. Title
    282   BX1390

    ISBN 0-900588-20-9

Printed in Great Britain by
Nene Litho, Earls Barton, Northamptonshire
and bound by Weatherby Woolnough,
Wellingborough, Northamptonshire.

TABLE OF CONTENTS

DEDICATED TO

St. Michael the Archangel
St. George of the Dragon
St. Christopher
St. Patrick
St. Philomena
and to all the other "mythological" characters
with whom I pray I may have the privilege
of spending eternity.

"Thus saith the Lord:

Stand ye on the ways and see,
and ask for the old paths
which is the good way.
And walk ye in it,
and you shall find refreshment for your souls.

And they said 'We will not walk'."

Jeremias vi:16

INTRODUCTION

"Many American Catholics over 30 remember living in that history-heavy church as if living in a spiritual fortress — comforting at times, inhibiting and even terrifying at others. But it was a safe and ordered universe with eternal guarantees for those who lived by its rules. THAT FORTRESS HAS CRUMBLED."

TIME Magazine, May 1976

Recent events within the Catholic Church have clearly resulted in great confusion, and if this ancient structure can no longer stand as a monolith in which each component part speaks "with one voice", there is little doubt but that the various factions that claim Catholicity would agree in stating that something is seriously wrong. In America alone some 10,000 priests and 35,000 nuns have abandoned their religious vocations. Annulments (referred to by some as "Catholic divorces") are approximating the level of 10,000 a year. Weekly Mass attendance has dropped to well below the 50% level and monthly confession below the 17% mark. The priesthood is no longer attracting youth to its ranks and many seminaries have been closed. Conversions which once approached the level of almost 200,000 a year in the United States are now virtually at a standstill. According to the "Boystown Project" from the Catholic University of America "nearly seven million young people from Catholic backgrounds no longer identify themselves with the Church" (National Catholic Register, Mar. 27, 1977). What is perhaps of even greater importance is that those who continue to call themselves "Catholic", are by no means unanimous as to what this term means. As Archbishop Joseph L. Bernadine, president of the U.S. Bishop's Conference has noted, "many consider themselves good Catholics, even though their beliefs and practices seem to conflict with the official teaching of the Church" (*Time*, May 24, 1976). This man speaks with both personal experience and authority, for he has also stated that it was his "belief that it was legitimate for theologians to speculate about the removal of doctrines that have already been defined, and to request the magisterium to remove such doctrines from the content of the Faith" (*The Wanderer*, St. Paul, Minn., June 17, 1976).

There are of course those who see in all this only signs of hope and "progress". They claim that those who have left are "deadwood", and that the Church is better off without them. They compare the Church to a grain of wheat that must die and be born again; that the *Angst* and chaos are essential if the Church is going to have "relevance" for modern man; that all that is happening is under the guidance of the "Holy Spirit" which desires to have the Church "adapt" herself to what is euphemistically called "the times". Having previously claimed that the changes were necessary "to bring the masses back to the Church", they now proclaim that they "are not interested in the numbers game". Others view the situation in a quite different light. They see in all the changes not so much an "adaption" as a "capitulation"; they do not see the world becoming Christianized, but rather, a Church becoming secularized; they do not see the "vines" as being pruned so much as their being uprooted and destroyed. They see the present situation as one that St. Paul predicted as preceeding the coming of the Antichrist — "for that Day shall not come, except there come a falling away first" (2 *Thes.* 2:3). They liken the present situation to that described and prefigured in Maccabees:

> "In those days went there out of Israel wicked men, who persuaded many, saying, Let us go and make a covenant with the heathen that are round about us; for since we departed from them, we have had much sorrow. Then certain of the people were so forward herein, that they went to the King, who gave them licence to do after the ordinances of the heathen . . . (and they) made themselves uncircumcised, and forsook the holy covenant, and joined themselves to the heathen . . ."

The great majority however remain bewildered and confused. Bred in an atmosphere which led them to accept with trust whatever came to them from their clergy, they tend to find excuses for all they do not understand. Like Paul VI, some admit that "the smoke of Satan has entered into the Church"; they however refuse to look for the source of the fire.

Now, whatever the causes of the present situation may be, it is certain that prominent among them must be the changes that have occured within the Church itself. These are clearly identified as those affecting the Liturgy (and especially the Mass), and the teachings (or, as they are called, the "new directions") that have resulted from the Second Vatican Council and the "Post-conciliar" Popes. The present book will attempt to discuss in some depth the nature of these changes and their implications.

Before doing so however, certain principles have to be understood that relate to the fundamental nature of the Church, her authority to "teach", and the manner in which she does so. Those who still believe in the possibility that God in His Mercy gave us a Revelation, will have no difficulty in accepting these concepts. Others who cannot, or will not accept such a premise, must, if they wish to understand what is happening to this Church, at least concede the existence of this premise, for if there is no Revelation, there is no Church. With this in mind we shall initiate our text with a study of the nature of the Church's teaching function. From there we will proceed to consider the sources of the Church's teaching and the manner in which they are conveyed to the faithful. It will be in the light of these basic facts that we then proceed to examine Vatican II, with its "new directions", and the liturgical changes that followed in rapid sequence.

It is hoped that as a result of this approach, even those who do not agree with the author's stance will come to see what even Louis Bouyer has called "The Decomposition of Catholicism" is all about. As St Gregory of Tours said, "Let no one who reads my words doubt but that I am a Catholic." Despite the fact that under normal circumstances it would be redundant, I must qualify this further by stating that my stand is that of a "traditional Catholic", (is there any other kind?) and not that of a "liberal", "modernist", or "Post-conciliar" one. To paraphrase the Abbé Guéranger, the reader should clearly understand that I am in no way trying to propagate any personal views of my own. I am only attempting to state the traditional Church's teaching as it has always been *(in saecula saeculorum),* and to show wherein the New Church has departed from this. If the reader does not happen to like what the Church has always taught, that is too bad. He will however, never understand the present situation unless he recognizes that, as Louis Evely has said:

> "The present crisis of the Church consists in its division between two irreconcilable groups: the 'old ones', who cannot or will not admit liturgical, disciplinary, and conceptual changes; and the 'young ones' who are repelled by the old ceremonies, beliefs, and practices. It is impossible to speak to both groups at once. Every priest today finds that his parish is really two parishes. What awakens faith, or at least stirs interest among young people, scandalizes their elders to the point that they lose what little faith they have left. And to lead older people from the traditional faith to one which is more personal requires so much time, so much patience and so many precautions that the young people have not the patience to listen to, let alone read anything about it (they read so little of anything, for that matter)".

If the Church is to Survive[1]

The reader is further assured that in the exposition of the teachings of the traditional Church, wherever direct quotation is not given, the statements have been checked and approved by competent authority.

---

1. Louis Evely is one of the most popular authors in the Post-conciliar Church, and according to Father Greeley's survey, one of the most frequently read authors by the modern clergy. A former priest, he is now laicized.

PART I

THE NATURE OF
THE CHURCH'S MAGISTERIUM

"The Church teaches and has always taught that there is a divine Tradition, that it is the sum of truths which, having been divinely revealed to the Apostles, has been handed down without error through the genuine magisterium of Pastors."

Tanquerey, *Dogmatic Theology*

When Christ first established His "visible" Church on earth, and sent out the Apostles — "Going therefore teach ye all nations . . . teaching them to observe all things whatsoever I have commanded you" (*Matthew*, xxviii: 19-20) — He told them that they should "feed His sheep", and do so "in His name". He established then a "teaching authority" that was to act on His behalf, and since that time this "Magisterium" or "teaching authority of the Church" has always taught that which He (and His Apostles) gave to them as a "deposit". Defenders of the "Post-conciliar Church"[1] often state that this Magisterium of the Church, to which all Catholics owe assent, resides "in the Pope and Bishops in union with him".[2] Now,

1. The term "Post-conciliar" was utilized by Paul VI's representatives sent to remonstrate with Archbishop Lefebvre at Econe to describe the "New" Church. Included in this category must be all those who accept the teaching of Vatican II and the man-originated rites of the *Novus Ordo Missae*. All such are "in obedience" to the New Church. Traditional Catholics, needless to say, will not accept anything in Vatican II that contradicts the traditional teaching of the Church, and refuse to accept the new "rites" which among other things dare to change the form of the Words of Consecration, the very words given us by Christ.
2. As the French Bishops stated in their Congress at Lourdes, 1976, a meeting convened to discuss the terrible crisis facing the Church in France,

such a statement must be understood correctly. Taken in isolation, and especially when used to defend the changes in doctrine and rites that this New Church has introduced, it is a classical example of *suppressio veri* and *suggestio falsi*. The statement is true, but it must be understood that the Pope and the Bishops in union with him are themselves, in their function as *depositi custodies* (guardians of the "deposit" of the Faith as in 1 Tim. vi:20) bound not to depart from or to go against that which was delivered to the Church by Christ and the Apostles. To speak of "Revelation" is to say that it is a "precious pearl" to be preserved.

The Church has always taught that an individual Pope can stray from sound doctrine in his personal and public life. Should this be the case prior to his election, the election is deemed invalid;[3] should he openly embrace doctrines that contradict this deposit after his election, he would become a public heretic, and as such he would no longer be Pope.[4] Such

---

"the unity of the Church comes before everything else and is guaranteed *only* (italics mine) by being at one with the Pope. To deny this is to exclude oneself from this Unity." The documents of Vatican II use a similar phraseology.

3. Paul IV, in his Apostolic Constitution *Cum ex Apostolatus Officio* (1559) states that "if ever it should happen that . . . a reigning Roman Pontiff, having deviated from the faith, or having fallen into some heresy prior to his nomination as . . . Pope . . , the election is null and void, even if all the Cardinals have unanimously consented to it. It cannot become valid . . . despite the crowning of the individual, despite the signs of office that surround him, despite the rendering of obeisance to him by all, and no matter how long the situation continues, no one can consider the election as valid in any way, nor can it confer, nor does it confer, any power to command in either the spiritual or temporal realms . . . All their words, all their actions, all their resolutions, and all that results from them, have no juridic power and absolutely no force of law. Such individuals . . . elected under such circumstances, are deprived of all dignity, position, honour, title, function and power from the very beginning . . ."

4. As Cardinal Saint Bellarmine says, *"Papa hereticus est depositus"*. A Pope may of course be in error on a given point, but may retract when his error is pointed out. (He has theologians to consult with so as to avoid such mistakes.) What is required is that he persist in an error after he knows it is heretical. This adds the sin of "obstinacy" to that of heresy. Several popes have been guilty of error, but most, thank God, have recanted prior to death. Pope Honorius I was condemned by the Third Council of Constantinople, the Sixth Ecumenical Council, in these terms: "After having taken account of the fact that they (his letters to Sergius and Sergius's writings) are not in conformity with Apostolic dogma, and the

is only logical since, from the moment he publicly embraced heresy, he would cease to be a member of the Church, and how could one who is not even a Catholic be the Pope, to say nothing of being Christ's representative and a "Pontifex" or "bridge" between this world and the next? The oft quoted maxim of St. Ambrose to the effect that "where Peter is, there is the Church" is valid only in so far as "Peter" remains rooted in orthodoxy or "pure faith and sound doctrine".[5] When he is not, then as Cardinal Cajetan taught, "Neither is the Church in him, nor is he in the Church." Cornelius Lapide, S.J. puts it bluntly: were the Pope

> "to fall into public heresy, he would *ipso facto* cease to be Pope, yea, even to be a Christian believer."

Thus the Pope and his function is limited precisely by that authority which is the basis of his own authority. As Christ's representative on earth his monarchical function and quasi-absolute power to command is limited by this very fact

---

definitions of the Holy Councils and all the Fathers worthy of approbation, and that, on the contrary, they uphold false and heretical doctrines, we reject them absolutely and denounce them as a grave threat to the salvation of souls . . . It is our judgment that Honorius, formerly Pope of Rome, has been cast out by God's Holy Catholic Church and made anathema . . ." Pope Leo (d. 683) on whom fell the necessity of confirming such statements, wrote: "We declare anathema those who instigated these new errors . . . (including) Honorius who was shown to be incapable of enlightening this Apostolic Church, by the doctrine of Apostolic Tradition, in that he allowed its immaculate faith to be blemished by a sacrilegious betrayal."

Pope Paschal II (1099-1118), having been imprisoned by the Emperor Henry VI, was forced to make concessions and promises that were impossible to reconcile with Catholic doctrine. When released, he failed to annul these statements (relating to investiture by temporal rulers), and St. Bruno, Guido of Burgundy, Archbishop of Vienne (the future Pope Callistus II), as well as St. Hugh of Grenoble (among others) stated to him "should you, in spite of our absolutely refusing to believe it possible, choose an alternative path and refuse ratification of our decision (that you must retract), may God protect you, for were this to be the case, we should be forced to withdraw our allegiance from you." The Pope retracted. Other examples could be given.

5. "Pure faith and sound doctrine" is the Catholic Encyclopedia's definition of the term "orthodoxy". The modernist attempt to paint orthodoxy as a sort of fanatical rigidity is to belie the fact that there are certain things about which we are meant to be rigid. If we were not meant to be rigid about the truth, we would not have had any martyrs.

and he must act, not on his own behalf (which would be
despotism), but on behalf of Christ, His Lord and Master. As
Vatican I teaches us in terms that are *de fide:*

> "the Holy Spirit is not promised to the successors of Peter
> so that, through His revelation, they might bring new
> doctrines to light, but that, with His help, they might
> keep inviolate and faithfully expound the revelation
> handed down through the Apostles, the deposit of
> faith . . ." *(Denzinger 1836).*

If we are to be in submission to the "teaching authority of
the Church", it is essential, in these latter days, when so many
of our shepherds are walking "after their own (pseudo-
intellectual) lusts", when they have become "men speaking
perverse things", "vain talkers and seducers . . . erring and
driving into error . . .",[6] that we define this and related
entities with clarity. Our failure to do so will only result in
our giving assent to what is false, or else in our ascribing to
"obedience" a false meaning that subverts truth itself.[7] The
Church has never asked us to give assent to error, or to submit
to illegal and sinful commands in the name of "obedience".
As St. Ignatius of Antioch stated in sub-Apostolic times:

---

6. These phrases are Scriptural, and are cited from the introductory
paragraphs of Pope Saint Pius X's Encyclical *Pascendi* against the
modernists. The *didaskaloi* (as in the Second Letter of Paul to Timothy)
have, to paraphrase St. Vincent of Lerins, "always been with us, are with
us now, and always will be with us."

7. As St. Francis de Sales said, "obedience is a moral virtue which depends
upon justice." (Faith, Hope and Charity are theological virtues, and
therefore of a higher order). Even the Jesuit vow of obedience states "in all
things, except what your conscience tells you would be sinful." As St.
Thomas Aquinas says, "it sometimes happens that the commands issued by
prelates are against God. Therefore, in all things are prelates not to be
obeyed . . . Not in all things are prelates to be followed, but only in those
things which accord with the rules which Christ has laid down". As St.
Catherine of Siena wrote to Pope Gregory XI: "Alas Holy Father, there are
times when obedience can lead directly to damnation". She proceeded to
quote to him the Scriptural passage — "If the blind lead the blind, they
shall both fall into a pit." *(Letters)*

"Do not err, my brethren . . . if a man by false teaching corrupt the faith of God, for the sake of which Jesus Christ was crucified, such a one shall go in his foulness to the unquenchable fire, as shall also he who listens to him."

Epistle to the Ephesians

THE MAGISTERIUM DEFINED

Donald Attwater defines the Magisterium as:

"The Church's divinely appointed authority to teach the
truths of religion, 'Going therefore teach ye all nations . . .
teaching them to observe all things whatsoever I have
commanded you' (*Matt.* xxviii: 19-20). This teaching,
being Christ's, is infallible . . ."[1]

This *Magisterium,* or "teaching authority of the Church", is
termed "solemn" or "extraordinary" when it derives from the
formal and authentic definitions of a General Council, or from
the Pope himself: that is to say, dogmatic definitions of
Ecumenical Councils, or of the Pope's teaching *ex cathedra.*[2]
Included under the category of solemn are "symbols or
professions of faith", such as the Apostle's Creed, the

---

1. *Catholic Dictionary,* Macmillan, New York, 1952.
2. It is only in his *ex cathedra* pronouncements that it is impossible for a
genuine Pope to teach heresy. (To claim that a Pope cannot be a heretic is
to state that he no longer has the use of his free will.) According to
Cardinal Newman, a Pope speaks *ex cathedra* or infallibly "when he
speaks, first, as the Universal Teacher; secondly, in the name and with the
authority of the Apostles; thirdly, on a point of faith or morals; fourthly,
with the purpose of binding every member of the Church to accept and
believe his decision". Further, Cardinal Newman states, "another limitation
is given . . . in the *Pastor aeternus* . . . the proposition defined will be
without any claim to be considered binding on the belief of Catholics
unless it is referable to the Apostolic depositum, through the channel of
either Scripture or Tradition . . ." *(Letter to His Grace, the Duke of
Norfolk).* It is pertinent that Paul VI himself has specifically excluded both
his *Novus Ordo Missae* and the documents of Vatican II from the realm of
ex cathedra teaching. (Sources of such statements are to be found later in
this text.)

Tridentine or Pianine Profession, and the Oath against Modernism required by Pius X since 1910 (and for obvious reasons no longer required by the New Church). Finally, included under theological censures are those statements that define and condemn heretical propositions *(Tanquerey, Manual of Dogmatic Theology)*.

The "ordinary" or "universal" Magisterium is that which is carried on daily through the continuous preaching of the Church and refers to the universal practices of the Church connected with faith and morals as exercised in the "unanimous consent of the Fathers, the decisions of the Roman Congregations concerning faith and morals, in the consensus of the faithful, in the universal custom or practice associated with dogma (and above all, in the Roman liturgy or traditional Mass), and in the various historical documents in which the faith is declared". It is termed "Pontifical" if the source is the Pope, and "universal" if it derives from the Bishops (in union with him). It is termed "living", not because it "evolves" in the manner that modern man erroneously ascribes to all living things, but because it exists today as a viable entity within what the theologians call the "visible" Church. Its sources, from which by definition it must not defect, are Scripture and Tradition. By these the Pope and the Bishops in union with him are bound. As a standard theological text puts it:

"The Pope is only the interpreter of this truth already revealed. He explains, he defines, but he makes no innovation."[3]

What is involved in our giving assent to the teaching authority of the Church is the recognition of the fact that, as Saint Catherine of Siena says, "the Church is no other than Christ Himself, and it is she who gives us the Sacraments, and the Sacraments give us life."[4] It is the recognition of the fact that Christ is God, that He gave us a Revelation, and that the Church preserves it intact. It is a conscious submission — not

---

3. *Exposition of Christian Doctrine* — Course of Instruction written by a seminary professor of the Institute of the Brothers of the Christian Schools. McVey: Phil., 1898.
4. Quoted by Jorgensen in his Life of St. Catherine of Siena. She is a doctor of the Church, a title bestowed only on some thirty of the saints.

blind, but with full awareness — to God Himself acting through the organization he established on earth. The Catholic Church is not a congregation of persons agreeing together; it is not a School of Philosophy; it is not a Mutual Improvement Society; it is not even *a* Church among other Churches. It is *the* Church Universal — the Living Voice of God, in Christ's revelation unto all people, through all time. It is for this reason, and this only, that it teaches as the Master taught — not as the Scribes and Pharisees, but as one "having authority". It is for this reason that it proposes for our belief not only those things that are *de fide* — that is to say, directly revealed by God and so defined by the Church, but also those things that logically result from what God has revealed. It is in God's name that the Church makes the awesome demand she does upon the faith of man — a demand that cannot be merely waived aside as being incompatible with the so-called rights of private judgment — unless one is prepared on the same principle to deny that there can be any authoritative revelation of God's truth at all.[5]

In the last analysis man must, in religious matters, rely upon some authority. Either this derives from himself and can be characterized as "private judgment", or else it is to be found outside of him, and then is dependent upon some objective "teaching authority".[6] Clearly the basis for the prevailing religious views of the modern world — be they Protestant or "modernist-Catholic" — is private judgment, which is to say, paramount authority resides in that which at any given moment commends itself to the individual or group

---

5. The statements of John-Paul I to the effect that the Catholic Church has no special rights (*Time*, Sept., 4, 1978) become absurd in the face of the above facts. Consider these words taken from Scripture: "Unless he hear the Church, let him be to thee as the heathen and the publican." What kind of "ambassador of Christ" is this who would concede and barter away "rights" that are not even his? If the Church's rights are to be equated with those of other churches and "ecclesiastical communities", then by what authority does the Church command our obedience? His statement is nothing but an affirmation of the Protestant principle of "private judgment" in religious matters.

6. It should perhaps be pointed out that atheists and those who deny there is any such thing as a "religious issue" are also exercising private judgment, or else blindly submitting to the private judgment of others — or to that of the state. It is no worse to follow the blind than to be blind oneself.

most strongly.[7] Now, such a principle by its very nature represents a revolt against the Church, for it proclaims that what the Church teaches and has always taught is not true simply because it is not what the private individual or group would teach and hold to be true. Private judgment always starts out by accepting some of the teachings of the established faith and rejecting others — it is only a matter of time before the "new" faith suffers in turn from the same principle. (As St. Thomas Aquinas said, "the way of a heretic is to restrict belief in certain aspects of Christ's doctrine selected and fashioned at pleasure" (*Summa* II—II, 1.a.1.). Soon sects give rise to other sects, and before long all truth and falsehood in religion becomes a matter of private opinion, and one doctrine becomes as good as another. Again, it is only a matter of time before all doctrinal issues become irrelevant (who can ever agree about them anyway?). What follows is that morality loses its objective nature, and being based on "social contract", can alter in accordance with social needs.[8] Man, not God, becomes the criteria for truth, and the center of the universe; doing "good" to others becomes his highest aspiration, and "progress" his social goal. The idea of "sin" is limited to what "hurts" our neighbour or the "state". What need is there for God, for truth, for doctrines, for authority, for the Church and for all the "claptrap" of the ages that has held man back from reaching his worldly "destiny". All that is asked of modern man is that he be "sincere", and that he do not disturb his neighbour excessively. If he has any

---

7. "Groups" or "ecclesiastical communities" may agree on broad issues, but never on detailed doctrine. The Protestant denominations early found it necessary to distinguish between "fundamental" and "non-fundamental" beliefs — the latter of which their followers were free to "pick and choose". It is this same basic idea that underlies the modern ecumenical movements: as long as we are "baptized in Christ", we are free to believe anything we want.

8. Consider the following statement given out in June 1978 by the Catholic Theological Society of America: Any form of sexual intercourse, including both homosexuality and adultery, could be considered acceptable, so long as it is "self-liberating, other-enriching, honest, faithful, socially responsible, life-serving and joyous". Far closer to the Catholic position is the statement of the Rev. Jesse Jackson, a black activist leader in Chicago. "One has to have an ethical base for a society. Where the prime force is impulse, there is the death of ethics. America used to have ethical laws based on Jerusalem. Now they are based on Sodom and Gomorrah, and civilizations rooted in Sodom and Gomorrah are destined to collapse."

religious sense at all, it is his "private affair". Man's "dignity", which traditionally was due to the fact that he was "made in God's image", now is said to derive from his independence of God. In reality, man has made himself his own God (as Paul VI said, "honour to man . . . king of the earth, . . . and today, prince of heaven!"); he lives by his own morality and only accepts the truths that he himself has established. (It used to be said of the Protestants that "every man was his own Pope"). A satanic inversion has occurred and man cries out as once did the Angel of Light — "I will not serve" any master other than myself.[9]

Of course, all this occurs in stages. What is remarkable is the similarity of pattern seen in all "reformation movements". What starts out as the denial of one or two revealed truths (or of truths derived from revelation), progressively ends up in the denial of them all.[10] Similar also are the various subterfuges by which this is achieved. Almost all reformers declare that they are "inspired by the Holy Spirit (who can, after all, argue with the Holy Spirit?) and end up by ignoring or denying His existence. All claim to be returning to "primitive Christianity", which is nothing other than Christianity as they think it should have been all along. All, or almost all, claim that they are adapting the Faith to the "needs" of modern man, which is nothing else than an appeal to the pride and arrogance of their followers. All quote Scripture, but selectively and out of context, and never those parts that disagree with their innovative ideas — thus it follows that

---

9. Doctrinal truths revealed by God are attacked in the name of "reason", and the responsibilities that freewill imposes on us are obliterated in the name of "grace". (What else is "justification by faith", but the denial of the need for "good works", those acts we "willfully" perform. Surely grace will abandon us in proportion to our refusal to cooperate with it.) Reason, once the "handmaid" of Revelation, having no "husband", becomes subservient to our "feelings". Those who have any "religious sense" left at all base it on their "feelings" — "welling up from the depth of the unconscious under the impulse of the heart and the inclination of a morally conditioned will" to use the jargon of the times. Feelings of course are easily manipulated, and when not under the control of reason, are simply "passions". What results is that religion, no longer being "super-natural", becomes "infra-rational". Man is truly reduced to the level of a beast.

10. "To refuse to believe in any one of them (the teachings of the Church) is equivalent to rejecting them all." Pope Leo XIII, *Sapaentiae Christianae*.

they reject the traditional interpretation given to the sacred writings by the Church Fathers and the Saints.[11] All mix truth with error, for error has no attractive power of its own. All attack the established rites, for knowing that the *lex orandi* (the manner of prayer) reflects the *lex credendi* (the manner of believing), once the latter is changed, the former becomes an embarrassment to them.[12] All use the traditional terms of religion: love, truth, justice and faith, but attach a different meaning to them. And what are all these subterfuges but means of introducing their *private* and *personal judgments* on religious matters into the public domain. Finally, none of the reformers fully agree with each other (except in their rejection of the "fullness" of the established faith), for error is "legion" and truth is one. As one mediaeval writer put it, "they are vultures that never meet together except to feast upon a corpse".[13]

The Church has of course always eschewed the use of "private judgment" in religious matters. Man's "liberty" lay not in his freedom to decide for himself just what was true or false, but in his freedom to accept or reject the truth that

---

11. Satan is the past master at quoting Scripture out of context as is illustrated by Christ's temptation in the desert.

12. Paul VI's statement to the effect that his *Novus Ordo Missae* "has imparted greater theological value to the liturgical texts so that the *lex orandi* conformed better with the *lex credendi*" is a frank admission that either the liturgical texts in use for hundreds of years by the Catholic Church did not possess the degree of theological value which was desirable, or that his New "mass" reflects a change in the *lex credendi*.

13. It is of interest to listen to Luther's own words on the nature of heresy, words he used prior to his open rupture with the Church, but at a time when he had already embraced and expressed certain opinions inconsistent with Apostolic teaching.

> "The principal sin of heretics is their pride . . . In their pride they insist on their own opinions . . . frequently they serve God with great fervor and they do not intend any evil; but they serve God according to their *own* wills . . . Even when refuted, they are ashamed to retract their errors and to change their words . . . They think they are guided directly by God . . . The things which have been established for centuries and for which so many martyrs have suffered death, they begin to treat as doubtful questions . . . They interpret the Bible according to their own heads and their own particular views and carry their own opinions into it . . ." (Theological lectures on the Psalms, Dresden 1876, quoted by J. Verres, *Luther*, Burns Oates, 1884: London).

Ex ore tuo te judico!

Christ taught. It is a saying of common wisdom that no man should be his own advocate or physician, lest his emotions should interfere with his judgments. If we are careful to obtain authoritative advice and direction in the management of our physical and economic well-being, it becomes absurd for us to relegate the health of our soul to the "whims" of our emotions. As Socrates said, — "Being deceived by ourselves is the most dreadful of all things, for when he who deceives never departs from us even for a moment, but is always present, is it not a most fearful thing?" As soon as we make ourselves, rather than God speaking through the Church, the criterion for truth, we end up by making man *qua* man the center of the universe and all truth becomes both subjective and relative. This is why Pope Saint Pius X said "we must use every means and bend every effort to bring about the total disappearance of that enormous and detestable wickedness so characteristic of our time — the substitution of man for God" (*E Supremi Apostolatus*).[14]

Those who see the futility of resolving religious issues on the basis of their personal and subjective opinions, and who seek objective and external sources for the Truth, must inevitably turn to the various "churches" for a solution to these problems. Of all the various "ecclesiastical communities" that hold out the possibility of finding objective truth, only one has consistently rejected "private judgment" as a source of truth. Only one proclaims that God Himself (through Christ and the Apostles) has revealed the Truth, and only one can demonstrate that it has retained this "deposit" intact from Apostolic times down to the present times.[15] This is of course, the "One, Holy Catholic and Apostolic Church".

---

14. There is of course an area in which "private judgment", or more correctly, theological opinion, can be legitimately used. The application of principles to a given situation, or areas where the Church has never specifically spoken and where it allows for differences of legitimate opinion are examples. It cannot however be used to abrogate the principles as such.

15. No Protestant Church can date its origin prior to the time of the Reformation. True they can point out earlier instances where "private judgment" has been proclaimed as a source of truth — after all, even in the Garden of Eden the serpent existed. On the basis of whose judgment did Judas act if not his own? The Protestants claim to be returning to "pure" and "primitive" Christianity. From where did they learn of Christ, if not in the documents that the Church so carefully preserved? Who, after all, preserved the Bible for the hundreds of years between the time it was

Oneness or "unity" exists as a characteristic of this Church because its members "agree in one Faith", the Faith established by Christ; all have "the same Sacrifice (rites)", and all are "united under one Head".[16] It is not the agreement of the faithful with any faith the hierarchy may teach, or their use of any rite the hierarchy may advocate, but rather the agreement of both the laity and the hierarchy (who one hopes are also to be numbered among the faithful) with the faith and the rites that Christ and the Apostles gave us. Deviations from orthodoxy on the part of even the majority of the hierarchy do not make up the "deposit", but rather, it is the "deposit" which the hierarchy is in existence to preserve. Authority exists to protect the deposit of the faith, and not the other way around. As Cardinal Newman said:

"The Church is founded on a doctrine — the gospel of Truth; it is a means to an end. Perish the Church Catholic itself (though, blessed be the promise, this cannot be), yet let it perish rather than the Truth should fail. Purity of faith is more precious to the Christian than unity itself".

"How to Accomplish It".

If we as Catholics owe assent to the "teaching Magisterium of the Church", it is precisely because the Church is teaching that which was entrusted to it by its Master. (It also teaches as true those things which are virtually revealed, that is to say, derived from what is revealed by the use of reason; and things that are true because they are connected with revelation and witnessed to as such by the Church Fathers and the Saints). Hence it logically follows that it is *de fide* that:

---

written and Luther came along? The same questions can be put to the Post-conciliar Church with regard to its brand of Christianity.

16. To refuse to obey a Pope who asks us to do what is against the laws of God is not to "attack" the Pope; it is rather, to "defend" the Papacy. Such unfortunately, however, is not the attitude of the present post-conciliar hierarchy. For example, when the Most Rev. Paul Grégoire, Archbishop of Montreal, deprived Father Normandin of his parish because he insisted on offering the traditional Catholic Mass. He said "My own conscience imposes serious obligations to obey my superior, the Pope. I prefer to be wrong with him rather than to be right against him." Either the Archbishop does not know his theology, or he is not a Roman Catholic.

"All those things are to be believed with divine and Catholic faith, which are contained in the word of God, written or handed down, and which the Church, either by a *solemn* judgment, or by her *ordinary* and *universal magisterium,* proposes for belief as having been divinely revealed."

Vatican I, Session III

THE NATURE OF REVELATION

What then are the primary sources to which we as Catholics owe assent, and with which the Popes and his Bishops must themselves be in union? They are the sources of Revelation, which are, according to a *de fide* statement, Scripture and Tradition. "It would be true in a sense, to say that there is but one source of Revelation (apart from God Himself), namely, divine Tradition — understanding thereby the body of Revealed Truth handed down from the Apostles . . . Nevertheless, since a great and important part of that tradition was committed to writing and is contained in the inspired books of Holy Scripture, it is the custom of the Church to distinguish two sources of Revelation: Tradition and Scripture".[1] Indeed, the fact that the books of the Old and New Testament are "inspired" at all, and the contents of the "canon" or list of books admitted as Scripture (as opposed to the Apocrypha), cannot be demonstrated from the Bible, and is entirely based on Tradition.[2] As St. Augustine said, "I should not believe the Gospel, unless I were impelled thereto by the authority of the Catholic Church".[3] It is only just that such should be the case, for the Church existed long before the Scriptures were written (St. Matthew's Gospel, the earliest, was written eight years after the death of Our Lord; the

---

1. Canon George D. Smith, *The Teaching of the Catholic Church*, McMillan: N.Y., 1949.
2. *Exposition of Christian Doctrine, op. cit.*
3. *Contra ep. fundament.*, c. 5: Protestants who claim that Scripture is the only source of the Christian revelation are put in the anomalous position of denying the very authority that gives Scripture its authenticity, namely Tradition and the "visible" Church which has "canonized" and preserved the sacred books intact. This occured in the year 317.

Apocalypse many years later), and as the Apostle John himself tells us, it was neither reasonable nor possible for every last word and action of Our Saviour to be committed to writing.[4] Cardinal Manning puts it well in saying:

> "We neither derive our religion from the Scriptures, nor does it depend upon them. Our faith was in the world before the New Testament was written."

The primacy of Tradition has been a constant teaching of the Church, and is indeed, as Tanquerey states, the "principal source of Revelation".[5] He summarizes this teaching by saying:

> "Tradition is more extensive than Scripture, and embraces truths which are not at all contained in Scripture or are contained there only obscurely; also Tradition is more essential to the Church than is sacred Scripture, for revealed truth at first was handed down orally by the Apostles, it was always proclaimed orally, always and everywhere it is to be proclaimed . . ."

Scripture is of course, one of the primary sources from which we can come to know the Christian tradition. As such it has always been greatly venerated by the Catholic Church. If the great hand-written and illuminated Bibles were in mediaeval times "chained" in the Churches, this is but similar to the practices today in any rare-book collection or library. If they were preserved in the Latin (Vulgate) original, this was but to prevent the introduction of error into the established text. They were from the earliest days of the Church read in both the liturgical language and the vernacular — this we know from the history of St. Procarp who was

---

4. "But there are also many other things which Jesus did; which if they were written, every one, the world itself, I think, would not be able to contain the books that should be written" (*John*, xxi:25).
5. It has been argued that the insistence on Tradition is a "post-Tridentine" phenomenon. Listen to the words of St. Epiphanius (circa 370): "We must also call in the aid of Tradition, for it is impossible to find everything in Scripture; for the holy Apostles delivered to us some things in writing and others by Tradition." St. Basil similarly speaks of dogmas being found — "some in doctrinal writings, others handed down from the Apostles . . . both of which have the same religious force."

martyred in the year 303, and whose function it was at Mass
to translate the sacred text into the spoken tongue — a custom
that prevails to this day wherever the traditional Mass is said.
Nor is it true, as Luther and the Protestants claim, that the
Church "kept the Bible from the laity". For example, there
were at least nine German editions of the Bible published
prior to Luther's birth and many more in Latin. The same
was true in other countries.[6] What the Church was and is
concerned about is that the translations be accurate lest any
distortion of the original deposit of the faith should creep in.[7]
And indeed, how wise she is! The "New American Bible", the
English version of the Scriptures that the New Church
advocates be used in all North American Churches (and which
is fully acceptable to the Protestants and carries the "Papal
blessing" of Paul VI) consistently translates the phrase
resurrexit and *surrexit* (active voice) as "Christ has been
raised", rather than the correct "Christ is risen".[8] The distinction may seem minor, but Christ was not raised by another.
"If Christ be not risen (being God, in and of Himself) . . .
then is our faith in vain" (1 *Cor.* xv). Her other concern is
that the obscure passages in Scripture be understood correctly
— that is, after the manner of the Fathers, the Doctors and
the Saints. How could she take such care to preserve the

---

6. cf. Catalogue of Bibles in the Caxton Exhibition at South Kensington in
England in 1877.

7. W. Walker, an individual hardly friendly to the Church, calls Luther's
translation "very free . . . judged by modern canons of accuracy". *(The
Reformation).* Zwingli was even more critical. "Thou corruptest O Luther,
the Word of God. Thou art known to be a notorious perverter of the Word
of God. How much we are ashamed of thee whom we had once so much
respected."

8. It is to be admitted that St. Paul uses the passive form in at least one
place. The defect in the new translation lies not in saying that Christ was
raised, but in suppressing the texts that say He rose by His own power.
Many other examples could be given such as translating *"He groaned in
the spirit and troubled Himself"* (John xi:33) by *"He shuddered with the
emotions that flared up within Him",* clearly suggesting that Christ was not
in control of his passionate nature. Those interested in the problem of the
false translations fostered on the faithful by the New Church are referred
to Ronald D. Lambert's "Experiment in Heresy", *Triumph* (Wash., D.C.)
March 1968, and Gary K. Potter's "The Liturgy Club", *Triumph,* May
1968. An excellent discussion by a non-Christian is to be found in "The
Survival of English" by Ian Robinson, Cambridge University Press,
Cambridge, England 1977.

Scriptures intact and not also be concerned about their proper use? How else would we have a loving Mother act?[9]

But Scripture is by no means the only channel through which Tradition is preserved and handed on to us. Other organs of the Magisterium also subserve this function — above all the Liturgy (the traditional Mass, the Breviary, the Sacramental rites and traditional prayers), the Councils, the writings of the sub-Apostolic Fathers and the historical documents of the Church. It is the "traditions" of the Church which, just as much as Scripture, preserve for us the original "deposit". Hence it follows that, as St. John of Damascus said, "he who believeth not according to the Tradition of the Catholic Church . . . is an unbeliever", and as St. Augustine said, "it is madness to quit the traditions of the Church." And how could these saints say otherwise when the Apostle himself instructs us:

> "Stand fast, and hold the traditions which you have learned, whether by word or by our epistle . . . Hold the form of sound words which thou hast heard of me in faith and in love, which is in Christ Jesus . . ."

---

9. It was after the fifteenth century Lollard (early Reformation) cry in England — "An open Bible for all!" — meaning by an "open Bible", the incorrect and mischievous translations being spread — that Arundel, the Archbishop of Canterbury at the Council of Oxford in 1406 stated that "no one on his own authority should translate into English any portion of Holy Scripture". Anyone with even a superficial knowledge of mediaeval sermons, knows how full of Scriptural quotations they were — many were indeed nothing but the stringing together of one passage after another taken from this sacred source. "This fancy", says St. Chrysostom, "that only monks should read the Scriptures, is a pest that corrupts all things; for the fact is that such reading is more necessary for you (the laity) than it is for them" (*In. Matth. Hom.* ii). The Church however taught: "Let the reader beware how he makes the Scripture bend to his sense, instead of making his sense bend to Scripture" (*Regula cujusdem Patris ap Luc. Hols. Cod. Reg.*). In passing, it is worthy of note that the English translation that Wycliffe used (d. 1384) was in fact a Catholic translation that existed prior to his movement. (This Bible is kept at the British Museum and the contention was proved by Cardinal Gasquet.)

JUST WHAT IS MEANT
BY THE WORD "TRADITION"?

Etymologically tradition simply means "that which is transmitted", or "handed on". According to the Catholic Encyclopedia (1908), "traditional truth was confided to the Church
as a deposit which it would guard and carefully transmit as it
had received it without adding to it or taking anything
away . . ." As to the hierarchy, as Cardinal Franzelin put it in
his work *De Divina Traditione et Scriptura*. "The Lord chose
a body of men to whom he entrusted his Revelation. He sent
them to preach this truth and he threatened punishment on
those who would not listen to them . . . Entrusted with this
mission, the Apostles and their appointed successors have
taught all generations the revealed truth which comes from
Christ".

It should of course be abundantly clear that the Christian
Revelation was complete with the death of the last Apostle.
There is no such thing as "ongoing revelation." The teaching
of the Magisterium is quite clear on this issue:

> "The Revelation made to the Apostles by Christ and by
> the Holy Spirit whom He sent to teach them *all truth* was
> final, definitive. To that body of revealed truth nothing
> has been, or ever will be added."

It should also be clear that this restriction on the hierarchy
applies as much to the Pope as it does to any other member
of the body of the faithful. As Cardinal Hergenrother states
(in the *Catholic Encyclopedia*), "He is circumscribed by the
consciousness of the necessity of making a righteous and
beneficent use of the duties attached to his privileges . . . He
is also circumscribed by the spirit and practice of the Church,

by the respect due to General Councils, and to the ancient statutes and customs." Now this Revelation is given to us in Scripture and Tradition, and is preserved for us in the writings of the "Fathers", and the "traditions" of the Church. It is passed on to us through the various "organs" of the Magisterium, of which the Pope himself is but one. It behoves us now to consider in greater detail, the nature of "tradition".

Almost all the theological texts initiate their discussion of this subject with the following *de fide* statement taken from the Council of Trent:

> ". . . Our Lord Jesus Christ, the Son of God, first pro-mulgated with His own mouth, and then commanded to be preached by His Apostles to every creature, as the fountain of all, both saving truth and moral discipline; and seeing clearly that this truth and discipline are contained in the written books, and the unwritten tra-ditions which, received by the 'Apostles themselves, the Holy Ghost dictating, have come down even unto us, transmitted as it were from hand to hand; (the synod), following the examples of the orthodox Fathers, receives and venerates with an equal affection of piety and reverence all the books of both the Old and the New Testament — seeing that one God is the author of both, — as also the said traditions, those appertaining to faith, as well as to morals, as having been dictated either by Christ's own word of mouth or by the Holy Ghost, and preserved in the Catholic Church by a continuous succession . . . If anyone . . . knowingly and deliberately condemn the traditions aforesaid; let him be anathema."

> *Session IV*

Despite the distortions that mistranslation and private interpretation leave Scripture open to, and despite the fact that the various Protestant sects reject certain of the Biblical books of the Catholic Canon (as Luther repudiated both the Epistle of St. James and the Book of Esther), the meaning of the term remains relatively clear.[1] Such however is not true

---

1. As St. Alphonsus Liguori, a doctor of the Church states, "Traditions are necessary that the Church may determine the true sense of the passages of Scripture." The "private" interpretation of Scripture is by no means a

of the term "Tradition" which has been used in such a wide variety of contexts, and with reference to different aspects of the divine *depositum*. There are those who would limit its use to the divinely revealed dogmas not contained in Scripture, while others apply the term to cover the whole spectrum of Catholic teaching and practice. In order to clarify the issue theologians have defined Tradition as *dogmatic* or *disciplinary* from the point of view of its subject matter, and *divine* or *divine-Apostolic* from the point of view of its origin. It is divine or divine-Apostolic to distinguish it, on the one hand from *ecclesiastical traditions*, which are the precepts and customs long observed in the Church, and which, even if they might be revelatory, can only be traced back to post-Apostolic times, and on the other hand, from human-Apostolic traditions which trace their origins to the Apostles indeed, but not in their capacity as channels of Revelation.[8]

"new" or even a "reformation" problem as is shown by the words of St. Irenaeus (circa 175) who notes that "others however retain the Scriptures, but are so conceited by their false knowledge that they alter their true sense." (*Adv. Her.* III, 12, 12).

The Church has traditionally taught that Scripture is to be understood in four ways. To quote Dante *(Convivio)*. "The first is called the literal and it is the one that extends no further than the letter as it stands; the second is called the allegorical, and is the one that hides itself under the mantle of these tales, and is a truth hidden under beauteous fiction . . . The third sense is called moral, and this is the one that lecturers should go intently noting throughout the scriptures for their own behoof and that of their disciples . . . The fourth sense is called the anagogical, that is to say 'above the sense'; and this is when a scripture is spiritually expounded." All this is but a scholastic summary of the saying of the ancient Jewish fathers to the effect that "Torah is like an anvil, when it is struck, a thousand sparks fly."

Protestant and modern exegetes with their pseudo-scholarship — replacing the understanding of the sacred with philology, historical criticism, psychological interpretations, to say nothing of the merely sociological and political expositions, would reduce Scripture to the level of modern profane literature on the level of a Dreiser novel. The youth of today in rejecting religion are often rejecting the absurdities that result from such "liberal" approaches to the sacred. Fundamentalists on the other hand, limit themselves to a narrowly "literal" interpretation only, a process that renders such texts as the Song of Songs almost unintelligible. Both groups would of course, as Hilaire Belloc notes, refuse to take such statements as "This is My body" in a literal sense.

2. Tradition is further classified as *objective* when referring to dogmatic truths, and *active* by some in reference to the "customs, precepts, disciplines and practices", and by still others when refering to the various organs of transmission such as the rites of the Church and the teaching Magisterium. It is called *constitutive* if it is established by the Apostles and *continuative*

Several points can now be made: First of all Tradition (with a capital T) as a source of Revelation refers to immutable things which cannot be rejected or changed. Second, such Traditions include both Truths and Disciplines which have as their source Christ and the Apostles. Third, it is extremely difficult if not impossible at this distance in time to distinguish between what is "sub-Apostolic" Tradition and what is truly divine-Apostolic, and between what is human-Apostolic and what is divine-Apostolic.[3] Thus, for example, in the Canon of the traditional Mass, apart from the words of Consecration, we are by no means sure which parts are of divine-Apostolic origin, and which parts can be considered human-Apostolic or ecclesiastical tradition. It must be remembered that, as Cardinal Bellarmine states in his *De Verbo Dei*, Tradition is called "unwritten", not because it was never written down, but because it was not written down by the first author. It may be reasonably assumed that the sub-Apostolic authors to whom "innovations" were anathema, codified many "customs, precepts, disciplines and practices" that were truly Apostolic in origin. Further, it must be stated that ecclesiastical traditions, while not carrying the same weight as Apostolic ones, certainly deserve our greatest veneration, and to reject them on the grounds that they are not "divine", is as absurd as to reject the canons of the Ecumenical Councils because they did not derive from Christ Himself.[4] Hence it follows that as St. Peter Canisius states in

---

if of later origin. With regard to its relationship with Scripture, it is termed *inherent* (if what is handed on is clearly stated in Scripture), *declarative* (only stated in an obscure manner in Scripture and needing the help of Tradition to be understood) and *constitutive* (if not in any way to be found in Scripture).

3. St. Clement, fourth Bishop of Rome, and travelling companion to St. Paul, was described by the early Fathers as "sometimes apostolic, sometimes apostle, sometimes almost apostle".

4. The Fathers of the Council of Trent were quite specific that "truths and disciplines are contained in the written books and in the unwritten traditions" but failed to specify these in an exact manner. The following passage from Rev. J. Waterworth's *Canons and Decrees of the Council of Trent* (Burns Oates. 1848) is pertinent:

"These regulations having been completed, the private congregations proceeded to consider divine and apostolical traditions — such doctrines that is, and practices, as, taught by Jesus Christ and his Apostles, have not been recorded in the sacred writings, but have

his *Summa Doctrinae Christianae*, "It behoves us unanimously and inviolably to observe the ecclesiastical traditions, whether codified or simply retained by the customary practice of the Church." All these points are summed up in the following, taken from a standard theological text:

> "There are many regulations which have been handed down with Apostolic authority, but not as revealed by God. They are merely Apostolic Traditions, in contradistinction to divine-Apostolic Traditions. This distinction, though clear enough in itself, is not easy of application, except in matters strictly dogmatical or strictly moral. In other matters, such as ecclesiastical institutions and disciplines, there are various criteria to guide us; e.g. (1) the distinct testimony of the teaching Apostolate or of ecclesiastical documents that some institution is of Divine origin . . .: (2) the nature of the institution itself — for instance the essential parts of the sacraments . . . Where these criteria cannot be applied and the practice of the Church does not decide the point, it remains an open question whether a given institution is of Divine right and belongs to the Deposit of the Faith. In any case, we are bound to respect such traditions, and also those which are merely ecclesiastical. Thus in the Creed of Pius IV (Creeds are part of the solemn magisterium — Ed.) we say: 'I most steadfastly admit and embrace Apostolic and Ecclesiastical Traditions and all other observances and institutions of the said Church . . . I also receive and admit the received

___

been transmitted in various ways from age to age. Numerous congregations, both particular and general were held on this subject. On the existence of such traditions all were agreed; but whilst some insisted that the received traditions should be distinctly specified, others were as urgent that they should be approved of in the most general manner possible, even to the exclusion of the distinctive term apostolical, for fear of seeming to repudiate such usages and rites as could not be traced to that source . . . In the general congregation of the 5th April, the Bishop of Chioggia raised a more intemperate opposition; regarding the traditions as laws, not as revelations; and pronouncing it impious to declare them as of equal authority with the written word. This sentiment had no approvers, but excited the indignation of the whole assembly . . ."

and approved ceremonies of the Catholic Church used in the solemn administration of all the Sacraments.'"[5]

Among the Traditions which are clearly of Apostolic origin are included "the inspiration of the books of the Old and the New Testament, the power of the sign of the cross, the determination of the precise number of the sacraments, the baptism of infants, the validity of baptism administered by heretics, the substitution of the Sunday for the Sabbath, the Assumption of the most Blessed Virgin, etc.,"[6] One can add to this list the "form" and "matter" of the sacraments, especially that of the Holy Mass, and the establishment of the Episcopate as the legitimate descendants of the Apostles. It is this latter act that carries with it the concept of tradition (with a small t), for the legitimate pastors of the early Church established the ecclesiastical traditions — the "precepts, customs, disciplines and practices", not as men establishing human customs, but either as codifying those they had received or learnt from the Apostles, or as members of that one body fashioned by God Himself, and animated and directed by His Holy Spirit. "Hence their testimony is not the testimony of men, but the testimony of the Holy Ghost."[7] As it states in the Epistle of Diognetus, Christians "have no earthly discovery transmitted to them, and are not careful to guard any mortal invention".

One is hardly surprised to find the majority of Church Fathers failing to make a clear distinction between what is Apostolic (strictly speaking) and what is ecclesiastical in tradition. Cardinal Tixeront in his text on *The History of Dogmas* states: "St. Leo uses the word Tradition in its primitive sense of teaching and custom transmitted by word of mouth or practice." He states elsewhere in the same text that St. John Damascene "like St. Basil . . . admits as a rule of faith, besides Scripture, certain unwritten traditions that have come down from the Apostles, and certain ecclesiastical customs that must be accepted as authoritative". St. Jerome also conceives of tradition in a broad context: "The traditions and customs of the Church can make up for the silence of

5. *A Manual of Catholic Theology,* based on Scheeban's "Dogmatic" by Joseph Wilhelm and Thomas Scannell, Kegan Paul: London, 1909.
6. *Exposition of Christian Doctrine,* op. cit.
7. *A Manual of Catholic Theology,* op. cit.

Scripture (on many points) as may be seen in many (of her) practices" (*Dialogus contra luciferanos,* viii). Such an understanding is also reflected in Father Barry's *"The Tradition of Scripture"* (1911) where he states: "Catholics assuredly mean by Tradition the whole system of faith and ordinances which they have received from the generations before them . . . so back to the Apostles of Christ."

The Councils also reflect the mind of the Church on this issue. Thus, Canon III of the Council of Carthage and Canon XXI of the Council of Gangra state that it is "insisted that the unwritten traditions shall have sway". The Seventh Ecumenical Council states that "if anyone disregards any ecclesiastical tradition, written or unwritten, let him be anathema", and "let everything that conflicts with ecclesiastical tradition and teaching, and that has been innovated and done contrary to the examples outlined by the saints and the venerable Fathers, or that shall hereafter at any time be done in such a fashion, be anathema".[8] The Second Council of Nicaea also condemned "those, who dare, after the impious fashion of heretics, to deride the ecclesiastical traditions and to invent novelties of some kind". Such also is the attitude of the saints and the popes. St. Peter Damian (a "doctor" of the Church) writes that "it is unlawful to alter the established customs of the Church . . . Remove not the ancient landmarks which thy fathers have set". St. John Chrysostom states, "Is it Tradition, (if so) ask nothing more." As Pope Benedict XV said, repeating almost verbatim one who held the Apostolic seat a thousand years before (Pope Sylvester), "Do not innovate anything. Rest content with the Tradition." Not one Church Father, not one saint or doctor of the Church, and not one Pope (prior to the present era) has ever decried or attempted to change the ecclesiastical traditions. All this is a far cry from the teaching of the New and Post-conciliar Church whose erstwhile leader, Paul VI tells us "it is necessary

---

8. It is pertinent to note that "The Profession of Catholic Faith from Converts" required by the traditional Church states: "I admit and embrace most firmly the apostolic and ecclesiastical traditions and all the other constitutions and prescriptions of the Church." (Collectio Ritum, 1964). St. John Fisher taught that "Those apostolic traditions which are not recorded in Scriptures must none the less be observed. In addition to these traditions, the customs received by the universal church must not be rejected by any Christian." (Life, E. E. Reynolds).

to know how to welcome with humility and an interior freedom what is innovative; one must break with the habitual
attachment to what we used to designate as the unchangeable
tradition of the Church . . ." (*La Croix*, Sept 4, 1970). Judas
could not have put it better!

In order better to understand the relationship between
Divine Tradition and *Ecclesiastical Tradition*, we may draw a
parallel between what is termed *de fide definita* or *fide
catholica* (truths divinely revealed by Christ or the Apostles
and declared by the Church to be such) and what is termed
de fide ecclesiastica or *proxima fidei* (revealed truths not as
yet formally so defined by the Church). As Father Faber has
said:

> "There are three kinds of faith, *human*, which rests on
> human authority, and as such is uncertain and obnoxious
> to error; *divine*, which rests on divine authority, and
> *ecclesiastical* faith, which rests on the authority of the
> Church defining anything with the assistance of the Holy
> Ghost, through which she is preserved from the
> possibility of error; and this faith is infallible with a
> participated and borrowed infallibility, inferior in degree
> to divine faith, but with a certitude raising it far above
> human faith. If therefore anything be shown to be
> *de fide ecclesiastica* it is not only entitled to our
> acceptance, but it even overrules all opposition, as a
> man, though not formally a heretic, would, to use the
> common phrases, be rash, scandalous, and impious if he
> asserted the contrary."[9]

Certain ecclesiastical traditions can of course be modified
by appropriate authority, but "modification" is vastly different
from the abrogations and changes that have of late been
introduced into the "Post-conciliar" Church. The true Church
and faith are characterized as "living", and the vine that

---

9. Listen to the words of St. Bruno: "With one evil will unanimously
against Christ, they make a covenant that they may destroy his tabernacles.
These are the transitory and fallible multitude of the Idumeans, the earthly
and blood-thirsty multitude of false Christians, who though initiated in the
ecclesiastical sacraments, are yet worldly . . . and cruel against the good
and true Ishmaelites *(Expos. in Ps.* lxxxii).

Christ established can always sprout forth new branches. It is not the newness of the leaf, but the "sap" that runs in its veins that maintains both spiritual health and traditional validity. The fact that the feast of Corpus Christi with public processions may have been established in the late Middle Ages (such was hardly a possibility in the times of Nero) changed nothing in the Revelation that Christ gave us. Our ways of showing respect and honour to the Sacred Species may be modified, but this in no way changes our traditional reverence for the Body of Christ. (Such an "introduction" is in no way to be compared to the distribution of the Eucharist by unconsecrated hands under modern circumstances, to the removal of tabernacles from altars, and to the promulgation of rites that allow for a Protestant understanding of the Sacrifice. Such acts represent no "flowering forth" of the vine, but rather desecrations and clear cut breaks with tradition.) Thus, customs can be introduced into the practice of the Church which are "traditional" such as the Feast of the Sacred Heart[10] or the Rosary. Such practices are in no way "innovations", for they have their roots in sound doctrine, and are as it were, the reverberations which the original deposit, like a stone cast into a quiet pond, inevitably sends forth.

A further extension of the concept of "tradition" is to be found in the various "organs" that are used to transmit the "customs, precepts, institutions, disciplines and practices" of the Church to our generation. Thus Franzelin, the papal theologian to the First Vatican Council, describes what is handed down as "objective tradition", and the process of handing it down as "active tradition". Primary among these "organs" are the Solemn Magisterium (dogmatic definitions of the Roman Pontiffs, of Ecumenical Councils, Professions of the Faith and theological censures); and the Ordinary and Universal Magisterium (which includes among other things

---

10. In writing of this Feast, Gerald Manley Hopkins said: "This is what the Church does or the Holy Ghost who rules the Church: out of the store which Christ left behind him he brings from time to time as need requires some doctrine or some devotion which was indeed known to the Apostles and is old, but is unknown or little known at the time and comes upon the world as new. Such is the case with the worship of the Sacred Heart." *(Sermons)*.

the universal customs or practices associated with dogma and
above all the traditional Roman Liturgy).[11]

Clearly the traditional Mass combines all these aspects of
tradition. Indeed, as Pope Pius XI said, "it is the most
important organ of the Ordinary Magisterium of the Church",
and of "the teaching of the Church".[12] It is a "theological
locus of the first importance in knowing the living tradition
of the Church".[13] Its content is partially of Divine origin,
partially of Apostolic origin and partially of Ecclesiastical
derivation. It has undergone various modifications throughout
the ages, but never changed its essential nature. As one
theologian has put it, "were any of the early Christians to rise
from their tombs in the catacombs, they would recognize in
the Catholic worship of our time (needless to say, one is
referring to the traditional Mass, and not the *Novus Ordo
Missae)*, not merely the elements, but also some details of the
form of worship to which they were accustomed".[14] Its Canon
is as the Council of Trent teaches, "Composed out of the very
words of the Lord, the traditions of the Apostles, and the
pious institutions of the holy Pontiffs." To quote Dr. Nicholas
Gihr *(The Holy Sacrifice of the Mass)*:

> "Christ's example was the norm for the Apostles at the
> celebration of the Sacrifice. They did, first, only that
> which Christ had done before. According to His
> directions and under the inspiration of the Holy Ghost,
> they observed other things besides, namely, according to
> circumstances, they added various prayers and obser-
> vances, in order to celebrate the Holy Mysteries as
> worthily and as edifyingly as possible. Those constituant
> portions of the sacrificial rite, which are found in all the
> ancient liturgies, incontestably have their origin from

11. Later theologians have labelled "objective" tradition as the "remote rule
of faith", and the magisterium or "active" tradition as the "proximate rule
of faith". Still others have reversed the terms "remote" and "proximate".
Pius XII used the phrase "proximate and universal norm for every
theologian" with regard to the Magisterium (A.A.S. XLII, 1950, 567),
but at the same time made it clear that the Magisterium is the "guardian
and interpreter of revealed truth", and not "a separate source of truth".
12. *Rev. Greg.* 1937, p. 79.
13. A. M. Henry, O.P., *An Introduction to Theology*, Fides, Ill., 1952.
14. *Ecclesia:* The Church of Christ; Ed. A. H. Mathew, Burns Oates,
London: 1906.

Apostolic times and tradition; the essential and fundamental features of the Sacrificial rite, introduced and enlarged upon by the Apostles, were preserved with fidelity and reverence in the Churches founded by them . . . certain ceremonies, for instance, the mystical blessings, the use of lights, incense, vestments and many things of that nature, she (the Church) employs by Apostolic prescription and tradition . . ."

No wonder then that the Abbé Guéranger states:

"It is to the Apostles that those ceremonies go back that accompany the administration of the sacraments, the establishment of the sacramentals, the principal feasts . . . The Apostolic liturgy is found entirely outside the Scripture; it belongs to the domain of Tradition . . ."

The Magisterium then, as a whole as well as in its constituent parts, is, as the *Catholic Encyclopedia* states, "the official organ of tradition". Our faith is totally dependent upon tradition and cannot under any guise depart from it. "Tradition is thus the faith that the Church (i.e., the Magisterium) teaches, for she has received it from the Apostles, and it is the norm of Truth."[15] And how could it be otherwise, for as Cardinal Saint Bellarmine says in his *De Verbo Dei*, one of the characteristics of tradition is that it is "perpetual — for it was instituted that it might be continuously used till the consummation of the world . . ." Among the customs of the Church that he lists as examples of "continuous usage" from the time of Christ to his day are "the rites of administering the Sacraments, the feast days (Easter, etc.), the times of fasting, the celebration of the Mass and the divine office, *et alia generis ejusdem*". Admittedly, Bellarmine takes little pains to distinguish between what is "divine" and what is "ecclesiastical" in tradition[16] — rather he describes it as an integral whole in which the distinctions are between the

---

15. *Dictionaire de Théologie Catholique*, Letouzey et Ane, Paris: 1911-49.
16. The faithful Catholic finds no need to make these distinctions because he is prone, almost by the very nature of his soul, to accept what is divine, divine-apostolic and ecclesiastical with the same reverence and love. He would no more think of changing his rites than would a devout Moslem, Hindu or Buddhist. Is the traditional Mass any less "Catholic" than Scripture?

"matter" and the "form" it takes. And indeed, the distinctions that we are forced to make between what is Divine, what is Apostolic and what is "merely" Ecclesiastical, have about them a certain air of artificiality. Thus it is that Bossuet defines Tradition as the "interpreter of God's law", and the "unwritten doctrine coming from God and preserved in the feelings and universal practice of the Church",[17] and Deneffe states that:

"In the nineteenth and twentieth centuries many theologians say it quite clearly: Tradition is the Church preaching . . . Indeed, some say, TRADITION IS THE CHURCH MAGISTERIUM."[18]

The "traditions" are not opposed to Tradition, but the legitimate offspring of it, and like Christ, the son is father to the parent. Thus it follows that one can speak of tradition in a still broader sense as the total influence of a Catholic society and culture upon the souls of its members. For example, however offensive it may be to modern eyes, the crawling of the Mexican peasant on her knees to venerate Our Lady of Guadaloupe can be called "traditional" with complete legitimacy. The Catholic Encyclopedia (1908) expresses this well. "This concept of tradition", it states, "is not always clear, but we endeavour to explain it to ourselves in the following manner: We are all conscious of an assemblage of ideas or opinions living in our mind . . . a common sentiment . . . a common spirit . . . The existence of tradition in the Church must be regarded as living in the spirit and the heart, thence translating itself into acts, and expressing itself into words and writings . . . This sentiment of the Church is peculiar in this that it is itself under the influence of grace. The thought of the Church is essentially a traditional thought." And why is this so? It is because those who are deeply steeped in their faith, whose patterns of life conform to the established and formal "traditions", find that their every act and thought is correspondingly influenced. Generosity, gentleness, courtesy, dignity and a whole host of similar qualities that reflect the divine virtues become a normal part of living. Such are not the qualities of the modern world, for

---

17. *Défense de la tradition des saints Pères.*
18. *Der Traditionsbegriff*, quoted by J. P. Mackey. *The Modern Theology of Tradition*, Herder: New York, 1963.

"the spirit of our times" derives from a very different source, an origin that can well be described as "anti-traditional".

Tradition then is a term that can be applied to the entire Christian ethos, and as such can be envisaged as a stately tree. Its roots are divine and are often not clearly seen. They blend into its trunk which is solid, firm and clearly visible — conforming to its "ecclesiastical" and "visible" nature. The branches can be likened to the various "organs" of the Magisterium through which the "sap" of the Holy Spirit constantly flows. The leaves, the flowers and the fruit complete the analogy — a living organism always changing with the seasons, always growing, occasionally losing a branch or bough, and yet always remaining essentially the same.

Now, if we have treated of the subject of Tradition at great length, it is because the present situation demands a deeper understanding of the concept. The New and "Post-conciliar" Church, despite its attempt to disguise the situation, represents a RUPTURE WITH TRADITION of almost APOCALYPTIC proportions. It is, to use the words of Pope Saint Pius X in his Encyclical *Pascendi* against the modernists, "using all its ingenuity in an effort to weaken the force and falsify the character of tradition, so as to rob it of all its weight and authority". In so far as this New Church teaches falsely (either by omission or commission) and replaces the "customs, institutions, precepts, disciplines and practices" of the traditional Church, not with alternative Apostolic actions, but with "forms" of purely human origin, it follows in the footsteps, not of Christ, but of the Protestant reformers such as Luther, Calvin and Cranmer. As to its Magisterium, it can hardly be the "official organ of tradition" when it sets out to introduce among the faithful, entirely new rites modelled after the heretical forms of worship such as are used by those who avowedly hate the true Church and deny her basic teachings. Nor can this "New" and "Post-conciliar" Magisterium proclaim as "true" what the traditional Magisterium has defined as "false" without in doing so denying the very possibility of truth, to say nothing of the inerrancy and indefectibility of the Church.[19] Where do we, and how do we

---

19. As might be imagined, it was the modernist Loisy who used the loophole of "modification" (the traditions can be modified, but not

demonstrate that a given Tradition is Divine (such as the Assumption of Our Lady), if it is not by means of the very "traditions"? To deny the traditions is to deny the inspired character of the Scriptures, to deny the rites of the Church, to deny the wisdom of the Fathers, the saints and the Popes, to deny many of the Sacraments, and indeed to deny all that is truly cultured in the present world.[20] Tradition is, as the *Dictionnaire de Théologie Catholique* states, "the faith that the Church teaches, for she has received it from the Apostles, and it is the norm of truth". "Even", as St. Athanasius stated many years ago, "if Catholics faithful to tradition are reduced to a handful, they are the ones who are the true Church of Jesus Christ." And such must be the case, for as St. Irenaeus taught, "the magisterium was not instituted to receive new truths, but to guard, transmit, propagate and preserve revealed truth from every admixture of error and to cause it to prevail." Tradition is what the Magisterium teaches and must for all times remain the "rule of faith". When doubt arises, the fathers and the saints have always turned to this source for clarification:

"I have often then enquired earnestly and attentively of very many men eminent for sanctity and learning, how and by what rule I may be able to distinguish the truth of the Catholic faith from the falsehood of heretical depravity; and I have always and in almost every instance received an answer to this effect: That whether I or anyone else should wish to detect the frauds and avoid

---

changed) to attack the unified concept of Tradition. To quote him, "What disquiets the faithful as far as Tradition is concerned is the impossibility of reconciling the historical development of Christian doctrine with the claim made by theologians that it (Tradition) is immutable." Let us have no illusions. The Faithful were not disquieted; Loisy was, as are the modernists in control of the New Church. Then as today, they claimed they were attacking Tradition in the name of the "faithful".

20. It is to be readily admitted that the "Post-conciliar" Church has retained many "traditions", as indeed, in fact, the Protestants also did. The point is that they have "picked and chosen" those which they retain which is nothing other than "private judgment" as to what should be kept. Listen to the words of Paul VI: "It is for the Pope, the College of Bishops (and) the Ecumenical Council (Vatican II) to decide which among the innumerable traditions must be considered as the norm of faith." Surely we should accept and revere all the traditions, and not just those we may personally find acceptable.

the snares of heretics as they arise, and to continue
sound and complete in the Catholic faith, we must, the
Lord helping, fortify our own belief in two ways: first by
the authority of the Divine Law, and then, *by the
tradition of the Catholic Church."*

St. Vincent of Lerins.

To argue that we need only accept what in tradition is
clearly "divine", is similar to arguing that Catholics need only
believe what has been proclaimed by the Church as being *de
fide* — a point to which we shall return later. It is to attack
the "trunk" of the tree and to presume that the "roots" will
survive in spite of this. To divorce tradition from custom is to
divorce faith from practice; to separate Christ's teaching from
His actions, to consider the Apostles and their immediate
spiritual descendants as inferior to ourselves in wisdom, and
to refuse to Truth its legitimate manner of expression. To
separate the Church from her traditions is to disrupt her
"unity", and to proclaim she is no longer to wear the "wedding
garments" that characterize her as the "Spouse of Christ". To
claim that we are other than traditional Catholics is to state
that we are not Catholic at all. Faced as we are with innovation upon innovation, let us always ask with St. Chrysostom:
"Is it tradition?" and let us also state with him that we "ask
for nothing more". Unless the New Church can claim and
proclaim with her founding Apostles *"Ego enim accepi a
Domino quod et tradidi vobis* — For I have received of the
Lord that which I have transmitted unto you . . .", then it is
not the Church that Christ founded. As Cardinal Cejetan has
said: "Note well that God's teaching alone is really the rule of
faith. Although the universal Church cannot err in her faith,
she is, however, not herself the rule of faith: the divine
teaching upon which she is founded alone is."

"And we charge you, brethren, in the name of Our Lord
Jesus Christ, that you withdraw yourselves from every
brother walking disorderly, and not according to the
tradition which they have received of me."

II Thes. iii:6

PART II

THE NATURE OF THE
CATHOLIC FAITH

We have to this point demonstrated that the Catholic "rule of faith" must be "the Bible and Divine Tradition", and that the Magisterium (whether seen as the "proximate" or the "remote" rule of Faith) can in no way depart from these primary sources. We have further demonstrated that the "traditions" of the Church are part and parcel of the Magisterium, for it is through them that the "teaching authority of the Church" is manifest. It behoves us now to consider the concept of Faith in greater detail. According to the *Catholic Encyclopedia,* Faith must be considered both objectively and subjectively. "Objectively, it stands for the sum of truths revealed by God in Scripture and Tradition and which the Church presents to us in a brief form in her creeds (and one might add, an excellent presentation of the creed is to be found in the famous Catechism of the Council of Trent — Ed.[1]); subjectively, faith stands for the habit or virtue by which we assent to these truths". According to St. Thomas, "the principles of the doctrine of salvation are the articles of faith" *(Commentary on* 1. Cor. xii:10), and St. Paul clearly teaches that "without faith, it is impossible to please God" (*Heb.* xi:6). "The entire foundation of the spiritual life is the faith . . . by faith we listen to God Himself,

---

1. This Catechism is a most remarkable one. It is unlike any other summary of Christian doctrine, not only because it is intended for the use of priests in their preaching, but also because it enjoys a unique authority among manuals. In the first place, it was issued by the express command of the Ecumenical Council of Trent, which also ordered that it be translated into the vernacular of different nations to be used as a standard source of preaching. Moreover, it subsequently received the unqualified approval of many Sovereign Pontiffs, including Pius V, Gregory XIII amongst others. Clement XIII said in a Papal Bull (June 14, 1761) that the Catechism

for it is not a human, but a divine teaching . . ."[2] This faith and the Revelation on which it is based has been given to us once and for all, and in a total manner. The teaching of the Magisterium is quite clear on this point:

> "The Revelation made to the Apostles by Christ and by the Holy Spirit whom He sent to teach them all truth was final and definitive. To that body of revealed truth nothing has been, or ever will be added. The duty of the Apostles and their successors was clear; to guard jealously the precious thing committed to their care and to transmit it whole and entire to posterity . . ."

Now, if the Catholic Church is *the one true Church,* and not just one Church among others, then also the faith she teaches is *the one true faith,* and not just one faith among others. What then does a Catholic understand by *"the* Faith"? In what must he place his belief? The answer is made clear by his traditional "Act of Faith":

> "O my God, I firmly believe in all that your Holy Catholic Church approves and teaches, since it is you, the Infallible truth, who has revealed it to your Church."

There may of course be certain Truths that the Church teaches that a given Catholic is unaware of. His attitude however is that of a person who wishes to think correctly, rather than of one who wishes to think for himself. (Imagine a mathematician computing the way he wished rather than correctly — he could come up with thousands of wrong answers in the place of the one right one). He therefore, when

contains a clear explanation of all that is necessary for salvation and useful for the faithful and that no other catechism could be compared with it. He called it "a norm of Catholic teaching and discipline". Pope Leo XIII recommended that every seminarian should possess it and considered it to be on a par with the *Summa Theologica* of St. Thomas Aquinas. Of the several people responsible for compiling it, six subsequently became canonized saints of the Church, including St. Charles Borromeo. One could go on endlessly giving testimony to its authority and excellence. As Father Hogan (former rector of the Irish College in Rome) has stated, "at the very least it has the same authority as a dogmatic encyclical".
2. Blessed John of Ávila, *Audi Filia,* translated from the French, Aubier: 1954.

faced with a doctrinal or moral question, hastens to ask "what does the Church teach?" The Church in turn, knowing that most individuals cannot be aware of all that she teaches, specifies some dogmas as being necessary for the possibility of salvation. These she categorizes as a knowledge of the means of salvation *(necessitate medii)*, and that which it is necessary to know because the Church commands it *(necessitate praecepti).*[3] In addition, there are still other truths that one would be required to know in order to lead a worthy Christian life in accord with the ordinary status of the faithful. Beyond this however, there are still other truths that the Church teaches and which the ordinary Catholic may be unaware of without thereby endangering his soul — truths nevertheless which he must believe implicitly — that is to say, giving assent to them because the Church proposes them for belief. It should be quite clear that these distinctions have nothing to do with the Protestant distinctions between *fundamental* (to be believed) and *non-fundamental* articles (which may or may not be believed according to the individuals choice). A Catholic must believe all the Truths that the Church teaches whether he knows them all or not. It goes without saying that a Catholic has an obligation to know those truths necessary to him in his particular station in life.

In the current situation where the New and Post-conciliar Church would teach us "New" and "Post-conciliar" Truths (such as the new teachings on the nature of "Religious Liberty") — and where it claims to have changed nothing that is *de fide,* — it becomes necessary for us to understand the various theological distinctions that relate to the certitude that the different Truths of the Catholic faith enjoy. Taken from Parente's *Theologica Fundamentalis,* the following categories are used:

1 Maximum certitude is to be found in formal dogma which is truth divinely and formally revealed and as such set forth either in the solemn or in the ordinary magisterium. This

---

3. There is some difference in theological opinion as to just what constitutes *Necessitate medii,* though certainly all agree that a knowledge of both the existence of God and of the fact that we will be judged for our actions is essential. Others also include a knowledge of the Incarnation and of the Blessed Trinity.

kind of truth is called *de fide definita* or *de fide catholica,* and to reject it is heresy.

2 Following closely on this is revealed truth, not as yet so defined by the Church, and which is refered to as *proxima fidei,* and to deny which is *proximum haeresi.*

3 The third level falls to truth that is virtually revealed *(virtualiter revelata),* which is to say, it is derived from what is revealed, but with the help of reason *(conclusio theologica)* or a theological conclusion. Such then are the truths of theological certitude *(theologia certa)* or pertaining to the faith *(ad fidem pertinens),* and these are so intimately connected with dogma that to deny them is a theological error or an error in faith.

4 Next are the non-revealed truths, but truths nevertheless connected with revelation which the opinion of the theologians *(sententia theologorum)* refer to as *communis* (common, general, universal, ordinary, usual), and to deny such is termed temerarious *(temeraria).*

At a still lower level are to be found theological censures that range from "equivocal, deceitful and scandalous, to pernicious and dangerous".

Now, for the theologians of the New Church to teach in effect that a Catholic need only believe in what is *de fide,* is in itself "deceitful, scandalous and pernicious". It is to tell us that we can be in proximate heresy — that is to say, that one can reject revealed truths simply because they have not as yet been so defined. It is to say that we can be in theological error and that one can freely hold to views that are contrary to the opinions of the saints, the doctors of the Church and teachings of sovereign Pontiffs, without placing oneself outside of unity.[4] It is to say that we can abandon ecclesiastical traditions, reject the canons of the Ecumenical Councils and deny the teachings of the Catechism of the Council of Trent while still remaining Catholic. We can, as Father Faber has said, hold to views that are "savoring of heresy, suspected of heresy, close upon heresy, schismatical, Jewish, pagan,

---

4. One can disagree with a saint about material facts, just as one can disagree with a living saint about the time of day. To disagree on theological issues is however quite another matter. The fact that St. Thomas did not know a currently accepted scientific fact does not make his theology either archaic or invalid.

atheistical, blasphemous, impious, erroneous, close upon error, savoring or suspected of error, scandalous, temerarious, seditious, ill-sounding, offensive to pious ears, lax, likely to seduce the simple, fabulous, lying, apocryphal, improbable and insane . . ."[5] Yet these are precisely the characteristics of the New and Post-conciliar Church, a Church that has abrogated "the most important organ of the Ordinary and Universal Magisterium" — the traditional Mass; a church that has directly contradicted the teachings of Popes Pius IX, Leo XIII, Pius X, Benedict XV, Piux XI and Pius XII by inserting into its official documents — the documents of Vatican II — statements that teach exactly those things which the "theological censures" of the *Syllabus of Errors* condemned. Should the New Church ever admit that she had gone against what was *de fide,* should she, as Archbishop Bernadine (see Introduction) seems to advocate, "remove such doctrines from the content of the Faith", she would lose that last vestige of seeming legitimacy to the claim that she still represents that Church which Christ established to guard, preserve and teach His Revelation.

One of the propositions that the *Syllabus of Errors* specifically condemned was that:

---

5. Introduction to his life of St. Alphonsus Liguori. He continues: "Now, it is clear that there are in the Catholic Church, independent of the dogmas which are actually *de fide,* and which a man must receive or become formally heretical, a great number of important doctrines which are so true, that it is a moot point among Catholic doctors whether they are not *de fide,* a number which are *proximae fidei,* a number which are certain because *de fide ecclesiastica,* as it is called, many which are commonly received, many which the greater number of Saints hold, many to which, expressed in certain devotions, the Church accords liberal indulgences, many which are symbolized in certain ritual acts authorized by the Church, many which form the groundwork of approved customs in religious orders, many the denial of which has been stigmatized by universities and theologians as scandalous and temerarious and savoring of heresy. Now how could a man be considered in harmony with the Church, supposing he rejected all or many of these things? . . . Can he (a Catholic) safely reject as false, or at least, not worth a thought, everything which is not positively *de fide?* Certainly not: it would be the most unreasoning indiscretion, the most impatient intellectual rashness that could be conceived. It would be the case of a man whose prime care was, not to be in harmony with the Church, but just to turn the corner of formal heresy by an adroit and perilous nicety." So much for the implication on the part of the Conciliar Church that only what is *de fide* should or must be retained.

"The obligation which absolutely binds Catholic teachers and writers is restricted to only those matters which are proposed by the infallible judgment of the Church as dogmas of the faith to be believed by all. (i.e. *de fide* statements — Ed.)"[6]

As Mgr. Van Noort states in his text on Dogmatic Theology, the belief that "one may reject or call into doubt any

---

6. The theologians of the Post-conciliar Church deny that the *Syllabus of Errors* is an infallible document, and hence argue that it is not binding on the faithful. John Courtney Murray, S.J. openly admits that Vatican II goes against the "censures" of this Papal document in his introduction to the Vatican II decree on *Religious Freedom* (Abbot's Translation). He should know, as he was one of the principle "periti" (experts) responsible for drawing up this document and also translated it into English. Among propositions condemned by the Syllabus, but approved by Vatican II, are the following:

"That every man is free to embrace and profess the religion he shall believe true, guided by the light of reason . . . That the eternal salvation may at least be hoped for, by all those who are not at all in the true Church of Christ. That Protestantism is nothing more than another form of the same true Christian religion; in which it is possible to please God as in the Catholic Church".

As for Catholics who remain "traditional", the *Catholic Encyclopedia* is quite specific. "All Catholics . . . are bound to accept the Syllabus. They must exteriorly neither in word nor in writing oppose its contents; they must also assent to it interiorly".

Theological "censures" are usually considered to be *de fide*, or at least as part of the "solemn Magisterium". (See section on the Magisterium above.) True, the Syllabus is not an Encyclical — it was issued by the Holy Office — which is the Roman Congregation that watches over the purity of Catholic Doctrine. Its contents however have been approved by all the Popes listed above in the body of this text. It was formerly ratified by Pope Pius X on July 4, 1907. In a *Motu Proprio* issued in the same year, he prohibited the defence of the condemned propositions under penalty of excommunication reserved ordinarily to the Pope. Further, in the "oath against modernism" which Tanquerey considers part of the solemn Magisterium, every priest of the traditional Church swore to "adhere wholeheartedly to all the condemnations, declarations and prescripts contained in the Encyclical *Pascendi* and the Decree *Lamentabili*" (Syllabus of Errors). (*Lamentabilis Sane* - published in 1907 by Pius X and listing 65 propositions of the modernists that were "condemned and proscribed"). It is sad to see modern theologians claiming to be "Catholic", who 20 years ago would never have dared to question the Syllabus, now proclaiming it not to be *de fide definita*, and hence instructing the faithful, not only to disregard it, but to believe precisely what it condemned! Intellectual honesty has never been a characteristic of the Reformers.

non-revealed truth one chooses, without committing sin or injuring the Catholic profession of the faith" is an "extremely serious error". He continues, "Some truths are so necessarily intertwined with revelation that to deny or doubt them would cause injury to revelation itself . . . Other truths are connected with revelation as a necessary consequence *(conclusio theologica)* . . . Finally, some truths are necessarily connected with revelation by reason of its goal (decisions relating to the universal discipline of the Church). Truths not formally revealed but bound up with Revelation in one of these three ways just pointed out look directly to the guardianship and practical application of the deposit of the faith; thus indirectly, they belong to the deposit itself and to Catholic faith."[7]

Another standard commentary on Canon Law, and specifically on Canons 1322, 23 and 24 that deal with the "deposit of the faith" states:

"The deposit of the faith is defined as comprising all the truths which are either implicitly or explicitly contained in the written word of God or in tradition and must be believed as revealed with divine faith . . . In a wider sense, the deposit of the faith comprises also those truths which, though not revealed, bear such an intimate relation to revealed truths that, without them, the latter could not be at least easily and fully preserved, expounded and defended."[8]

The author of this commentary further continues to discuss those truths that are not directly and explicitly contained in Revelation, but only virtually *(virtualiter)* deduced therefrom by logical reasoning: "Some writers have asserted that they must be believed *fide ecclesiastica* only . . . Even the so-called *fides ecclesiastica* requires not a mere servile silence, but a real assent, elicited by the will, although the formal reason, the *auctoritas Dei loquentis* (the authority of God's spoken word) may not be implied".

The argument that only what is *de fide definita* is sacrosanct is by no means new. Not only was it condemned by

---

7. Mgr. G. Van Noort, *Dogmatic Theology,* Vol III, "Divine Faith" Newman, 1960.
8. Rev. Chas. Augustine, O.S.B., D.D. *A Commentary on the New Code of Canon Law,* B. Herder, 1929.

Pius IX in the *Syllabus;* Pius XI spoke to the issue in his Encyclical *Mortalium Animos:*

> "In matters of faith it is not permitted to make a distinction between fundamental and so-called non-fundamental articles of faith, as if the first ought to be held by all, and the second the faithful are free to accept or not. The supernatural virtue of faith has as its formal cause the authority of God the revealer, which suffers not such a division."

> "Not because the Church has defined and sanctioned truths by solemn decree of the Church at different times, and even in times near to us, are they therefore not equally certain and not equally to be believed. For has not God revealed them all?"

He continues later in the same Encyclical to state that the Church

> "has the duty to proceed opportunely in defining points of faith with solemn rites and decrees, when there is a need to declare them to resist more effectively the errors and the assaults of heretics or to impress upon the minds of the faithful clearer and more profound explanations of points of sacred doctrine. However, in this explanatory use of the teaching authority nothing is invented nor is anything new added to the sum of the truths that are, at least implicitly, contained in the deposit of divine revelation that was entrusted by God to the Church. Instead points of faith are defined that could by chance still seem obscure to some, or truths are established as matters of faith that for the first time were called into question."

This then is the teaching of the Church! This has always been the teaching of the Church, and if the New and Post-conciliar Church departs from this teaching, it departs from "unity". As St. Vincent of Lerins stated:

> "To announce to Catholic Christians a doctrine other than that which they have received (from the Apostles

and their immediate descendants) was never permitted, is nowhere permitted, and never will be permitted. It was ever necessary, is everywhere necessary, and ever will be necessary that those who announce a doctrine other than that which was received once and for all, be anathema."

Commonitoria, IX

Thus St. Thomas Aquinas instructs us:

"Hold firmly that our faith is identical with that of the ancients. Deny this and you dissolve the unity of the Church."

Disputations Concerning Truth[9]

And further, one must believe all that Holy Mother Church teaches. If we are to reject any of the truths of the Catholic faith, we will end up by rejecting them all. As Pope Leo XIII said in his Encyclical *Sapaentiae Christianae:*

"To refuse to believe in any one of them is equivalent to rejecting them all."

And as Pius XII said in his address to the Bishops of the Sacred Congregation in 1949:

"The Catholic doctrine must be set forth and taught completely and entirely. One cannot allow that anything should be omitted or veiled in ambiguous terms . . ."

Such then in summary is the "objective" nature of the Catholic faith which comes to us through the various organs of the teaching Magisterium. It is to these truths that we give our assent. As St. John Fisher put it, "The faith of the Church is not made by our faith, but by our assent, which assent cometh

---

9. Such has always been the attitude of the faithful. For example, the unanimous statement of the prelates at the Council of Cloveshoe (England) in the year 552:

"Know that the faith we profess is the same as was taught by the Holy and Apostolic See when Gregory the Great sent missionaries to our fathers."

of us, and is the work of our soul". The individual must have, as the theologians say, *the pious will to believe*. A person may know that what the Church teaches is true, but he still has a will that is free, and hence he may choose to act against what he knows to be right. As Vatican I states:

> "Faith itself and in itself, even if it does not work through charity, is a gift of God, and its act is a work pertaining to salvation; by it a man offers to God Himself a *free* obedience insofar as he consents and cooperates with His grace which he *could* refuse . . ."

We must not be confused by the statement that faith is a "gift", as if those who do not possess this gift are therefore free of responsibility. As with any "gift", we must be willing to accept it — it cannot be forced upon us. God would not, "in charity", hold back from any soul the necessary grace required. As St. Augustine teaches us in his commentary on the passage "no one can come to me (by faith) unless the Father who sent me draw him", says:

> "And yet no one comes (to the faith) unless he wills to. He is drawn therefore, in marvellous ways to will by Him who knows how to work interiorly in the very hearts of men; not that men — something which is impossible — should believe unwillingly, but that from unwilling they should be rendered willing . . . God acts with persuasions that we may will and believe; what is more, God brings Himself about in a man, the very will to believe."

The fact that *the* faith is a "gift", that the will must be under the influence of supernatural grace, in no way removes from man the obligation of preparing himself to receive the necessary grace. Since Scripture tells us that "without faith it is impossible to please God", and since God cannot desire other than our salvation, it clearly follows that as Mgr. Van Noort states, "The vocation to the faith . . . is a free gift of God, which, just as it is denied to no adult except through his own fault, cannot be merited by any natural work."

Since Vatican II, there has been in the New Church, a great deal of talk about "faith". There is in this institution an "open" attitude — if some Catholics want to believe in the traditional way, it is acceptable, providing they also tolerate the new "pluralism" and don't insist upon participating in the traditional rites, and providing they don't insist that others maintain the same standard. Others are equally free to call themselves Catholic while denying fundamental tenets of *the* Catholic faith. An excellent example of this is provided by the statement of the entire French hierarchy which, after the publication of Paul VI's *Humanae Vitae* forbidding artificial methods of birth control, stated that any couple could use contraceptive methods providing that to do so was in their conscience a "lesser evil" than obeying God's law! (Of course, they put it in far more euphemistic terms — however, the idea that the faithful can choose a "lesser evil" in direct disobedience of God's commands, or can formally cooperate in an intrinsically evil act, is simply not Catholic). What is more extraordinary about this is that Paul VI telegraphed to them his thanks for "so clearly interpreting his thinking" on the issue!

Faith is described by modernist theologians with considerable vagueness as "man's response to God's Revelation", as an "encounter with Christ", as a "birth in the Spirit", as a "personal" or "religious experience", and in a variety of similar phrases.[10] As Archbishop Bernadine, president of the U.S. Bishop's Conference admitted, "many consider themselves good Catholics, even though their beliefs and practices seem to conflict with the official teaching of the Church" (*Time*, May 24, 1976). He of course finds this in no way objectionable, for when he was asked how a person like Avery Dulles S.J. could publicly deny the Immaculate Conception and the Assumption of Our Lady (thus declaring himself a "depraved

---

10. To quote Avery Dulles himself, "Vatican Council II, in its Constitution on Divine Revelation, moves away from the Counter Reformation view of faith as a sheerly intellectual assent to revealed truths. Through His revelation, we are told in Article 2, 'the invisible God out of the abundance of His love speaks to men as friends'. In accordance with this view of revelation as an offer of friendship, the Council looks upon faith as a personal engagement involving loyalty and self-commitment. It is an act of the whole man, 'an obedience by which man entrusts his whole self freely to God' (5)". (*Doctrines do Grow*, Ed. John T. McGinn, CSP., Paulist Press: N.Y. 1972). Again, Vatican II states: "The People of God believes that it is led by the Spirit of the Lord, who fills the earth. Motivated by this faith, it labours to decipher authentic signs of God's presence and purpose . . ."

heretic", and outside the traditional Church) and could continue to teach theology at the Catholic University of America, the Archbishop stated that it was his "belief that it was legitimate for those theologians to speculate about the removal of doctrines that have already been defined, and to request the magisterium to remove such doctrines from the content of the Faith" (*The Wanderer,* June 17, 1976). Those who would defend the "orthodoxy" of the New Church will argue that such is an "abuse". But "abuses" have become "normative" and have the full approval of the hierarchy. When Cardinal Suenens declared himself a Pentecostal, he stated (somewhat later) that if the Pope were to ask him to deny the "Pentecostal creed", he would do so at once. Paul VI never made such a request, and has indeed given his blessing to the Pentecostal movement.[11]

What results from all this "openness" is a sort of "visceral Christianity" in which the individual is freed from the accusation of heterodoxy and at the same time is free to believe anything he wants. Such, according to Andrew Greeley's statistical study of the priesthood, is the position of the majority of the clergy in the New Church.

> "69 percent of the bishops and only 45 percent of the priests agreed that 'faith means essentially belief in the doctrines of the Catholic Church', whereas 46 percent of the bishops and 69 percent of the clergy would agree that faith is 'primarily an encounter with God and Jesus Christ rather than an assent to a coherent set of defined truths'."

This is a most remarkable statement, for it demonstrates that 46 percent of the bishops (remember, this is in 1973) and 69 percent of the clergy have declared themselves outside the unity of the faith. To state that their faith is an "encounter" with God might possibly allow for an orthodox interpretation — but to state also that it is this *rather than an assent to a coherent set of defined truths* means they are no longer

---

11. To the leaders of the Charismatic movement Paul VI said: "We are very interested in what you are doing. We have heard so much about what is happening among you. And we rejoice." (*L'Osservatore Romano*, Oct. 11, 1975).

Catholic![12] Our faith is "no simple sublimating aspiration", no "experiential" sort of "encounter with Jesus" such as any Protestant can claim, no sort of "personal understanding", "commitment", or "feeling". No indeed! It is, to use the words of St. Thomas Aquinas, "the act of the intellect assenting to a Divine Truth owing to the movement of the will, which is itself moved by the grace of God" (*Summa* II-II, iv, a.2). Consider the words of the Oath against Modernism, once required of every priest, and according to Tanquerey's criteria, part of the "solemn" Magisterium:

> "I hold with certainty and sincerely confess that faith is not a blind impulse of religion welling up from the depth of the unconscious under the impulse of the heart and the inclination of a morally conditioned will, but the genuine assent of the intellect to a truth which is received from outside . . ."

Our faith then is essentially a belief in the doctrines of the Catholic Church, and is based on a Truth that is entirely independent of our personal feelings or emotional reactions, a truth given us by Christ and the Apostles and one constantly upheld and preserved by the traditional Church throughout her existence. One must reject the concept taught by Vatican II that in matters of faith "man is to be guided by his own judgment, and he is to enjoy freedom". Rather, man is to be guided by the teachings of the Church, and his freedom exists in his ability to accept or reject this guidance. Faith is

---

12. One can give example upon example of the abuses that this "existential" view of the Faith results in. A classical case is that of Bishop Milvaine of the Diocese of Pocahontas who recently stated (*The Wanderer*, Jan. 26, 1978) that: "The Faith is not a collection of abstract propositions to be memorized. Faith is an encounter with Christ. It should be a deep experience. For several generations we have made a serious mistake in making catechesis mainly a matter of religious instruction (almost 2000 years — Ed.) and religious instruction a watered-down theology course. We must be aware that the central goal of catechesis is to strengthen faith. To accomplish this we must build up vibrant faith communities." *The Wanderer* then proceeds to describe the "faith community" of Pocahontas as "priests and nuns in rebellion against the Pope; heresy in the Catechisms; immorality passed off as virtue in the confessional: all apparently with the Bishops approval!" Surely one may be permitted to ask in what parishes of the United States such abuses are not the rule?

never "blind", for it involves the assent of the intellect to truths revealed by Christ and taught by the Church. The intellect is by its very nature a faculty that functions to "see" the truth and does not operate in the "dark".[13] Faith moreover is never unreasonable though it may accept what is beyond the grasp of reason. Faith is always free, for it cannot be coerced. In giving our assent to "the teaching Magisterium of the Church" we give our assent to that Truth which Christ and the Apostles gave to the Church to preserve. It is in this act that the possibility of freedom lies, for it frees us from our own subjectivity. Our refusal to give assent makes us slaves of our own "personal judgments", and in the last analysis, to our own passionate nature.

> For thus doth our faith teach, that is the true, the right Catholic faith, gathered not by the opinion of private judgment, but by the witness of the Scriptures, not subject to the fluctuations of heretical rashness, but grounded upon Apostolic truth . . ."
>
> St. Augustine, *Sermons* xxxiv

And if man is free to reject this faith, it must be remembered that his freedom is never without responsibility, for the eternal salvation of his soul depends upon how he exercises it. The stakes are rather high!

---

13. "Blindness" unfortunately has characterized much of the faith in the New and Post-conciliar Church. Blind obedience to a hierarchy that has departed from unity and blind obedience to the Post-conciliar Popes. In this manner many of the faithful have been led down the "primrose path" of modernism and heresy.

CAN TRADITION "EVOLVE"?
CAN DOCTRINE "DEVELOP"?

Post Vatican II theologians of every shade of persuasion readily admit that on multiple issues the teaching of the Church has changed.[1]

Now, if the faith was revealed in its fullness by Christ and the Apostles, and if the Church has as part of its function, the preservation of this "deposit of the Faith" unchanged, how then can we explain its "changing" positions? The modernist answer is that doctrine "evolves" and "develops". To what extent is such a concept Catholic?

The application of doctrine to various circumstances and the drawing forth of its implications as time passes can be seen as a "development", as indeed can the necessity of making explicit what was, in an earlier age, only implicit. But doctrine and the tradition that is its vehicle, cannot *develop* or *evolve* in some Darwinian manner any more than can that Truth which was given us by Christ and the Apostles. The concept as promulgated by Vatican II that "the tradition of the Church is a tradition of progress in understanding the truth", can never be accepted by a faithful Catholic as the modernists would interpret it. Dogma may become clearer to us; it may be more tightly defined by the teaching magisterium (as part of its function of preserving what was revealed, and this usually in response to a heresy that challenges a given truth), but *it does not and cannot change*. Moreover, the manner in which the teachings of the Church have been defined has always been explicit and clear, and the only possible reason for anyone wishing to rephrase or re-word them is to introduce into them an element of ambiguity such

---

1. See p. 113.

as would allow for multiple interpretations. It should be clear that either Truth is important, and doesn't change, or it changes and then is of no importance. After all, the truth as a whole is eternal, incapable as such of any improvement or advancement. And moreover, it is one of the patent absurdities of our times to suppose that our minds have improved since the time of Christ, or that we have developed or evolved greater insight into truth than our Lord and the Apostles had.[2] As Cardinal Newman has said:

"The holy Apostles would without words know all the truths concerning the high doctrines of theology, which controversalists after them have piously and charitably reduced to formulas, and developed through argument."

Essays and Discourses

---

2. The teaching of Vatican II clearly departs from traditional thinking on this point. To quote the documents directly:

"To a certain extent, the human intellect is also broadening its dominion over time; over the past by means of historical knowledge; over the future by the art of projecting and planning. Advances in biology, psychology and the social sciences . . . bring man hope of improved self-knowledge."

Of course, if this position is now to become part of the Post-conciliar Magisterium, then it logically follows that the documents are correct in teaching:

"Let them (the faithful) blend modern science and its theories and the understanding of the most recent discoveries with Christian morality and doctrine."

One has only to observe the present scene to see how insightful are the words of Pius XII in his Encyclical *Summi Pontificatus:*

"They boasted of progress, when they were in fact relapsing into decadence; they conceived that they were reaching heights of achievement when they were miserably forfeiting their human dignity; they claimed that this century of ours was bringing maturity and completion with it, when they were being reduced to a pitiable form of slavery."

Human weakness may alter its style in the course of history, but not its nature, and the sanctity achieved by a St. Thomas Aquinas is in no essential way different from that achieved by St. Theresa of Lisieux, or St. Iranaeus. It is not religion, but these false ideas of "progress" and "evolution" that are the opiate of the people. That the New Church should buy and teach this mess of pottage is extraordinary!

At the risk of stressing the obvious, it should be clear that, once the teaching Magisterium takes a clear cut stand on a doctrinal issue, no later or alternative organ of Tradition can contradict it. One cannot have two contradictory statements that both agree with a single principle derived from Revelation. And this is as true for the ordinary universal magisterium as it is for the solemn. That truth can change is against the doctrine of the indefectibility of the Church *(Behold, I am with you all through the days that are coming, until the consummation of the world" Matt.* xxviii, 20), and those who hold otherwise are in fact saying that either the Church previously taught error or is now teaching error. No wonder the New and Post-conciliar Church desires to hide behind the screen that she is changing nothing that is *de fide definita* — it is the same smoke screen that claims tradition only relates to dogmatic fact. The idea that the Church can change her constant teaching on any issue is that she can "adulterate" her teaching. It is to say that the Spouse of Christ can become a harlot! — a blasphemy and a sacrilege. If the magisterium is under the guidance and protection of the Holy Spirit, one must remember that the Holy Spirit, being Truth itself, cannot contradict Itself. He would hardly have given to the Apostles a teaching that was to last "until the end of time" — and then change it before this end had occured. We are warned in Scripture of those who would teach us a "new gospel", other than the one "received" — that there would be *didaskalai "a continuous succession of new teachers"* teaching *"as the whim takes them",* and seeking to satisfy *"itching ears".* Surely, we cannot as reasonable men, believe other than, as St. Augustine says, "Wisdom uncreate is the same now as it ever was and ever will be". This is the constant teaching of the true Church, for as St. John of the Cross says:

"Since He has finished revealing the faith through Christ, there is no more faith to reveal, nor will there ever be . . . Since there are no more articles to be revealed to the Church about the substance of our faith, a person must not merely reject new revelations about the faith, but he should out of caution, repudiate other kinds of knowledge mingled with them . . ."

Ascent of Mount Carmel

The "Oath against Modernism" remains for ever an expression of the traditional *faithful* Catholic's attitude. It is credal in nature:

> "I sincerely accept the doctrine of the faith which was handed down to us in the same meaning and always with the same purport from the Apostles through the orthodox Fathers. I therefore entirely reject the heretical theory of the evolution of dogmas, viz. that they change from one meaning to another, different from the one which the Church previously held."

Clearly then, we must refuse to accept the teaching of Vatican II to the effect that "as the centuries succeed one another, the Church constantly moves forward towards the fullness of divine truth until the words of God reach their complete fulfillment in her.[3] This teaching, in so far as it contradicts the fundamental principle that the fullness of the Faith was given us by Christ and the Apostles, and in so far as it implicitly denies the coming of Anti-Christ when only a "remnant" will keep the faith, must be totally rejected by a Catholic. True there is always a need to reply to new questions, and new forms of ignorance can always arise (the truth is one, but error by its very nature is legion); one can and must explain the sacred doctrine, but never at the expense of that which gives it *raison d'être* — that is to say, never at the expense of truth and effectiveness. Adapting (a modernist euphemism for "altering") the teachings of the Church so as to make them acceptable to the "world" is to forget that the so-called modern world is intrinsically opposed to that "kingdom of heaven" that the Church envisages; by its very nature, it represents a rupture with traditional values — that is to say, it is founded on principles that reflect a basic infidelity to Christ — it has replaced the fire of love with the arson of rebellion. The Church cannot be adapted to this infidelity,

---

3. As Avery Dulles, S.J. states, "While stressing that God's self-revelation reached its unsurpassable fullness in Christ, the Council left ample room for development in the Church's assimilation of that fullness in new and unpredictable ways. Without using the term "continuing revelation", Vatican II allowed for something of the kind. Echoing a favorite term of John XXIII, it spoke repeatedly of the need to discern the 'signs of the times' through which God continues to address his people". *(op. cit.)*

and those who attempt to do this commit spiritual adultery; they call upon themselves all the strictures that Jeremias laid upon the Jews that had become a "generation of harlots". The absurdity of the adaptationist position can be seen more clearly if we compare it to the proposition that the father of the "prodigal son" should go and eat husks with the swine. (It is just these "husks" that the faithful are choking on in the New Church). The Church can only kill the fatted lamb when modern man returns to the fold and the bosom of the Father. Clearly, it is modern man that must adapt himself to the teachings of the Church, and his failure to do so is manifest in the consequences that are evident all around us. To depart from such a basic principle is to adapt truth to error and to falsify the Magisterium. It is to substitute for legitimate development, *change* — a procedure clearly condemned by the Canons of Vatican I.

> "The meaning of the sacred dogmas must always be retained which Holy Mother Church has once taught, nor may it ever be departed from under the guise of or in the name of deeper insight . . . If anyone shall say that, because of scientific progress, it may be possible at some time to interpret the Church's dogmas in a different sense from that which the Church understood and understands, let him be anathema!"

> "The doctrine of the faith which God has revealed has not been proposed to human intelligence to be perfected by them as if it were a philosophical system, but as a divine deposit entrusted to the Spouse of Christ to be faithfully guarded and infallibly interpreted."

This is the *de fide* teaching of the Church. This has always been the teaching of the Church. As Cardinal Newman states:

> "A development, to be faithful, must retain both the doctrine and the principle with which it started . . . Such too is the theory of the Fathers as regards the doctrines fixed by Councils, and is instanced by the language of St. Leo: 'To be asking for what has been finished, to tear up what has been laid down, what is this but to be unthankful for what is gained?' St. Vincent

of Lerins, in a like manner speaks of the development of Christian doctrine as *perfectus fidei, non permutatio* (as the perfection of the faith, and not its alteration."

All this is well summed up by St. Albertus Magnus, the teacher of St. Thomas Aquinas: "Development", he states, "is the progress of the faithful in the faith, not of the faith within the faithful."

THE ATTITUDE OF THE MAGISTERIUM
TOWARDS INNOVATION

Semper Idem ("Always the Same")
Motto of Cardinal Ottaviani

Webster's dictionary defines "innovation" as a "change or novelty, especially in customs, manners or rites", and reminds us that a more obsolete usage equates the term with "revolution and insurrection". The traditional Catholic Church has always been strongly opposed to all innovation. Even prior to the coming of Christ, we find Plato calling the innovator "the worst kind of pest" in any society, and stating that it was "our own irrational impulses which yearned for innovation".[1] In Rome also, Sallust describes the innovator as an "unprincipled character, hating the established order of things . . . bent on general upheavel, turmoil and rebellion".[2]

Certainly, our Lord did not put himself forth as an "innovator". He clearly stated that *"My doctrine is not mine, but His that sent me"* (*John* viii:16) and further stated *"I am not come to destroy, but to fullfil the law"* (*Matt.* v:17). The warnings of St. Paul against those who would teach us a new kind of gospel *("even though an Angel")* are quite clear. This attitude was preserved by the early saints with care. Thus St. Papias (whom Irenaeus describes as a "hearer of the Apostle John") says, "I do not take pleasure as many do . . . in those who relate foreign precepts, but in those who relate the precepts which were given by the Lord to the faith and came

---

1. Plato speaks out against "innovators" in several passages, and especially with regard to those who would innovate in matters pertaining to ritual and music.
2. We are not of course speaking of those who would make a "better mouse-trap", but about those who would replace what is traditional with "novelties". One must be aware of the Platonic distinction between "new songs" and "a new kind of music".

down from truth itself", and Tertullian said "I do not accept what you introduce on your own authority."

The Church fathers maintained this attitude with clarity. St. Vincent of Lerins said, "The more a man is under the influence of religion, the more prompt is he to oppose innovation." St. Augustine taught "for thus doth our faith teach, that is the true, the right Catholic faith, gathered not by the opinion of private judgment, but by the witness of the Scriptures; not subject to the fluctuations of heretical rashness, but grounded upon Apostolic truth." St. Basil the Great said, "We accept no new faith, written out for us by others, nor do we proclaim the results of our own cogitation, lest mere human wisdom should be accounted the rule of faith; we communicate to all who question us that which the holy fathers have taught us." St. John Climacus in his famous "Ladder of Ascent" states, "We should constantly be examining and comparing ourselves with the holy fathers and lights who lived before us," and further says, "this I ask, that you should not imagine that we are inventing what we write, for such a suspicion would detract from its value." Pope Sylvester declared "Let there be no innovations", and about one thousand years later his words were reflected in the declaration of that great scholar, Pope Benedict XIV who said: "Do not innovate anything, rest content with the tradition." The Master of the Sentences, Peter Lombard, states in the prologue that "truly whenever and whatever we speak, it is the voice of the Church fathers that is heard, nor will we go beyond the limits they have set". St. Bernard taught that "it suffices us not to wish to be better than our fathers", and M. Olier, the founder of the Sulpicians says: "God forbid that I should ever innovate anything in religious matters." St. Francis de Sales said "I have said nothing which I have not learned of others", and in doing so reflected the very words of Cassian: "I am not inventing this teaching, but simply passing on what I have learned from others." St. Vincent de Paul decried "the novel opinions which are spreading more and more", and St. Alphonsus Liguori spoke out against those "who taught not the gospel, but their own inventions". And such has ever been the seemingly monotonous plainchant of the Church that sees her function as one of preserving that Truth which Christ entrusted to her. As Mgr. Van Noort states, "the point is hammered home more forceably by *Tradition* which from the very earliest days was willing to follow only the doctrine of the Apostles, and always considered any innovation in matters of the faith to be a clear hallmark of heresy." Not one saint, not one Pope from a previous era, and not one line of Holy Scripture can be brought forward in defense of innovation. This attitude is well summarized by St. Bonaventura who said:

> "Preachers should discover nothing new in their hearts, for Our Lord did not create new loaves to feed the crowd. He multiplied the five loaves that were at hand. So it is that true doctrine must be drawn out and multiplied through prayer which rises up to heaven, through devotion which blesses, through meditation which breaks the bread, and through preaching which distributes it."[3]

Such is by no means the attitude of the Post-conciliar Church. Indeed, Paul VI would instruct us that "it is necessary to know how to welcome with humility and an interior freedom what is innovative"; and praises the "renewal" that has been achieved in his Church since Vatican II in the following terms:

> ". . . that of renewal conceived in correct terms, and according to the 'good spirit' promised by the heavenly Father . . . We could by the grace of the Lord, give many proofs, and not trivial ones either, that seem to us convincing . . . If we think of the SUM TOTAL OF INNO — VATING MEASURES THAT HAVE BEEN PUT INTO EFFECT IN THIS PERIOD, PARTICULARLY IF WE CONSIDER THE LITURGICAL REFORM — A GREAT INNOVATION INDEED!"
>
> (*General Audience*, August 4, 1971).

---

3. The Law of the Church with regard to the Canonization of Saints as promulgated by Pope Urban VIII states:

> "A most diligent inquiry be made as to whether the servant of God whose canonization is sought wrote any books, tracts, meditations, or the like; for if any such have been written, no inquiry is to be carried on until such books are carefully examined by the Congregation to see whether they contain any errors contrary to faith or morals, *or any novel doctrine* opposed to the sound and pure teaching of the Church."

And indeed, he dares to state elsewhere that the "Chief innovation affects the Eucharistic prayer . . ."

The problem with innovations is that they are the essential background to the introduction of heresy — indeed, the Church fathers frequently join the two terms in a single phrase: As St. Augustine said with regard to the teaching of the Church on original sin: "It is not I who devised the teaching of the Church which the Catholic faith holds from ancient times, but you who deny it are undoubtedly an *innovating* heretic." *(De Nupt.* II). If the Church functions to preserve the deposit of the faith, she has an absolute obligation to speak out and expose those who would dilute or distort this deposit, and she has an absolute obligation to try and prevent such heretics from misleading the faithful. As Pope Saint Pius X in his Encyclical *Editae Saepe* states, quoting the words of St. Charles Borromeo: "It is a certain, well-established fact that no other crime so seriously offends God and provokes His greatest wrath as the vice of heresy."

The idea that it is not necessary for those in authority to condemn heretics was condemned as "scandalous" by Pope Alexander VII in 1665 *(Denzinger* 1105). Pope Leo confirmed the Conciliar condemnation of Pope Honorius I on the grounds that "he was wanting the vigilance expected from him in his Apostolic office and thereby allowed heresy to make headway which he should have crushed in its beginnings". During the rite of Ordination of Bishops, the following words are read: *"I have made thee a watchman to the house of Israel"* (*Ezech.* iii: 17), and the very next sentence goes on: *"If thou declare not to be wicked his iniquity, I will require his blood at thy hand"* (*Ezech.* iii:18). Canon law states (2316) that "he is suspect of heresy who spontaneously and consciously helps in any way with the propagation of heresy". Pope Felix III stated: "Not to oppose error, is to approve of it, and not to defend truth is to suppress it, and indeed, to neglect to confound evil men, when we can do it, is no less a sin than to encourage them".[4]

Now, these "anti-heretical" attitudes on the part of the traditional Church can, as one would expect, be defended on

---

4. Vatican II, under the heading of "Religious liberty" would concede to all religious sects, and to non-religious political organizations, the right to propagate their views, no matter how heretical, and even in situations where the Church could prevent it. This is, the Council teaches, to be

Scriptural grounds. Christ himself warned us that *"many false prophets shall arise, and shall seduce many . . ."* He further stated that *"he who is not with me is against me . . . and he who will not hear the Church, let him be to thee as the heathen and the publican"*. He was not ambiguous when he said *"he who believeth not shall be condemned"*. The Apostles spoke in a similar vein. St. Paul warned us against those *"who would teach us a gospel besides that"* which we had received of him. St. John calls the heretic *"a seducer, an antichrist, a man who dissolves Christ"*, and instructs us *"to receive him not into the house, nor say to him, God speed you"*. St. Peter, with his characteristic ardour, calls the heretics *"lying teachers who shall bring in sects of perdition, and deny the Lord who bought them; bringing upon themselves swift destruction"*. He called them *"clouds without water and clouds tossed in whirlwinds, to whom the mist of darkness is reserved"*. St. Jude speaks in a similar strain throughout his whole Epistle. And St. Paul tells us how to act with regard to heresy. He instructs Timothy to *"war on them a good warfare, having faith and good conscience, which some rejecting have made shipwreck concerning the faith . . ."* He exhorts the ancients of the Church at Ephesus to *"take heed to yourselves, and to the whole flock, wherein the Holy Ghost hath placed you*

"guaranteed" as a "civil and legal right". What father would ever allow such in his family?

In passing, the accusation that the Church "burned" heretics is false. Heretics, especially anarchists and satanists, were considered enemies of the state. The Albigensians denied all civil as well as all spiritual authority. The Church and her "inquisition" functioned to determine whether or not they were in fact heretics, and always insisted that they be given a chance to "recant". Our modern "jury" system is an outgrowth of the Inquisition as all evidence had to be presented, not to a jury of "peers", but to one of experts. In many situations, the inquisition functioned to "protect" the faithful from the state. It was those who clearly were attempting to destroy the civil order who were turned over to the state for punishment. That abuses occured is unfortunately true, but these were surprisingly few in number. Those who are interested in an unbiased view of this institution are referred to William Thomas Walsh's *Characters of the Inquisition*, Kennedy: N.Y., 1940.

The Church has always taken the position that error can under certain circumstances be "tolerated", but never one that gives it approval or treats it on an "equal footing" (to use a Vatican II phrase). Thus while forced conversions are clearly forbidden by Canon Law, she has always done all in her power to prevent the faithful from being seduced by heretical teachings. Convinced of her sacred function and duty, how else should she behave?

Bishops, to rule the Church of God . . . I know that, after my departure, ravening wolves will enter in among you, not sparing the flock, . . . therefore watch." "Beware of dogs", He writes to the Philippians, the "dogs" being the same false teachers as the ravening wolves. Is it any wonder then that St. Jerome calls the congregations of the heretics "synagogues of satan" and says that their communion is to be avoided "like that of vipers and scorpions"? As St. Bernard warns, "It is not safe to sleep near serpents."

And what do we have today in the New and Post-conciliar Church? As Frank Sheed has said, "Every week brings news of some revolutionary-sounding denial by some theologian somewhere — and not a sound out of their hierarchy! . . . There is hardly a doctrine or practice of the Church that I have not heard attacked by some priest." Who are the great theologians of the New Church? Surely no one will balk at the names of Bernard Haring, Karl Rahner, Hans Küng, Joseph Suenens, Edward Schillebeeckx and Yves Congar, to give a few whose names are almost household words — and everyone of these has denied one or another of the Church's teachings. They were well known to Paul VI — some were personal friends — not one of them has been declared to be heretical. Every one of them is or has taught Catholics at Catholic institutions. And in fact, what did Paul VI do in the face of the "smoke of satan" that he claimed surrounded him? Let me tell you. He abolished the index;[5] he effectively abolished the Holy Office, one of the primary functions of which was to prevent heretics from doing harm, and finally, he publicly stated:

> "We are going to have a period of greater liberty in the life of the Church, and hence for each of her sons . . . Formal discipline will be reduced, all arbitrary judgment will be abolished, as well as all intolerance and absolutism."

Now such a statement from a person who claimed to be a reigning Pontiff — Christ's representative on earth, can only

---

5. The Index dates back to the Council of Nicea in 325 where the works of Arius (specifically, his book *Thalia*) were condemned because the Author's views that the Word of God was a creature were "set forth in a loose, free style, reminding one of the works of Sotades". The "loose free style" was not invented by the "periti" of Vatican II.

be termed extraordinary. First of all, the judgments of the Church have never been "arbitrary", but based on sound doctrine, and often taken after years of careful study. Secondly, the Church must be intolerant of error. After all, she is here to proclaim Christ's truth. Now either she is the Church that Christ founded, and therefore has, whether the world accords her recognition or not, special rights and privileges, or she is only one Church among many others. Either she teaches the absolute Truth, or there is in her eyes, no absolute truth. What parent would ever fail to censor the reading and activities of his children or children entrusted to his care? What government in power has ever allowed seditious organizations the freedom to undermine its structures? — and heresy, for the Church of Christ, is sedition. What physician would ever allow disease to play havoc with his patient when he was in a position to prevent it?

It should by now be quite clear to the reader that the New and Post-conciliar Church has departed from unity with the traditional Church, the "Church of All Times", the Church that Christ founded, the Roman Catholic Church as she exists now, and existed in far greater numbers prior to the Second Vatican Council. To those who argue that all such departures are in the nature of "abuses", let it be stressed that throughout this book, almost all examples of the RUPTURE WITH TRADITION are taken from either statements of the Post-conciliar "popes", the documents of Vatican II, or the *Novus Ordo Missae*. No Post-conciliar Catholic can refuse to accept these three sources without defeating his own argument. He cannot "pick and choose" just what he will accept in the New Church without declaring that it is in fact his own "private opinion" that is the basic authority for his decision. The "Post-conciliar Catholic", no matter how "sincere", is plainly and simply, NOT a Roman Catholic.

THE RUPTURE OF "UNITY" ON THE PART
OF THE "POST-CONCILIAR CHURCH"
AND THE ISSUE OF OBEDIENCE
TO THOSE RESPONSIBLE

"Unity", being an essential quality of God, is bound to be reflected in His Church. Anyone familiar with his Penny Catechism knows that this "unity" subsists in three things, unity of *faith,* unity of *worship and rites,* and unity *under one head,* the Pope, who is Christ's representative on earth. When the Church speaks of "unity of faith", she is not speaking of anything else than the acceptance of that faith which Christ and the Apostles revealed, and which "is believed always, by all, and everywhere". The same of course applies in the realm of worship, for the essential features of the Mass are divine and not of human origin. No one can dispute but that there has been, in the true and traditional Catholic Church, a perfect continuity in the unity of belief and worship among Catholics from Apostolic times down to the present day. As to unity under the Pope, this is essentially a unity with the Papacy. Thus, if an individual "pope" departs from unity of faith and worship, he can no longer be Christ's representative on earth, and Christ can no longer say of him, "he who hears you, hears me". As Vatican I put it:

"The Holy Spirit is not promised to the successors of Peter so that, through His revelation, they may bring new doctrines to light, but that, with His help, they may keep inviolate and faithfully expound the revelation handed down through the Apostles, the deposit of faith . . ."

(*Denzinger* 1836)

This has of course always been the Church's teaching. As St. Bernard said to Pope Eugene in his "Five Books on Consideration":

"You have been entrusted with stewardship over the world, not given possession of it. Leave possession and rule to Him; you take care of it. This is your portion: beyond it do not stretch your hand. You should not think that you are excluded from those about whom God complains, (when He says in *Hos.* viii:4) 'They have reigned, but not by Me; princes have arisen, but I do not recognize them'."

The Church has always taught that it was possible for a Pope to become a bad pope, and that, should such be the case, we are not to give him our total obedience. Listen to her theologians and the teaching Magisterium:

"Although it clearly follows from the circumstances that the Pope can err at times, and command things which must not be done, that we are not to be simply obedient to him in all things, that does not show that he must not be obeyed by all when his commands are good. To know in what cases he is to be obeyed and in what not . . . it is said in the Acts of the Apostles: 'One ought to obey God rather than man:' therefore, were the Pope to command anything against Holy Scripture, or the articles of faith, or the truth of the Sacraments, or the commands of the natural or divine law, he ought not to be obeyed, but in such commands, to be passed over *(despiciendus).*"

Cardinal Turrencremata (Summa de Eccl.)

"It is lawful to resist him (the Pope) if he assaulted souls, or troubled the state, and much more if he strove to destroy the Church. It is lawful, I say, to resist him by not doing what he commands and hindering the execution of his will."

Cardinal Saint Bellarmine (de Rom. Pont)

"If the Pope, by his orders and his acts, destroys the Church, one can resist him and impede the execution of his commands."

Francisco de Vitoria

"If the Pope lays down an order contrary to right customs, one does not have to obey him . . ."

Suarez

Now these quotations clearly show that there are certain circumstances under which we are free — nay even obliged — to resist the evil commands and actions of a Pope. But a Pontiff can go even farther on the path of error. Again, we turn to the theologians:

"One (a Pope) also falls into Schism if he departs himself from the body of the Church by refusing to be in communion with her by participating in the sacraments . . . The Pope can become schismatic in this manner if he does not wish to be in proper communion with the body of the Church (the Church of All Times — Ed.), a situation which would arise if he tried to excommunicate the entire Church, or, as both Cajetan and Torquemada observe, IF HE WISHED TO CHANGE *ALL* THE ECCLESIASTICAL CEREMONIES, FOUNDED AS THEY ARE ON APOSTOLIC TRADITION."

Suarez

And which ceremony and Sacrament has not the Post-conciliar Church changed with full "papal" approval? Going still further, and bearing in mind the fact, as pointed out in an earlier section of this book, that Popes can fall into (obstinate) heresy, let us consider still further documents of the traditional Church:

"By disobedience the Pope can separate himself from Christ despite the fact that he is head of the Church, for above all, the unity of the Church is dependent on its relationship with Christ. The Pope can separate himself from Christ by either disobeying the laws of Christ, or by commanding something that is against the divine or natural law. By so doing, the Pope separates himself from the body of the Church because this body is itself linked to Christ by obedience. In this way, the Pope could without doubt, fall into Schism.

"The Pope can also separate himself from the Church and her priests if he so wishes to do and without any specific reason. (i.e., by the exercising of his free will — Ed.). He also does this if he refuses to do what the Universal Church (the Church of All Times — Ed.) does, based as these things are, on the Tradition of the Apostles; or again, if he does not observe those precepts which the Holy and Ecumenical Councils or the Holy See have determined to be of universal application (i.e. the solemn or universal magisterium). Especially is this true with regard to the divine liturgy, as for example, if he did not wish personally to follow the universal customs and rites of the Church. Such would be the case if he did not wish to celebrate Mass with the sacred vestments, or with candles, or if he refused to make the sign of the cross in the same manner as other priests do. The same holds true for other aspects of the liturgy in a very general fashion, and for anything that might go against the perpetual customs of the Church as incorporated in the Canons *Quae ad perpetuum, Violatores, Sunt quidem,* and *Contra Statua.* By separating himself from the observance of the Universal customs of the Church, and by so doing with obstinacy, the Pope is able to fall into schism. Such a conclusion is only just because the premises on which it is based are beyond doubt. For, just as the Pope can become a heretic, so he is also able to do so with the sin of obstinacy. Thus it is that Innocent states *(De Consuetudine)* that, it is necessary to obey a Pope in all things as long as he does not himself go against the universal customs of the Church, but should he go against the universal customs of the Church, he need not be followed . . ."

Jean de Torquemada

As Cornelius Lapide, S.J. puts it:

> "Wherefore, under no circumstances can he (the Pope) be deposed by the Church, but can only be declared to have fallen from his Pontificate, if for the sake of example, he should chance (which God forbid!) to fall into public heresy, and should therefore, *ipso facto*, cease to be Pope, yea, even to be a Christian believer."

Because "obedience" has become the crux of much of the debate between the Traditional and the New Church, it would be of great value to consider the teaching of St. Thomas Aquinas on this subject.[1] Since all authority in the last analysis comes from God, all obedience in the last analysis is given to God. "It sometimes happens that the commands issued by prelates are against God. Therefore not in all things are prelates to be obeyed. For those under them are bound to do so only in those matters in which they are subject to their superiors, and, in which those same superiors do not oppose the command of a Power higher than themselves" (*Summa* II-II, Q. 104, Art. 5). Elsewhere he says, "Anyone should be subject to a lower power only in so far as it preserves the order established by a power higher than itself; but if it (the lower power) departs from the order of the higher power, then it is not right for anyone to be subjected to that lower power — for example — if a proconsul ordered something to be done, when the emperor above commanded the contrary." *(Summa* II-II Q. 69, Art. 3). He is quite specific with regard to the Pope and the Bishops: "We however pay no regard to the successors of the Apostles except in so far as they proclaim to us those things which the Apostles left behind in their writings" (*De Veritate*, Q. 14, Art. 10). Now, it would be irrational to expect the teaching of the Church to be other than this, for in obedience, as St. Thomas says, "not only is promptitude required, but also discernment". (*Commentary*

---

1. To quote *L'Osservatore Romano*, January 7, 1971, "St. Thomas is named by the (Second) Vatican Council in the most explicit way, as the teacher to be followed in specifically theological thought, that is thought seeking the understanding of the mysteries, as far as is possible, and in contemplating the connection between the revealed truths. This is tantamount to recognizing the superiority of St. Thomas in certainty and depth of doctrine." See *Document on Priestly Formation*, Paragraph 16.

on the Epistle to Titus iii:1). *Blind* obedience is as foreign to the magisterium as is *blind* faith![2]

To summarize, it is only to God and the laws of God that a Catholic gives unconditional obedience. As to human authority, be it civil or ecclesiatic, he obeys only in so far as what is commanded is not against the laws of God. This is the faith! However, as it is in a "blind" obedience that the erstwhile faithful Catholic is being asked to follow the Post-conciliar Church, it behoves us to examine in detail just what this Church teaches, and just where it departs from tradition. This will be discussed under three headings: The post-conciliar "Popes", the Second Vatican Council, and finally, the *Novus Ordo Missae,* with some reference to the other Sacraments.

---

2. It is worth while to consider some of the statements made by Freemasons on the issue of "obedience". They have always dreamed of a Pope "according to our needs, not a scandalous Pope like Borgia, (some historians consider Alexander VI to have been a victim of falsification), but a Pope open to outside fluctuations . . ." As they stated in 1861, the "obedience" of the faithful to such a Pope would be the means that allowed them to destroy the Church: "In a hundred years time . . . Bishops and priests will think they are marching behind the banner of the Keys of Peter when in fact they will be following our flag . . . The reforms will have to be brought about in the name of Obedience" (Quotations taken from the documents of the Masonic organization entitled *Alta Vendita* that by accident fell into the hands of the Church and were published by Pope Pius IX). The attitude of Freemasonry towards the New Church will be discussed later, but for the present, to quote Yves Marsoudon, (State Master, Supreme Council of France, Scottish Rite): "The sense of universalism that is rampant in Rome these days is very close to our purpose for existence . . . With all our hearts we support the 'Revolution of John XXIII'."

PART III

THE POST-CONCILIAR "POPES"

Pope Pius XII was certainly aware of the threat that Modernism posed to the Church; not only did he complain about it being taught covertly in seminaries, he more than once was known to have stated that, even though he was the last Pontiff to hold the line on innovation, he would hold it firmly. How prophetic such a stance was is only now obvious. In 1958 when Roncalli was elected to the throne of Peter, and this despite the fact that, as Trevor informs us, he was dismissed from a teaching position at the Lateran University barely one term after he had been appointed professor of Patrology ("a curious proceeding"), and despite the fact that, as he himself admitted, there was a dossier on him in the Holy Office labeled "Suspected of Modernism", no one expected any great cataclysm. He was, however, the individual responsible, for initiating the Revolution.[1]

He was characterized by the liberal press as a "simple peasant", a "man of the people". Robert Kaiser, the *Time* correspondent accredited to Vatican II and an intimate of John XXIII described him as "a political genius", and a "quiet and cunning revolutionary". History will bear stronger witness to this latter assessment.

His personal views were influenced by Teilhard de Chardin and the current belief of the modern world in evolution and progress. "Divine Providence", he said, "is leading us to a

---

1. Robert Blair Kaiser, *Pope, Council and World*, Macmillan, New York, 1963; Lawerence Elliott, *I will be called John*, Dutton: N.Y., 1973; M. Trevor, *Pope John*, Doubleday: N.Y., 1967. Trevor goes so far as to say that some would see John XXIII's activities as being "Machiavellian", but then tries to assure us that this was only in appearance and not actually the case.

new order of human relations, which by man's own efforts, even beyond their very expectation, are directed towards the fulfillment of God's superior and inscrutable designs . . . Everything, even human differences, leads to the greater good of the Church . . . All the discoveries of science will assist progress and help to make life on earth, which is already marked by so many other inevitable sufferings, ever more delightful." He desired to work for peace and the eventual "unity of all mankind . . . in brotherly love, under the same Father"; according to Kaiser he saw Christian unity as but the first step in this direction. He was a "humanist", and when speaking of peace, saw it as directed "to the increasing of respect for the human person and to the procuring of a just freedom of religion and worship, a peace that nourishes harmony between nations". He again speaks of religious liberty in the Encyclical *Pacem in Terris,* where he taught that every human being had a right "to worship God in accordance with the right dictates of his own conscience and to profess his religion both in private and in public". Now, if this proposition is accepted and taught by Christ's representative on earth, then it follows that the Church should not be critical of "false" forms of religion and worship. Indeed, one is even led to question if such exist. Thus it followed that one of John XXIII's close aids described his attitude in these words: "The Church is not a dam against Communism. The Church cannot and should not be against anything. It should be positively for something." The Communist weekly in Rome described his "open" attitude under the title "No more Crusades". *Il Borghese,* another Roman paper put it into better perspective: "This policy means the end of *la chiesa cattolica romana.*"

Roncalli also initiated the post-conciliar policy of frequently breaking with Papal tradition — a policy that has gone so far under the guidance of those who followed in his footsteps, that by the time John-Paul II came along, there were almost no Papal traditions left for him to break. He put aside his Papal Tiara on state occasions, had Peter's throne lowered, and instructed those around him not to use his (really Peter's) honorific titles. All these actions will of course appeal to modern man, but the problem is that John XXIII was not an ordinary man, he was allegedly Christ's representative on earth. To put such actions into clearer perspective, one might try to imagine the Queen of England divesting herself of her royal robes to disco-dance with her subjects on state occasions. Hardly a dignified scene. Finally, if any doubt remains about Roncalli's attitude towards the Church he was commissioned to preserve, and towards his predecessors to whose stance he was indefectibly tied, let me give you the response he is reported to have given a friend who asked him how he managed to follow in the footsteps of so great a man as Pius XII. "I try to imagine what my predecessor would have done, and then I do just the opposite."

John had a problem, however. These private "liberal" views could never come to fruition unless they were introduced into the fabric of the Church. The solution was a Council — John's "toy" as Cardinal Tardini called it from the start. When he first informed a gathering of Cardinals of his intention, they were speechless. "To convoke a Council", as Cardinal Pallavicini had stated many years ago, "except when absolutely by necessity, is to tempt God." John described their reaction to his "divine inspiration" as a "devout and impressive silence". Needless to say, the Curia dragged its feet. John's reaction was to insist, and in order to overcome their resistance, he led them to think that they would have control over the entire affair. Thus it was that some 800 orthodox theologians spent three years in drawing up the various schemes for discussion. Meanwhile, John established, under Cardinal Bea, the "Secretariat for Promoting Christian Unity", an organization that functioned outside the Curia's control.[2] "You will be

---

2. It is of interest to note that prior to all this John XXIII had asked several of the Cardinals to relinquish their positions as heads of Congregations in order that they might be replaced by younger men who thought more like himself. These men, imbued with the idea that their sacred duty was to preserve the deposit of the Faith, refused to comply. Xavier Rynne (Letters from Vatican City) informs us that John was as amazed as he was enraged. "They refused!" he kept repeating. "Never in my life did I think anyone would refuse the pope . . ." When they later voiced their objections more openly, he called them "Prophets of doom".

John, in turning to Marrano Bea, knew well what kind of man he was choosing. This individual had been rector of the Biblical Institute in Rome for some two decades. Prior to the death of Pope Pius XII, the Holy Office had investigated this Institute, and was planning to reorganize it entirely as it was known as a den of modernists. When the death of Pius XII made this impossible, they published the pertinent information in an article in the December edition of Divinitas. When John XXIII heard of this he was furious and told his secretary to call the new rector of the Biblical Institute

more free", as he said to Bea, "and less bound by tradition if we keep you out of the normal Curial channels." He then proceeded to use this "front" with consummate skill to subvert the Council and to undermine the forces of tradition which the Curia represented. Bea, in turn, organized the "liberal" forces, and attached to his Secretariat (always pointing out that it was established for "union", and not for the "re-union" of Christians) such individuals as Jan Willebrands, Gregory Baum, and others of similar outlook. These individuals lectured widely, were responsible for sending representatives to the World Council of Churches, for inviting the non-Catholic observers to the Council, and for a variety of similar activities.[3] Whenever the Curia objected to their machinations, John XXIII came to their defense. He had in effect established his own private Curia. In addition, he called to Rome, in a variety of other positions, ecclesiastics of similar persuasion. Thus Montini, once "banished" to Milan by Pius XII — the first individual in hundreds of years to hold this ancient See without a Cardinal's hat — returned to be, in effect, his personal assistant. Having set the stage, John patiently waited for the Council to open.

With the opening of Vatican II, he published the "rules of procedure" and invited all shades of opinion to be expressed. He established another 10-member "Council Presidency" that balanced liberal and conservative forces, to direct the activities of the conclave. He created a new Secretariat "For Extraordinary Affairs" under his trusted lieutenant Cardinal Cicognani consisting of nine progressives and one conservative, and then announced to the world his "progressive" program of *aggiornamento.* (Meanwhile, Bea's legions were in Moscow inviting the Communists to come with promises that their ideology would not be condemned at the Council). What happened at the Council will be discussed in detail later, but

and say "the pope" had complete confidence in the school's orthodoxy. Next, he forced Cardinal Pizzardo (one of the authors of the article) to write what amounted to an apology to Cardinal Bea. (*Letters from Vatican City,* Farrar Straus, New York: 1963).

3. As one theologian stated, "When those thirty or forty or fifty observers show up at the Council, they'll have a role that will be psychologically more important than the rest of the Fathers put together." While Paul Etoga, the native bishop of M'Balmayo in the Cameroons, had to "hitchhike" from Le Havre, the Protestant and Communist "observers" were royally entertained and housed at John XXIII's expense.

suffice it to say, the liberals acted to a great extent under John XXIII's direction, and with his approval. For example, before the first great victory of the "Northern Alliance", and prior to the liberal challenge that led to the rejection of the Curial nominations for the individuals that were to sit on the various commissions, as well as the rejection of the various prepared schemas, the entire plan was cleared by phone with Roncalli. John sat back and watched the affair by television, only intervening when he felt it necessary to maintain the modernist orientations he saw as necessary. As E. E. Y. Hales said, he gave the Bishops of the Council "the clearest and most positive guidance as to the way they should approach their task".[4] He clearly saw *aggiornamento* as a means "of its presentation of the truth, which will have to be brought into harmony with the modes of life and thought of a new age". And finally, as a parting gesture, he introduced the first change into the Canon of the traditional Mass in over 1,500 years, a most effective way of telling the Fathers that the Mass could be changed. His life was terminated after he gave his approval to the "Constitution on the Sacred Liturgy", and Montini was "elected" to the chair of Peter.

With Montini, who incidentally is said to have written most of his predecessor's speeches and Encyclicals, we have a much clearer picture of what Roncalli intended. The rupture with tradition becomes much more obvious and much more emphatic. It was easy to be fooled by John's seeming simplicity, but with Paul VI, an active process of self-delusion becomes necessary.

At the start (1963), Montini was involved primarily with bringing the Council to its full potential. A careful reading of Father Wiltgen's book, *The Rhine Flows into the Tiber,* as well as Archbishop Lefebvre's *J'accuse le Concile* shows that he continued John XXIII's policy of appearing neutral while strongly abetting the "progressive forces" of the innovators. He spoke much of "Ecumenical Dialogue", "Openness to the World", "Reforms", and "Changes", while at the same time speaking of "Faith", "Tradition", and "the striving for spiritual perfection". Nevertheless, even in his early days, and prior to his election, a careful study of his statements makes it

---

4. E. E. Y. Hales, *Pope John and His Revolution,* Doubleday: N.Y., 1965.

clear that change and novelty rather than tradition were given pride of place in his thoughts, and that both his acts and his words reflect a spirit that was incompatible with the true Catholic faith. With time this became more obvious. An excellent exposition of all this is given by the Abbé Georges de Nantes in his well documented *Liber Accusationis in Paulum Sextum* ("Book of Accusation against Paul VI"), a book to which the New Church has made absolutely no response.[5]

Space does not allow us to do more than give a few of Paul VI's statements, and to review but a few of his acts. No matter how much he attempted to disguise his true nature and intentions, they are sufficient to make the issues clear. And in passing, let it be noted that those who claim to be "in obedience" must be in obedience, not only to his seemingly "orthodox" statements, but also to those which are clearly heterodox. In point of fact, it is totally impossible to be "in obedience" to this self contradictory individual, for to do so is to embrace both truth and error simultaneously. Nevertheless, obedience was a favourite theme of his.

"All must obey him (the Pope) in whatever he orders if they wish to be associated with the new economy of the Gospel" (*Allocution*, June 29, 1970). And just what is the "new economy of the Gospel"? Just what are some of the teachings that Paul would foist on us in the name of the Post-conciliar Magisterium? Here is a fair sampling! "The order to which Christianity tends is not static, but an order in continual evolution towards a higher form . . ." (*Dialogues, Reflections on God and Man*); he has further stated that "we moderns, men of our own day, wish everything to be new. Our old people, the Traditionalists, the Conservatives, measured the value of things according to their enduring quality. We instead, are actualists, we want everything to be new all the time, to be expressed in a continually improvised and dynamically unusual form" (*L'Osservatore Romano*, April 22, 1971). And hence it follows, as he says, "it is necessary to know how to welcome with humility and an interior freedom what is innovative; one must break with the habitual attach-

---

5. Available from "The Catholic Counter-Reformation", 31 Wimbotsham Road, Downham Market, Norfolk PE38 9PE, England. This represents a most important document. Unfortunately, subsequently to this, the Abbé has acted in a strange and inconsistent manner, and come to some kind of "accommodation" with the New Church.

ment to what we used to designate as the unchangeable tradition of the Church . . ." (*La Croix,* Sept 4, 1970). He is critical of those who refuse to go along with the changes — they have what he calls a "sentimental attachment to habitual forms of worship", and are guilty of "inconsistency and often of falsity of doctrinal positions" (quoted in O'Leary's *The Tridentine Mass Today).*[6] As for those who find such statements heterodox, he had stated while still in Milan that "the exigencies of charity frequently force us outside the bounds of orthodoxy" (quoted by Monteilhet in *Pape Paul VI — L'Amen-Dada).*[7]

Paul VI's break with tradition, and his teaching of doctrines that are opposed to those of the Church of All Times, comes to a head in his so-called "humanism". While still Archbishop of Milan, he stated that "we must never forget that the fundamental attitude of Catholics who wish to convert the world must be, first of all, to love the world, to love our times, to love our (non-Catholic — Ed.) civilization, our technical achievements, and above all, to love the world" (Bodart's *La Biologie et l'avenir de l'homme).* This theme of "loving the world" was repeated again and again. With regard to the Council he stated: "And what was the Church doing at that particular moment? The historians will be asking; and the reply will be: the Church was filled with love . . . The Council puts before the Church, before us in particular, a panoramic vision of the world; how can the Church, how can we ourselves, do other than behold this world and love it . . . The Council is a solemn act of love for mankind . . . love for the man of today, whoever and wherever they may be, love for all . . ." (Abbé of Nantes, *op. cit.*). Now, if the world is to be indiscriminately "loved", it can hardly be criticized. Religious liberty and "freedom of conscience" must therefore be proclaimed, but not only religious liberty — one must also proclaim the "rights" of man to ignore God entirely. (We will

---

6. The attachment of traditional Catholics to their "rites", does not reflect a "sentimental attachment to habitual forms of worship", as Paul VI has said but a legitimate sentimental attachment — indeed, a nostalgia, for the "sacred". The so-called "falsity of doctrinal positions" has never been specified.

7. The idea that Charity can exist outside the bounds of "true doctrine and right belief" (as "orthodoxy" is defined) is highly absurd. Was Christ lacking in Charity? Did St. Thomas More lack sufficient charity towards his family when he refused to compromise his faith? Are we to tell lies and dissimulate rather than offend our neighbour, or the truth? Hardly.

note in passing that this love of mankind was curtailed by the decision not to criticize Communism at the Council, as it was in the new doors created by this "Pontiff" for Saint Peter's — doors which depicted slavery throughout the world, but not of course in Communist countries). Now, it is one thing for an atheist to demand such "rights", but it is quite another for a person who claims to be Christ's Vicar to proclaim them. Yet this is precisely what Paul VI did at the United Nations on October 4, 1965 — that is, before the Council itself had so proclaimed them. Speaking to this Assembly which he referred to as "the hope of the world", (for a Catholic, Christ is the "hope of the world"),[8] he stated: "It is your task here to proclaim the basic rights and duties of man, his dignity and liberty, and above all, his religious liberty. We are conscious that you are the interpreters of all that is paramount in human wisdom. (Incredible! coming from the "pope" and to the United Nations!) We would almost say: of its sacred character. For your concern is first and foremost with the life of man, and man's life is sacred: no one may dare to interfere with it." Now anyone who has read the proclamations of this Assembly knows that it asserts in its "wisdom" that man is free, and that this freedom is sacred; that nothing on earth is greater, that no God on high can impose His Rule on man's liberty, nor any man exercise authority over another, to teach or govern, to judge or even to punish him in the name of God. This is why Paul VI rescinded various excommunications and refused to pronounce further ones. This is why heresy under the guise of "pluralism" and "openness" has become rampant in his Church. (The words of Scripture are forgotten: "Put not your trust . . . in man, in whom there is no salvation" Ps. 145). This is why the need for priests to say the *Anti-Modernist Oath,* ordered by St. Pope Pius X in 1910, as well as the *Profession of Faith of the Council of Trent* introduced by

---

8. "The peoples turn to the United Nations as their last hope for peace and concord . . . Your characteristic (i.e. the UN) is to reflect in the temporal order what our Catholic Church is in the spiritual order . . . Nothing higher on the natural plane can be imagined in the ideological edifice of humanity. (The goals of the UN) are the ideal that mankind has dreamed of in its journey through history. We would venture to call it the world's greatest hope — for it is the reflection of God's design — a design transcendent and full of live — for the progress of human society on earth; a reflection in which We can see the gospel message, something from heaven come down to earth."

Pius IV and in force ever since, was eliminated during his "Pontificate".

The "confidence in man" of the Post-conciliar Church was another favourite theme of Montini. "We have faith in Man. We believe in the good which lies deep within each heart, we know that underlying man's wonderful efforts are the motives of justice, truth, renewal, progress and brotherhood — even where they are accompanied by dissension or sometimes even, unfortunately, by violence . . ." (*Address to the journalists in Sydney, Australia,* Dec. 1970).[9] Indeed, as the *L'Osservatore Romano* quotes him as saying, "There are no true riches but MAN" (August 5, 1969). "Honour to Man, honour to thought, honour to science, honour to technique, honour to work, honour to the boldness of man, honour to the synthesis of scientific and organizing ability of man who unlike other animals, knows how to give his spirit and his manual dexterity these instruments of conquest. Honour to man, king of the earth, and today Prince of heaven . . ." (*Doc. Cath.* No. 1580, January 21, 1971).[10] Now, lest there should be any doubts left about Montini's "humanism" and his CULT OF MAN, let us listen to his words addressed, not in a moment of gushing enthusiasm to some secular gathering, but to the entire assembled body of the Fathers at the Council on December 7th, 1965:

"The Conciliar Church has also, it is true, been much concerned with man, with man as he really is today, with

---

9. The Church would teach with Genesis (viii:21) that "the imagination and thought of man's heart are prone to evil". Anyone familiar with the modern business world where the "law of the sharks" prevails, must surely see this as the height of naïveté. It is of interest to quote Montini's speech in Bombay: "Mankind is undergoing profound changes and searching for guiding principles and new forces which will show it the way in the world of the future . . . We must come closer to one another, not merely through the press and radio, by boat or jet aircraft, but with our hearts, by mutual understanding, esteem and love." At no time during this talk was truth and obedience to God's laws offered as a basis of human relations. And how can a "pope" make such a statement about seeking "guiding principles" without offering those that Christ gave us — or at least those based on the "natural law"?

10. This *litany* was occasioned by the landing of the astronauts on the moon. Paul VI was greatly enamoured with science and progress. "Will not modern man gradually come as a result of scientific progress to discover the realities hidden behind the inscrutable face of matter; will he not lend

living man, with man totally taken up with himself, with man who not only makes himself the centre of his own interests, but who dares to claim that he is the end and aim of all existence . . . Secular, profane, humanism has finally revealed itself in its terrible shape and has, in a certain sense, challenged the Council. The religion of God made man has come up against the religion (for there is such a one) of man who makes himself God. And what happened? An impact, a battle, an anathema? That might have taken place, but it did not. It was the old story of the Samaritan that formed the model for the Council's spirituality. It was filled only with an endless sympathy. Its attention was taken up with the discovery of human needs — which became greater as the son of the earth (*sic*) makes himself greater . . . Do you at least recognize this its merit, you modern humanists who have no place for the transcendence of the things supreme, and come to know our new humanism: We also, we more than anyone else, have the cult of man".

We are, it would seem, to play the Good Samaritan, even to the devil! As Paul said elsewhere, "Man is both giant and divine, in his origin and his destiny. Honour therefore to man, honour to his dignity, to his spirit, and to his life." How often Montini breaks forth in the form of a Litany to praise his idol. And how easy to forget that Christ once said to Peter, *"Get thee behind me Satan, thou art a scandal to me: for thou dost not mind the things of God, but those of men"*. (Matt. xvi:23).[11]

---

an ear to the marvellous voice of the Spirit that vibrates in matter? Will not this be the religion of today? Did not Einstein himself catch a glimpse of the religion of the universe spontaneously . . .? And is not (scientific) labour itself already engaged in a course that will eventually lead to religion?" (*Doc. Cath.* 133, 1960).

11. Admittedly these are selected quotes. One can quote Paul VI on both sides of almost any issue — and further, he is a master of equivocation and ambiguity. We have already cited the example of where he congratulated the French hierarchy for its rejecting of his orthodox teaching in the Encyclical *Humanae Vitae*. Another case in point is his appointing Cardinal Samore to be "Prefect of the Sacred Congregation for Discipline in Sacramental Matters" two months after this Cardinal had distributed Communion to a motley of Protestants — with full awareness on his part that they did not believe in the "Real Presence". This fact received a great

And what are some of the actions of the "Pope" wherein he puts into practice what he preaches? He is personally responsible for the promulgation of the Documents of Vatican II, in which the teachings of the "New Economy of the Gospel" are, at least in broad form, outlined. As he said, "from the start, the Council has propagated a wave of serenity and optimism, a Christianity that is exciting and positive, loving life, mankind and earthly values . . . an intention of making Christianity acceptable and lovable, indulgent and open, free of mediaeval rigorism and of the pessimistic understanding of man and his customs . . ." (*Doc. Cath.* No. 1538). He is also responsible for the promulgation of the *Novus Ordo Missae* and the various other Post-conciliar sacraments of dubious validity. But even beyond this, he has taken an extraordinary lead in breaking with Papal traditions. One of his first acts was to give up the Papal Tiara, symbolic of giving up the rights of Christ's representative to have precedence over the Kings and Princes of this world. He was crowned with a tiara of his own design (looking like a space rocket), and not in Saint Peter's, but outside the sacred precincts. While spending a fortune on some of the most trivial and ugly modern art known to mankind, he made a great show of selling this Tiara and giving the money to the poor. He then proceeded to give his Shepherd's Crook and Fisherman's Ring *(his?)* to U Thant (Is there perhaps something symbolic in this? U. Thant was head of the United Nations.), again to be sold for the poor, and began to carry what must be one of the world's ugliest crucifixes in its place. (Normally, a crucifix is carried in front of a Pope to remind him constantly of who he really is.) He then proceeded to ask the various Bishops of the world to give up their traditional rings, and gave each of them a new gold ring symbolic of the Post-conciliar Church. And what about the expense of these new rings? Could not that money have been given to the poor? (It was his "new" ring that he placed on the finger of Archbishop Ramsey, head of the Anglican Church — a Church Paul VI calls a "sister Church" — when he asked this heretic to bless the Catholic faithful in St. Peter's Square.)

---

deal of publicity in the French press, so much, in fact that Paul VI was led to deplore "the acts of intercommunion that went against the proper ecumenical guidelines" (Doc. Cath. 68-141). In such a manner are the perpetrators of sacrilege rewarded. Truly, as someone has said, "pale faith speaks with forked tongue!"

However, Montini reaches the apogee of scandalous example with his visit to Fátima. Here we see a Pope who spent time "meditating" in the "meditation room" at the United Nations, a room replete with Freemasonic significance and containing an altar dedicated to "the faceless God"; here we see a man who received with respect the members of the B'nai B'rith at the Vatican;[12] here we see a man who has promised to pray for the success of Mrs. Hollister and her "Temple of Understanding" (which according to Cardinal Bagnozzi's comments to Paul VI, is "an occult enterprise of the Illuminati whose aim is the founding of 'the World Religion of Human Brotherhood'); here we see a man who has taken part in "the Ecumenical Celebration of the Town Hall in Sydney, Australia" (*Doc. Cath.* Jan. 17, 1971); here we see a man who has joined with Cardinal Willebrands in "the common prayer at the World Council of Churches" (*ibid,* June 10, 1969); here we see the man who claims to be the head of the Catholic Church, Christ's representative on earth, finally visiting one of the most sacred shrines in Christendom. And what does he do? With the whole world watching on television, he says mass in Portuguese (an act offensive to many of the traditional Catholics of this country and in a language that but a small percentage of those watching could understand), and then proceeds to give a series of audiences including one to the "representatives of the non-Catholic Communities". Not one Hail Mary did he say! He made no visit to the shrine at the Cova de Iria where the apparitions took place. According to the Abbé de Nantes, he even refused to talk privately with Sister Lucia, fifty years a nun, and one of the Children of Fátima, who claimed to have a private message from the Virgin for his ears.

Much more could be said about this enigmatic individual, about his communist leanings, about his dastardly treatment of Cardinal Mindszenty, one of the most heroic and saintly figures of the 20th century (broken promises and lies), about

---

12. The B'nai B'rith is held by many to be the Freemasonic order of Judaism. In passing, let us listen to a representative of traditional Judaism. High Rabbi Kaplan of Paris recently said "If I had been a Catholic, I would have been an 'integriste' (traditional Catholic). If Judaism is alive and authentic in this day, it is because her ministers have never raised doubts about her real nature. We have but one disagreement with the (post-conciliar) Bishops — but it is a most important one. While they are trying to *adapt their religion to man,* we put forth all our efforts to *adapt man to religion".* The Imam of the Mosque in Paris has gone so far as to invite Catholics who are seeking an *unchanging* religion, to embrace Islam!

his doing nothing to support the struggles of five million Ukranian Catholics[13] in their struggle for the faith, about his allowing and fostering the spread of heresy within the Church, about his refusal to condemn the Dutch Catechism, but space does not allow. I leave you then with Paul VI, the individual most responsible for what he himself terms, the "auto-destruction of the Church". Far more an "Iago" than a "Hamlet".

We shall pass over the subsequent "popes" quickly. John-Paul I was known to be a liberal and a favourite of Cardinal "innovator" Benelli. He had obtained his Doctorate in Theology by defending Serbati Rosmini (1797-1855), a man who had 40 propositions from his writing condemned by the Holy Office in 1887. He was an ardent feminist as is shown by his letters to playwright Carlo Goldini in his now famous book entitled *Humbly Yours*. He was prone to making surprising theological statements, such as one that would appeal to theologian Rosemary Reuther (teacher at a Jesuit University and an ardent proponent of the theory that God is a woman!): "God is our Father — even more, God is our Mother". He refused to be crowned as Pope and was "invested" as "Bishop of Rome" (a title recognized by the Anglicans of Reformation time, who by referring to the pope under this "title" wished to proscribe his other sacred functions, and place him on the same level as the "Bishop of London"[14]). He planned to melt

---

13. Paul VI is not known to have criticized the slavery imposed by Russia on its citizens — yet he took almost every opportunity to call attention to abuses of human rights in the Western nations. Perhaps one of his most offensive statements to those who are aware of the some 30 million Chinese "liquidated" by Mao-Tse Tung, is the following. "The Church recognizes and favours the just expression of the historical phase of China and the transformation of ancient forms of esthetic culture into the inevitable new forms that rise out of the social and industrial structure of the modern world . . . We would like to enter into contact once again with China in order to show with how much interest and sympathy we look on at their present and enthusiastic efforts for the ideals of a diligent, full, and peaceful life." (Congregation For the Evangelization of the Peoples (formerly *De Propaganda Fide*), 1976). One is reminded of Father Barry's (Fordham University) teaching the faithful that Mao Tse-Tung's famous trek across China is an exact parallel to Moses' leading his people out of Egypt!

14. Both John-Paul I and John-Paul II were shown on television as being "invested" with the "pallium". Now, according to Rev. L. O'Connell *(The Book of Ceremonies*, Bruce: Milwaukee, 1956), the pallium is "a wide circular band of white wool with a pendant attached to the front and back,

the Tiara down and sell it for the poor. Of course, as a historical monument and work of art, this "crown" would have fetched much more on the art market — but then, a subsequent Pope might have bought it back. He left us rather suddenly under circumstances that are hardly clear.

John-Paul II, the present "pontiff," provides us with little hope for change. He is by no means an "unknown" that arrived on the scene unexpectedly, for he has moved in Vatican circles since the time of the Council. It was Bishop Garonne of Toulouse, later Cardinal, and the chief inquisitor of Archbishop Lefebvre, that recommended this young Polish prelate to the Vatican just as preparations for the Council were getting under way. Bishop Wojtyla proceeded to bring his "personalist" and existentialist ideas, what has been described as his "Heidegger-Husserl-Scheler concepts," to the key conciliar document entitled *Guadium et Spes*. Contacts established at this time led to his rapid rise in the hierarchy. In 1964 he was made Metropolitan of Krakow, and in 1967 Paul VI made him a Cardinal and bestowed upon him the Pallium. He was one of the three European Bishops appointed as permanent members to the Vatican's Episcopal Synod, the "collegiate" organ established after Vatican II. Finally, according to *Time* magazine, it was Cardinal Benelli, whose anti-traditional stand is well known, that engineered his election to the chair of Peter. With such a background, it is little wonder that he chose as his name, "John-Paul," or that, like his predecessor, he refused to be crowned with the Tiara. [15]

---

and with six black crosses stitched on it . . . Symbolic of the plentitude of the Episcopal power, the pallium is worn by the Pope at all times. It is worn by archbishops also as a mark of their participation in the Pope's supreme pastoral office . . . It is a mere honorary dignity". It is even occasionally conferred upon Bishops. As such, it denotes no function beyond that of being "Bishop of Rome".

15. While it is true that a (valid) pope is pope from the moment he is elected and accepts, it is of interest to know the words of the traditional ceremony: "Receive the Tiara of three crowns, knowing you are the father of princes and kings, the guide of the faithful and the Vicar of Christ on earth." Instead these words were used: "Be blessed by God who has chosen you as supreme pastor of the whole Church, confiding in you the apostolic ministry. May you shine gloriously during many years of life until called by your Lord to be covered with immortality at the entrance of the heavenly kingdom."

Instead, he was once again invested as "Bishop of Rome" with the Pallium, and proceeded to address the faithful, not as his "children," but as his "brothers and sisters." (All this refusal to be crowned at a time when the Communist government of Hungary was so anxious to have the crown returned to its country to give its illegal government some vestige of legitimacy!).

Despite his seeming turn to "orthodoxy" with the condemning of Hans Küng ("He is not a Catholic Theologian."),[16] Edward Schillebeeckx and the Dutch Hiearachy, one thing is quite clear — he intends no departure from the principles established by his three predecessors and the Second Vatican Council. Thus, in his first encyclical, *Redemptor Hominis,* he makes it quite clear that the "inheritance" which he accepts in coming to the chair of Peter is that "unique inheritance left to the Church by Popes John XXIII and Paul VI." It is this "inheritance" which Wojtyla intends to "develop." They are the "threshold from which he intends to continue, in a certain sense, together with John-Paul I, into the future." He speaks of their "profound wisdom," and their "constancy and courage" on many and diverse occasions. As *The New York Times* commented in reviewing this text, his stand "on key issues . . . is little different from that of his predecessor, Pope Paul VI." (March 16, 1979). Moreover, John-Paul II extends this "inheritance" to include the dubious pronouncements of Vatican II — "this inheritance has struck deep roots in the awareness of the Church in an utterly new way, quite unknown previously, thanks to the Second Vatican Council . . . The ways on which the council of the century has

---

16. Hans Küng has denied the divinity of Christ, the Virgin Birth, the indefectibility of the Church, and the infallibility of the pope. The penalty he has incurred for his apostasy from the faith was the repudiation of his status as a "Catholic theologian," and an attempt to have him removed from the university faculty at Tübingen. The censure does not denounce him for heresy, and does not declare him to be excommunicated, suspended or under interdict. Thus, Hans Küng remains a "priest in good standing" in the Conciliar Church. This is, canonically speaking, but a slap on the wrist compared to the "suspension" of Archbishop Lefebvre.

set the Church going, ways indicated by the late Paul VI in his first encyclical, will continue to be for a long time the ways that all of us must follow . . . through the Church's consciousness, which the council considerably developed . . ."

This veneration for his post-conciliar predecessors reaches its apogee in the General Audience which he gave on the anniversary of Montini's death. He calls him the "pope of Vatican II," and suggests that his death on the feast of the Transfiguration was evidence of God's approbation of his life and actions. He describes him as "the pope of that deep change which was nothing but a revelation of the face of the Church, awaited by the man and the world of today!" Is not such a statement an admission of "ongoing revelation," to say nothing of being an accusation against the Holy Spirit of having been somewhat tardy in revealing the true face of the Bride of Christ? John-Paul then goes on to describe a new "charism," one previously absent throughout the entire history of the Church! "The charism of transformation!" Here are his words: "The Lord, having called Pope Paul to Himself on the solemnity of this (feast of the) Transfiguration, permitted him, and us to know that in the whole work of transformation, of renewal of the Church in the spirit of Vatican II, He is present, as He was in the marvellous event which took place on Mount Tabor . . . John XXIII and after him, Paul VI, received from the Holy Spirit the charism of transformation." Not once, at least to date, has Wojtyla voiced any criticism of Paul VI, or any determination to undo those transformations which Montini was responsible for. What then of his "orthodox" stand that has so endeared him to conservative Catholics? For one thing, it is little stressed that the condemnation (if such it can be called) of Hans Küng and Schillebeeckx was the culmination of a process initiated by his predecessors. As Mary Martinez, an accredited reporter to the Vatican has noted, "Already during the 1977 Synod (on 'catechesis') there were indications that certain of the most influential bishops were aware of the fact that the rythm of Conciliar change would have to slow down. In addition to the visible laceration that traditionalists represented, there was the alarming increase in defectors, people who were simply bored with the new rites and were quietly walking away. If, as several major Synod interventions indicated, there was an awareness that things had gone too far too fast, then conservative gestures on the part

of whoever would become pope could have been expected."
What is expected of a true pontiff is that he should be
orthodox in all things, both doctrines and rites. With regard to
doctrine, anyone who accepts the evolutionary basis on which
much of Vatican II is based, anyone who accepts *communicatio in sacris* and seeks "full communion" with other
Christians, (Billy Graham, the evangelist, has spoken to the
faithful at St. Ann's Church in Cracow at Wojtyla's invitation),
anyone who upholds the false concepts of religious liberty and
freedom of conscience that Vatican II proclaims, and anyone
who believes in ongoing revelation and the manifestations of
new charisms, by definition departs from the constant teaching
of the Church. As St. Thomas Aquinas states:

> "To reject but one article of faith taught by the Church is
> enough to destroy faith, as one mortal sin is enough to
> destroy charity; for the virtue of faith does not consist in
> merely adhering to the Holy Scriptures, and in revering
> them as the Word of God; it consists principally in sub-
> mitting our intellect and will to the divine authority of the
> true Church charged by Jesus Christ to expound them."

Despite his desire to see nuns back in their habits and despite
his support of priestly celibacy and of Paul VI's encyclical on
birth control, John-Paul II hardly fulfills the criteria for
orthodoxy in matters of faith. Indeed, let us for a moment
consider just how he defines this key concept. In a statement,
not made before a social gathering of laymen, but to a group of
theologians meeting in Rome he said:

> "To enter into dialogue with God means to allow oneself
> to be won over and conquered by the luminous figure of
> the Revealed Jesus, and by the love of the Father who sent
> him. *It is in precisely this that the faith consists.* In faith,
> man interiorly enlightened and attracted by God, goes
> beyond the limits of purely natural knowledge, and
> *experiences* God in a manner that would otherwise be
> impossible."

Despite the fine phraseology, no modernist, indeed no
Protestant, no Seventh Day Adventist and no Mormon would
have any difficulty in assenting to such a statement. Nor is this

an isolated quote. Consider the following proclaimed before the Bishops of Venezuela on Dec. 17, 1979:

> "This is the final aim of all catechesis: the vital, conscious and personal meeting with the Christ of faith, the Christ of history, the one Redeemer and hope of man . . . I encourage you to continue and redouble your efforts in a field so vital for the Church, since it is only with systemic catechetical work, in depth, that your Christian communities will be able to arrive at complete *experience* of the message of salvation and at bearing witness personally and collectively to the deep reasons of their hope in Christ."

It is well known that Wojtyla is a world-renowned "phenomenologist," described by *The New York Times* as "a technique for discovering what is hidden in appearances by looking at the world through the eyes of an infant . . . the search for essences that cannot be revealed by ordinary observation." George Williams, a Unitarian Divinity professor at Harvard University who has known the present "pope" for some sixteen years, describes this philosophical system as being derived "from the Bohemian-born Jew, Edward Husserl (1859-1938)," and notes that it "has led to such recent permutations as the hermeneutic phenomenology of Martin Heidegger and Jean-Paul Sartre." It is pertinent to note in passing that it is Heidegger who specifically dethrones the intellect and puts in its place *experience*. Now, the present Pontiff, as Williams tells us, "thought it would be possible to use the methodology of one phenomenologist, Max Scheler, as a starting point for rebuilding a Christian ethic." (Why do we have to rebuild it?) Let us also note that Scheler, born a Jew, became a convert and then went on to leave the Church. This effort resulted in Wojtyla's Doctoral thesis entitled "The Possibilities for Building a System of Christian Ethics on the Basis of Max Scheler," written at the Marxist-controlled Jagiellonian University in Poland. Anna Tymieniecka, who has translated the Pope's book *The Acting Person* into English, and who is his personal friend, summarizes his "complex thought" in the following terms. "He stresses the irreducible value of the human person. He finds a spiritual dimension in human interaction, and that leads him to a profoundly humanistic conception of society" (*Time*, Oct. 30, 1978). It is of interest that Wojtyla has encouraged the publishing of all his works but one — his doctoral thesis in theology written under the direction of the saintly and orthodox Garrigou-Lagrange. This has been "locked up" in the Vatican archives as "no longer reflecting his current views."[17] It is not surprising then to find Wojtyla welcomed among what George Williams calls "a circle of philosophers of various thrusts who are collectively called phenomenologists." Among his other friends, one must include Karl Rahner, who as Philip Trower states, "has done for existentialism what Teilhard de Chardin did for evolutionism." This same Karl Rahner, the darling of modernist Catholic intellectuals and probably the most influential theologian in the new church, was condemned by Pius XII, rehabilitated by Paul VI and is a personal friend of John-Paul II. He has been a private guest of the present pontiff at the Vatican on more than one occasion. Another of Wojtyla's intellectual heroes is Teilhard de Chardin. In his Retreats given at the Vatican under Paul VI *("The Sign of Contradiction")* he respectfully compares the insights in Genesis to those of this dubious "philosopher." If some of this seems at variance with what we would expect from one who sits on Peter's throne, let us remember that, as he told the Polish faithful on the Feast of Corpus Christi in 1978, he "respects all ideologies."

One may be permitted to question the "heroic" role in which Wojtyla is cast during his student days. He is pictured to us as a university student who worked after class in a chemical plant (all Polish chemical plants were geared to help the German war effort), and who still found the energy to spend long evenings rehearsing and performing leading rolls in a quasi-professional theatrical company. *Time* and the *National Review* have even gone so far as to suggest that he was also involved in underground activities reminiscent of James Bond for which he was wanted by the authorities. What seems more in keeping with reality is that this individual who proclaimed that he "respected all ideologies," managed to get along with the communist authorities quite well. How else would it have been possible for him to travel freely all over the world, publishing books and lecturing at international philosophical congresses,

---

17. This has subsequently been published by Ignatius Press under the title *Faith According to St. John of the Cross.*

while ten per cent of the clergy in Poland (mostly those who refused to say the new "mass") were being imprisoned or exiled. Anyone familiar with the methodology of communist tyranny knows that his freedom to travel throughout the world, to say nothing of his being allowed to exist at home, is entirely dependent upon his being in the graces of those in authority, or at least, on their seeing him as "useful" to their purposes. Certainly, he was no Mindszenty! And indeed, Mary Craig, in her biography *(Man From a Far Country)* tells us that when he worked as a parish priest in Poland, he kept a "low profile . . . steering clear of politics (even to mention 'good' and 'evil' could bring down the wrath of the authorities . . .)." Clearly he is a believer in *detente,* and when he was installed as "Bishop of Rome", Polish government officials, beginning with the ambassador to Italy, were glowing in their praise of him and the minister of state, Jablonski, came to Rome with a large entourage. Apart from his granting a long audience to Gromyko, one of his first acts was to appoint Cardinal Agostino Casaroli, the architect of *Ostopolitik* as his Pro-Secretary of State. It is of course true that Wojtyla has criticised communist methodology. What is striking however is that on no occasion has he ever criticized Communism as such. Indeed, most of his statements would indicate that he is perfectly at home with socialist ideology and would only seek to temper communist theory with — to use a phrase of Teilhard de Chardin — "the warmth of Christian love."

This ambiguity towards communist ideology is best demonstrated during his tour of Mexico. Prior to the opening of the Episcopal Conference in Puebla, he met with Alvarez Icaza in a private audience. This individual, who probably had known Wojtyla since the time of the Council, was a member of the Prague-based communist-sponsored Christians for Peace Congress, the president of which was the infamous Nikodim, Metropolitan of Leningrad.[18] He along with IDOC member Gary MacEoin was responsible for setting up the flourishing left-wing press bureau CENCOS which provided Marxist-line literature and two liberation theology press conferences daily throughout the period. Despite John-Paul's criticism of

---

18. When Nikodim died in the arms of the pontiff, the two Russian Orthodox Churches in Rome refused to allow him to be waked on their premises. Needless to say, this privilege was granted him by the post-conciliar Church, and he was waked within the Vatican.

"liberation theology" (which is nothing but communism disguised under a veneer of Christian phraseology), such criticism is almost always accompanied by a parallel condemnation of the excesses of capitalism. When he was in Oaxaca he went so far as to state there must be no hesitation when it comes to the expropriation of private property, "correctly carried out" providing it is for the common good. But nowhere does he say who is to decide what is for the common good, or what "correctly carried out" means. And even more important, nowhere does he point us back to the Encyclicals of Leo XIII and the teachings of the traditional church on sociology and economics — wherein are to be found the answers to all the false panaceas that plague the modern world. What resulted from the Puebla conference in Mexico is that both sides claimed a victory, and the forces of subversion were enabled to continue their activities throughout this essentially Catholic sub-continent. The communists would certainly prefer to have no religious problems to deal with. But Catholicism is a fact, both in Poland and in South America. Such being the case, Pope John-Paul II is certainly to be prefered to a Pius XII.[19]

Finally, it is quite obvious that the most pressing matter in the current Catholic scene pertains to the issue of the sacraments, and above all, the banning of the traditional Mass. More than sufficient time has passed for him to have given us some indication of his intentions with regard to this problem. Granted this would require not only the approval of the Mass of All Times, but also the re-ordination of all the clergy "raised to the table" since the middle of 1968; but such is by no means an impossibility. Nothing short of this can return the church to "unity," and nothing short of this can satisfy the traditional Catholic. John-Paul II, despite his condemnation of those who, to use the words of Cranmer, "would run ahead too fast," has given us no indication that he will satisfy this requirement, and indeed, he has made it abundantly clear that he is committed to the "reforms" of Vatican II. Should we have any doubts about this, they are removed by his statement to the traditional Catholics of Mexico:

---

19. This material and much more is documented in Mary Martinez's *From Rome Urgently,* (Via Sommacompagna 47, Rome 00185).

"Those who remain attached to incidental aspects of the Church, aspects which were valid in the past, but which have been superseded, cannot be considered the faithful."

Here we hear, not the voice of Peter, but the voice of Paul VI. Since when are the Mass and Sacraments "incidental aspects of the Church"? And why are some Catholics still attached to them? The answer is quite clear. We have not received the "charism of transformation." We have not been "blessed" with "the renewal of the Church in the spirit of Vatican II." And the price he tells us we must pay is that we "cannot be considered the faithful." We may not be faithful to Wojtyla's post-conciliar church, but this church is no longer "The Church of All Times," the Church that Christ established.

*   *   *

It should be quite clear to the reader that in "attacking" the strange antics of the Post-conciliar "popes," one is in no way intending to attack the papacy itself. On the contrary, it is the papacy which we would defend. The distinction between Sedes and Sedens (the Seat, and he who is sitting in it) was made, following Justinian, at the Council of Chalcedon in 451. There is a doctrine of "indefectibility" in the church which states that the teachings of our Holy Mother do not change. Anyone who desires to be "in obedience" to some two hundred and sixty popes that legitimately held the chair of Peter since it was established, and to the many encyclicals that they promulgated, must of necessity declare himself to be "in disobedience" to these latter-day modernists wherever they depart from their predecessors' teachings. Finally, a comment is in order as to what would satisfy the traditional Catholic. The answer is quite simple, and though it has been alluded to previously, it must be once again reiterated. It is a return to sound doctrine and true belief — the affirmation of the entire "depositum" of the Faith; and the re-introduction of the true and proper liturgy of the church. Apart from this, all else is dissimulation and talk. Pray God that we may see such a day before we die.

PART IV

VATICAN II

Before considering Vatican II in detail, it is necessary to understand just what an Ecumenical or General Council is. It is, as Hubert Jedin defined it in 1960:

> "An assembly of Bishops and other specified persons invested with jurisdiction, convoked by the Pope and presided over by him, for the purpose of formulating decisions on questions of Christian faith, or ecclesiastical discipline. These decisions, however, require papal confirmation . . . It has always been the highest duty of a council to assure the proclamation of the faith by delimiting the Catholic doctrine from contemporary errors. There have been councils which issued no disciplinary canons, but none at which some error was not rejected."[1]

Vatican II as an ecumenical council was unusual in several ways. It was the first "ecumenical" council that invited "observers" to participate in its proceedings.[2] It was the first such council to be declared "pastoral" and not "dogmatic".[3]

---

1. Hubert Jedin, Ecumenical Councils of the Catholic Church, Herder: N.Y., 1960.
2. The presence of "observers" from the various Protestant sects, even if not preventing the Fathers from speaking out forcefully on issues that might offend, certainly must have been inhibiting. This may have been very significant with regard to the presence of Russian Orthodox Observers (from Moscow) who only came with the understanding that Communism would not be criticized — a fact reported by various authors.
3. Every time orthodox fathers wished to define more clearly what was being ambiguously stated, they were informed that the Council was "pastoral" and not "dogmatic". (c.f. Arch. Lefèbvre's "J'accuse le Concile")

It was the first such council that neither delimited Catholic doctrine from contemporary errors, nor issued disciplinary canons.[4] It was the first such council that clearly departed from the teaching of previous ecumenical councils — so much so that Cardinal Suenens has stated that it was like the French Revolution in the Church, and theologian Y. Congar likened it to the October (1917) Revolution in Russia.[5] Finally, in closing the Council, Paul VI stated: "The teaching authority of the Church, even though not wishing to issue extraordinary dogmatic pronouncements, has made thoroughly known its authoritative teaching . . . All that has been established synodally (by Vatican II) is to be religiously observed by all the faithful." In so putting it, he removes the contents of the documents from the realm of *de fide* doctrine, and yet at the same time "binds" the Catholic by obedience to acceptance.

As to the documents themselves, there are sixteen of these, and all sixteen are considered to be "established synodally" — that it to say, agreed upon by the Fathers present at the Council. Now, these sixteen documents are entitled as "Constitutions", "Decrees" and "Declarations". Despite the fact that some of the "Constitutions" are qualified as being "dogmatic", Vatican II as a whole is by decree "Pastoral". Being Pastoral, it is "non-dogmatic" and is at most a kind of instruction, a sort of sermon, which of itself does not involve infallibility. Hence it is that Cardinal Felici, former secretary for the Curia and Secretary-General of the Council stated that the documents of the Council are *de jure,* and not *de fide.*[6] Despite this, Paul VI has on several occasions referred to this Council as "the greatest of all Councils", even greater than the Council of Trent (which is of course *de fide*). He is however by no means satisfied with what the Council achieved, for he states "the conciliar decrees are not so much a destination as a point of departure towards new goals . . . The seeds of life planted by the Council in the soil of the Church

---

4. Requests by hundreds of the Council Fathers for the condemnation of Communism were sidetracked by those in control as Father Wiltgen points out.

5. In a similar manner, Santiago Carrillo (the head of the Spanish Communist Party) has called, "Euro-communism" "our Aggiornamento, our Vatican II". (*Itineraires,* May 1977).

6. Quoted by D. Von Hilderbrand, *"Belief and Obedience: the Critical Difference", Triumph,* March 1970.

must grow and achieve full maturity." As Cardinal Suenens has said, "Vatican II is a stage, and not a terminus." Yet, even as a "stage", it represented "a French Revolution within the Church".

Few will deny that the "new directions" that the Post-conciliar Church has taken find their roots in this Council. As Avery Dulles says,

> "Vatican II adopted a number of positions which had been enunciated by the Reformation Churches, e.g. the primacy of Scripture, the supernatural efficacy of the preached word, the priesthood of the laity, and the vernacular liturgy."[7]

Nor is this an isolated opinion. Cardinal Willebrands, Paul VI's legate to the World Lutheran Assembly at Evian stated in July 1970:

> "Has not the Second Vatican Council itself welcomed certain demands which, among others, were expressed by Luther, and through which many aspects of the Christian faith are better expressed today than formerly? Luther gave his age a quite extraordinary lead in theology and the Christian life."

To quote Cardinal Suenens again:

> "It is possible to draw up an impressive list of theses which Rome has taught in the past and up until yesterday as being the only valid ones, and which the Council Fathers have thrown out."

One must ask how it was that in an "unchanging Church", such drastic changes could come about. There are of course many who claim that such statements are exaggerated; that there have been no significant changes, and that it is not Vatican II, but the modern theologians with their "abuses", that are to blame. It is said by these that the statements of the

---

7. Rev. Ralph M. Wiltgen, *The Rhine flows into the Tiber,* Hawthorn: New York, 1967, recently republished in paperback by the Augustine Publishing Co., Devon, England, 1978.

Council are misinterpreted and many fine and orthodox statements from the documents are brought to bear in defense of this contention. The answer to both these issues is however not difficult. Father Wiltgen who was "international publicity director in Rome" for the Council and who "founded during Vatican II an independent and multilingual Council News Service", has written a history of the proceedings entitled *The Rhinè flows into the Tiber*. Inasmuch as he approves of what the Council achieved, his text has become a valuable source of information. His information moreover is confirmed by numerous other sources. We have as a result, a "play by play" description of how the "liberal" theologians captured the Council. What was proclaimed by the world press as a "spontaneous outbreak of liberal sentiment", was in fact, as several authors have pointed out, part of a pre-determined plan to subvert the Council.

We have already called attention to the role that John XXIII played in setting the stage. Most of the Fathers were not well read theologians, and came "psychologically unprepared" (Cardinal Heenan) and "feeling their way" (Bishop Lucey). Other "hierarchies came to the Council knowing what they wanted and having prepared a way to get it" (Bishop Lucey). The takeover was surprisingly easy. As Cardinal Heenan stated, "the First General Congregation had scarcely begun when the northern bishops went into action." As Brian Kaiser states, "Cardinals Suenens, Alfrink, Frings, Doepfner, Köenig, Lienart and Bea conferred by phone" the night before, and received assurances from the Pope that their plans had his approval. Within fifteen minutes of the opening of the first session, the years of preparatory work and the suggested list of individuals for the various commissions were thrown out. This has been called by several "The First Victory" of the "European Alliance", and was characterized in newspapers as "Bishops in Revolt".[8] What followed has been described as a *Blitzkrieg* (Michael Davies) and a

---

8. As E. E. Y. Hales says: "On the face of it Pope John was allowing the Council to take shape in a way that seemed certain not to produce the *aggiornamento* of the Church which he wanted. One explanation of this paradox is that he was subtly allowing the Curia to think that it was going to be *their* Council, so as to ensure that they would not try to thwart it, while he himself knew very well that once it met, it would cease to be theirs, that he (and it) would take over from the Curia." (Pope John and His Revolution, Doubleday: N.Y., 1965).

"demolition exercise" (Henri Fesquet). It was only a matter of time and manœuvre before the liberal element took over the ten commissions that controlled the various schemas presented for voting. The "Council Presidency" established by Roncalli was helpless — and this was as he intended. Instead of intervening on the side of "tradition", he allowed things to proceed exactly as he wished, only intervening when it was necessary to support the "democratic forces".

Initially, any individual Father could rise to voice objection to the statements of the various schemas. Soon this was limited to ten minutes. As opposition gathered to the modernist clique, those in control required that five Fathers had to agree and speak in conjunction. Before long the number was raised to 70. Soon all objections had to be submitted in writing to the various commissions which in turn allowed for considerable behind-the-scenes machinations and the suppression or "re-wording" of those objections that could not be ignored. A petition signed by over 400 Fathers asking for the condemnation of communism was simply and conveniently lost. Complaints made directly to the Pope were ignored,[9] and on occasion the Pope directly intervened to force through a given vote. Both the press and the various liberal organizations within and without the Church carried on heavy propaganda in favour of the "liberalizing" of the Church. Cardinal Frings and Liniert and the members of the "Northern Alliance" were the "heroes", while Ottaviani and the conservative members of the Curia were the "villains" standing "in the way of progress". The majority of the Fathers present were Church dignitaries rather than theologians, and hence were heavily dependent upon the "periti" or experts who almost invariably were in the "neo-modernist" camp. A list of these "periti" would include almost all the well known heretical theologians of the Post-conciliar Church. Adequate time was frequently not given for proper discussion of the issues, and many of the Fathers admitted to having voted along with the majority without having read the schemas or amendments in question at all. As Dr. Moorman, leader of the Anglican delegation has stated, "there was a very real division among

9. Archbishop Lefèbvre's *J'accuse le concile* documents a letter sent to Paul VI signed by several Cardinals, and Superior Generals of Religious Organizations, and the manner in which he dismissed their contentions.

the fathers, a deep feeling that two big forces were coming to grips and that this was not just a clash of opinions, but of policies and even of moralities". But, as we have pointed out, the traditional forces were "psychologically unprepared", and the liberal forces "came to the Council knowing what they wanted and having prepared a way to get it". Things were pushed along very rapidly, and it was only towards the end of the Council that the orthodox Fathers were able to get organized, but by the time the *Coetus Internationalis Patrum* became a cohesive force, it was far too late.

Only one major problem remained. The liberals in the Council had to express their views in a manner that was not clearly and overtly heretical. (This would have created much stronger opposition and resistance.) The solution was the ambiguous statement. Whenever protests were raised against such tactics, the objector was informed that the Council was "pastoral", and not "dogmatic". What resulted has been described in Archbishop Lefebvre's words as "a conglomeration of ambiguities, inexactitudes, vaguely expressed feelings, terms susceptible of any interpretation and an opening wide of all doors". There are of course many statements in the documents that appear good, for it is characteristic of heresy that it comes cloaked in the garb of orthodoxy. The documents themselves are prolix, full of vague phraseology and psychologisms. Terms are frequently used (such as "salvation history"[10]) that are capable of being defined in a variety of ways. Statements made in one paragraph are qualified several paragraphs later so that multiple interpretations become possible. In fairness to the liberals, some of the "periti" such as Yves Congar and Schillebeeckx disapproved of such methods and wished to state the liberal viewpoint openly and clearly. They were of course, overruled. Lest the reader feel this opinion is unjust, I shall quote Professor O. Cullmann, one of the most distinguished Protestant observers at the Council:

---

10. "Salvation History", one of the favourite phrases of the innovators, and one clearly implying that Salvation is a historical process, is particularly offensive. Salvation is an "individual" process. Further, in accord with the Gospel story of the eleventh-hour labourer, salvation today is no different than it was in the days of Abraham.

"The definitive texts are for the most part compromise texts. On far too many occasions they juxtapose opposing viewpoints without establishing any genuine internal link between them. Thus every affirmation of the power of bishops is accompanied in a manner which is almost tedious by the insistence upon the authority of the Pope ! . . This is the reason why, even while accepting that these are compromise-texts, I do not share the pessimism of those who subscribe to the slogan that: 'Nothing will come out of the Council!' All the texts are formulated in such a manner that no door is closed and that they will not present any future obstacle to dis-cussions among Catholics or dialogue with non-Catholics, as was the case with the dogmatic decisions of previous councils."

It is then the ambiguity of most of the statements that allows for any interpretation one wishes. Those who would subscribe to the most liberal and extreme theses of modernism can do so on the basis of Vatican II, while those who are inclined towards orthodoxy can quote passage after passage to show that the Council "changed nothing". As Michael Davies says of the Dogmatic Constitution on the Church, it "contains a great deal of traditional and orthodox Catholic terminology well calculated to inspire confidence. Such confidence is likely to be weakened, however, when it is realized how pleasing the document is both to Catholic 'ecumeniacs' as well as to Protestants. If the document is as sound as it appears then why do those who reject Catholic teaching praise it?" And how could it be otherwise when, as Cardinal Heenan says, the various commissions were in a position to "wear down opposition and produce a formula patent of both an orthodox and modernistic interpretation". What resulted, to use the words of Bishop McVinney in discussing the Pastoral Constitution on the Church, was a doubtful compromise with everything which lies at the basis of the evils now affecting humanity".[11]

---

11. Ambiguity is always the refuge of the scoundrel who wishes to lie, not only to his neighbour, but also to himself. How does a naughty child respond to an accusing mother from whom he wishes to hide the truth while not clearly telling a lie? He equivocates. He departs from the Scriptural injunction to "say yea for yea and nay for nay". The modernist has basically

And even apart from the actual statements, there is an "animus" to the documents which is "offensive to pious ears". There is, as Cardinal Suenens has said, "an internal logic in Vatican II which in several cases has been grasped and acted on, showing in everyday practice the priority of life over law. The spirit behind the texts was stronger than the words themselves".[12] It is this undercurrent that has flowed forth as "the Spirit of Vatican II", a "spirit" that accepts almost all the modernist concepts — "progress", "dynamic evolution", and "universalism". As Avery Dulles, S.J., one of the "periti", has said, "without using the term 'continuing revelation', Vatican II allowed for something of the kind". Donald Campion, S.J., another "periti", and translator of the Pastoral Constitution on the Church Today has said: "Here, as elsewhere, it is easy to recognize the compatibility of insights developed by thinkers such as Teilhard de Chardin in his *Divine Milieu* with the fundamental outlook of the Council . . ."[13] Finally, let it be noted that as the Protestant observer Dr. McAfee Brown states, these sixteen documents are prolix in the extreme, and as Michael Davies says, much of them "consists of little more than long series of the most banal truisms imaginable".[14] They run to some 739 pages of small

---

lost his faith in Revelation, and if he wishes to remain within the visible Church, he must either change the meaning of certain words, or else change the words so that they can mean one thing to him, and another to the faithful. Thus, as one modernist put it, "one learns the use of the double meaning, the tortuously complex sentences and paragraphs which conceal meaning rather than reveal it." The existential theologian has a positive dislike for clarity. As Father Daley said of Tyrell: "He believed that clearness was a snare for the unwary, and that snare was avoided as long as one distrusts clearness and recognizes it as a note of inadequacy." As Pope Saint Pius X said in his Encyclical *Pascendi,* the writings of the modernist clique appear "tentative and vague", while those of the Church are always "firm and constant". He said further, "It is one of the cleverest devices of the Modernists (as they are commonly and rightly called) to present their doctrines without order and systemic arrangement, in a scattered and disjointed manner, so as to make it appear as if their minds were in doubt or hesitation, whereas in reality they are quite fixed and steadfast."

12. *Doctrines do Grow,* Ed. John T. McGinn, CSP, Paulist Press: N.Y., 1967.

13. *The Documents of Vatican II,* Ed. Walter M. Abbott, S.J., Guild: N.Y. 1968.

14. Consider the following Conciliar statement: "The widespread reduction in working hours, for instance, brings increasing advantages to numerous people. May these leisure hours be properly used for relaxation of spirit

print in translation (as opposed to 179 of large print for the Council of Trent and 42 for Vatican I). It is virtually impossible for the average Catholic to read them through with care, even if he is supplied, as Father Houghton has remarked, "with a sufficient supply of anti-soporifics".

In order to understand the real nature of Vatican II the reader must recognize that what occurred was not a "debate" between the conservative and liberal factions of the Church — as if there is a spectrum of opinion from which the faithful can choose — but rather a fight between those who felt it was their obligation to preserve intact the entire "deposit of the Faith", and those who were bent on adapting Christianity to the contemporary world; a battle waged between those who see the Roman Catholic Church as the "visible" Church founded by Christ, and therefore a Church that was entitled to certain privileges (whether the world accorded them to her or not), and those who felt that "all those baptized in Christ . . . had access to the community of salvation", that credal differences were irrelevant, and who dreamt of an ecumenical "union" of "all men of good will" in a "rejuvenated Christianity". The Church of All Times lost this battle at the Council, but the fight still continues, sometimes in minor skirmishes, and sometimes in open warfare. Scripture informs us of the final outcome to be anticipated.

It is with these facts in mind that we shall examine some of the Conciliar documents in greater detail. Consider the following quotations, taken mostly from the Pastoral Constitution on the Church, the document that Paul VI considers one of the most important, and one in which he personally played an important role:

"The human race has passed from a rather static concept of reality to a more dynamic, evolutionary one." (Para. 5)

---

and the strengthening of mental and bodily health. Such benefits are available through spontaneous study and activity and through travel, which refines human qualities and enriches man with mutual understanding. These can help to preserve emotional balance, even at the community level, and to establish fraternal relations among men of all conditions, nations and races." This from a document of an Ecumenical Council!

"She (the Church) likewise holds that in her most benign Lord and Master can be found the key, the focal point, the goal of all human history." (Para. 10)[15]

"It is a fact bearing on the very person of man that he can come to an authentic and full humanity only through culture, that is, through the cultivation of natural goods and values. Wherever human life is involved, therefore, nature and culture are quite intimately connected." (Para. 53)

"In every group or nation, there is an ever-increasing number of men and women who are conscious that they themselves are the artisans and the authors of the culture of their community. Thus we are witnesses to the birth of a new humanism, one in which man is defined first of all by his responsibility towards his brothers and towards history." (Para. 55)

"The culture of today possesses particular characteristics. For example, the so-called exact sciences sharpen critical judgment to a very fine edge. Recent psychological research explains human activity more profoundly. Historical studies make a signal contribution to bringing men to see things in their changeable and evolutionary aspects . . . Thus little by little, a more universal form of human culture is developing, one which will promote and express the unity of the human race to the degree that it preserves the particular features of different cultures." (Para. 54)

"Man's social nature makes it evident that the progress of the human person and the advance of society itself hinge on each other. From the beginning, the subject and goal of all social institutions is and must be the

15. The phraseology here is strikingly Teilhardian. Those who see the world as progressing towards some "point *Omega*", instantly ignore the fact that Our Lord is both the *Alpha* and the *Omega*. The premise that the human race has in some way changed is totally erroneous. It is radically false to suppose that our ancestors were intellectually or spiritually our inferiors. Human weakness may alter its style in the course of history but not its nature.

human person, which for its part and by its very nature stands completely in need of social life.

This social life is not something added on to man. Hence through his dealings with others, through reciprocal duties, and through fraternal dialogue, he develops all his gifts and is able to rise to his destiny." (Para. 25)

"Thus, through her individual members and her whole community, the Church believes she can contribute greatly towards making the family of man and its history more human. In addition, the Catholic Church gladly holds in high esteem the things which other Christian Churches or ecclesiastical communities have done or are doing cooperatively by way of achieving the same goal." (Para. 40)

"It has pleased God to make men holy and save them not merely as individuals without any mutual bonds, but by making them into a single people, a people which acknowledges Him in truth and serves Him in holiness. So from the beginning of salvation history He has chosen men not just as individuals, but as members of a certain community. God called these chosen ones "His People" . . . This communitarian character is developed and consummated in the work of Jesus Christ." (Para. 32)

"The Church further recognizes that worthy elements are found in today's social movements, especially in an evolution towards unity, a process of wholesome social-ization and of association in civic and economic realms. For the promotion of unity belongs to the innermost nature of the Church, since she is, by her relationship with Christ, both a sacramental sign and an instrument of intimate union with God and of the unity of all mankind." (Para. 42)

"Because the human race today is joining more and more in civic, economic and social unity, it is much more necessary that priests, united in concern and effort under the leadership of the Bishops and the Supreme Pontiff, wipe out every ground of division, so that the whole human race may be brought into the unity of the family of God." (Para. 43)

Such then is a selection of statements — and each of sufficient length to make the accusation of having taken them out of context implausible — which post-Conciliar Catholics must "religiously observe" if they wish to consider themselves in "obedience". What evidence is there for the claim that "the human race has passed from a rather static concept of reality to a more dynamic evolutionary one"? And how Christian is the "new humanism" which we are witnesses to the birth of, when it is defined "first of all by man's responsibility towards his brothers and towards history"? Surely man's first responsibility is towards God, his Creator. And since when does man "rise to his destiny" through reciprocal duties and fraternal dialogue" alone? Where in scripture does it instruct us that we are saved "as members of a community", rather than as individuals? And since when has the Church's function been to make "the family of man and its history more human"? And what is all this talk of "unity", the "process of wholesome socialization" that "belongs to the innermost nature of the Church" and permits the "wiping out of every ground of division" that should impede it? No wonder that the Protestant observer Dr. McAfee Brown said that "there are even occasional hints that the Council Fathers have listened to the gospel of Marx as well as the Gospel of Mark." Truly, as Father Campion, the translator of this document states, "Theological 'aggiornamento' means more than a rephrasing of conventional theological teaching in contemporary terminology."

Now there are many areas in which Vatican II departs from the traditional teaching of the Church. Consider the following statements which are in direct contradiction to the Syllabus of Errors:

"Religious freedom has its foundation in the dignity of the human person. This right of the human person to religious freedom is to be recognized in the constitutional law whereby society is governed". (Decree on Religious Freedom). "The brethren divided from us also carry out many of the sacred actions of the Christian religion. Undoubtedly, in ways that vary according to the condition of each Church or Community, these actions can truly engender a life of grace and can be rightly described as capable of providing access to the community of salvation" (Decree on Ecumenism). "Witness to the unity of the Church very generally forbids common worship to Christians, but the grace to be had from it sometimes commends this practice . . . Most valuable to this purpose are meetings of the two sides especially for discussion of theological problems — where each can treat with the other on an equal footing." (Decree on Ecumenism).

Following the "internal logic" of the Document, Father Avery Dulles S.J., Professor of Theology at the Catholic University of America, a "peritus" of some distinction, and a translator of the documents in question, has stated:

"Does God reveal himself in other ways than through the world's religions, thus making it possible for "non-believers" to make an act of faith? The documents of Vatican II, while not directly answering this question, open up the possibility of an affirmative answer. The Dogmatic Constitution on the Church, after discussing the opportunities for salvation in the various religions, adds that this possibility holds even for the sincere atheist or the conscientious agnostic: 'Nor does divine Providence deny the help necessary for salvation to those who, without blame on their part, have not yet arrived at an explicit knowledge of God, but who strive to live a good life, thanks to His grace'. The Constitution on the Church in the Modern World confirms this doctrine by asserting that grace works in an unseen way in the hearts of all men of good will. In these and similar texts, Catholic theologians find an official recognition by the Church that an act of saving faith is possible without any explicit belief in the existence of God or any religious affiliation."[16]

Now even if we do not carry things so far as to state that "an act of saving faith is possible without any explicit belief in the existence of God", the various teachings of the Documents on Religious Liberty have far reaching consequences. The "animus" of the documents is that other Christians (and communities) are good people. If they are baptized in Christ — "all those justified by faith through baptism are incorporated into Christ. They therefore have a right to be honoured by the title of Christian",[16] and must be treated on an "equal footing" whose only defect is that they have not joined in the "visible unity" of the Church, often because of historical or political reasons.[17] The Church must therefore make every effort to bring them into that unity so that we can all happily progress towards that time when "the whole human race may be brought into the unity of the family of God". This means that doctrinal divergences are to be suppressed — "wiping out every ground of division", — and all that is required is "sincerity" and "good will". Clearly, since even atheists "have access to the community of salvation", it follows, as the documents teach, that "man is to be guided by his own judgment and he is to enjoy freedom" in his religious decisions. No "coercion" is to be used in dealing with man (implying "physical", but saying nothing about other forms of coercion that the modern world is quite familiar with); and every religious sect is free to propagate its own views. Even those nations that are totally Catholic are to invite in Protestants and Communists and give them the right — both civil and legal — to propagate their anti-Catholic teachings freely.[18] Yes indeed, as the Document states, "He Himself (Christ), noting that cockle had been sown amid the wheat, gave orders that both should be allowed to grow until the harvest time which will come at the end of the world." The "cockle" then, or heresy which it symbolizes, is to be allowed to grow — not opposed, not uprooted from the Christian faithful. Finally, not content with conceding all this, the faithful are instructed that they should engage in active *communicatio in sacris* — that is to say, should join in common worship with heretics. Now, how can an organization that believes it was founded by Christ, that believes its rites are of divine origin, and that believes its very existence is tied to its function of preserving this depositum, encourage its members to join in forms of worship that are of purely human origin? Active

---

16. Avery Dulles, S.J. *Doctrines Do Grow, Op. cit.*
17. Passages in quotation marks are taken from the documents.
18. "The Christian faithful, like other men, should enjoy on the level of the state, the right of in no way being hindered from leading their lives according to their conscience. It is entirely in accord with the liberty of the Church and the freedom of religion that all men and all communities should have this right accorded to them as a civil and legal right."
(Vatican II).

communicatio in sacris has always been forbidden to Catholics. Canon law forbids it as a mortal sin (Canon 1258). It is further forbidden by St. Paul:

> Bear not the yoke with unbelievers. For what participation hath justice with injustice? Or what fellowship hath light with darkness? And what concord hath Christ with Belial? Or what part hath the faithful with the unbeliever?

> II Cor. vi:14

Above all, active *communicatio in Sacris* on the part of a Catholic involves him in FALSE WORSHIP and as such is theologically considered to be against the First Commandment. And if we allow the principle that the rights of Truth are to be sacrificed for some lesser good — that "the exigencies of charity force us outside the bounds of orthodoxy" (as Paul VI has said), then we concede all to the "private judgment" of the individual. Divorce, abortion, murder for social expediency, genocide and all the horrors of the modern world will follow rapidly.

As for the Church treating those who disagree with it theologically on an "equal footing" as Vatican II teaches — how can those who speak with the words of St. Augustine, St. Thomas Aquinas and Cassian deal on an *equal footing* with economic determinists, communists and village atheists? Nor can the hierarchy be true to the Church if it allows for the spreading of heresy in places where it is in a position to prevent it. "Not to oppose error is to approve it and not to defend the truth is to suppress it." The idea that "liberty of conscience and worship is the proper right of every man, and should be proclaimed and asserted by law in every correctly established society . . ." was specifically condemned by Pope Pius in his *Quanta Cura* and was referred to by Pope Gregory XVI as "insanity". The Church is bound by her very nature to support and foster that state which openly embraces the Catholic faith. She may herself, or in the rulers she approves of, tolerate or allow error to co-exist, but never in such a way as to give the impression that there exists such a thing as a God-given right to commit sin or to embrace falsehood. She must clearly stand forth as holding and teaching the "fullness of the faith" that Christ endowed her with, and use all reasonable efforts not only to convince others of the correctness of her position, but also take appropriate measures to prevent others from corrupting her doctrines and confusing the faithful. When the hierarchy fails to do this, it fails to show charity both to those within her fold and to those outside. And if this is true for the Church, it is equally true for the family. And if the New Church concedes to other "sister Churches", and to any "ecclesiastical community" an equal status to her own, how can she any longer claim the right, nay the obligation, to effect conversions? She can only do this because she believes she is the one true Church, and the means established by our Lord for the salvation of men. As there is only one true Saviour, there is only one true Church, outside of which there is no salvaton.[19]

Tied in with these false ideas on ecumenism are several "catch-words" that recur with considerable frequency throughout the documents of the Council, and are subsequently found in the mouthings of the post-conciliar clergy. Such phrases as "freedom of conscience", "liberty", and "the dignity of the human person", have about them an almost "superstitious" aura for the modernist and the liberal. It should be quite clear to a Catholic that the dignity of a person in no way consists in his liberty. For liberty is a means; liberty is good in so far as it is regulated by what is good and true. This is why Our Lord said *"the Truth shall make you free"*, and not "freedom shall lead you to the Truth". In so far as a person uses his intellect badly, or misdirects his will, he loses his dignity (and acts in an undignified manner). Our dignity derives from the fact that we are made "in His image", but to be dignified, we must conform to this image. Our failure to do so, even if we are not culpable (as in the insane), can never be dignified. Finally, it must not be forgotten that most people who use the phrase "freedom of conscience" in practice really mean "freedom not to have a conscience". (Was it "freedom

---

19. This is not to be interpreted as it was by Father Leonard Feeney who among other things, denied the possibility of invincible ignorance as well as Baptism by Blood and Desire, and who incidentally had his "excommunication" lifted by Paul VI even though he never recanted from his erroneous and heretical position. The problem of salvation "outside" the Church is too complex for brief discussion, but to quote Archbishop Lefebvre, "one may be saved within Protestantism . . . within any religion whatsoever, but one cannot be saved by that religion! The difference is enormous. One is not saved by error". (*A Bishop Speaks*, Scottish *Una Voce:* Edinburgh, Scotland).

of conscience" that lead to the martyrdom of the English Catholics, or to Luther's breaking his vow of celibacy — a vow he gave to God and not to the Church?) If we are truly to be "free" and "dignified", we must have one will and intellect and be guided by what is "good" and "true". And this is why the Church must be intransigent and absolute in instructing and guiding us. It is also why the Church cannot itself depart from the traditional teachings handed down from the Apostles, for it in turn must be guided by what is "good" and "true" which is Christ Himself. If man was in fact meant to "use his own judgment" in religious matters, then it must be asked "Why did Christ come down from heaven and die on the Cross? Why did Christ found a 'visible' Church and instruct it to preserve His teaching? Why was an Apostolic succession established?" What greater departure from the traditional teaching of the Church can there be than this open proclamation of "private judgment" as a source of truth? Yet despite this we hear the soothing words from the Conciliar Church: "Nothing *de fide* has been changed." Nothing *de fide* has been left. For the New Church to proclaim that man is to "use his own judgment" in religious matters is for it to state that man has no obligation to listen to God and His Church. As soon as the Post-conciliar Church accedes to the "rights" of "private judgment" in religious matters, she must accept and even bow to those who challenge her authority on such grounds, or else she must become an "open" Church that allows for a plurality of mutually exclusive theological opinions within her ranks. Neither alternative is acceptable to the Church founded by Christ.

It is of course impossible for us to consider all the implications that follow from the ambiguities, if not outright errors, that are found in Vatican II. We cannot however pass over one of its fundamental theses without comment — namely the idea that man has *evolved* and *greatly progressed* since the primitive era of the Apostles. "The human intellect is also broadening its dominion over time; over the past by means of historical knowledge; over the future by the art of projecting and planning. Advances in biology, psychology, and the social sciences . . . bring man hope of improved self-knowledge . . . Thanks to the experience of past ages, the progress of the sciences, and the treasures hidden in the various forms of human culture, the nature of man himself is more clearly revealed and new roads to truth are opened". And all this being so, the faithful are instructed to:

> "blend modern science and its theories and the under-standing of the most recent discoveries with Christian morality and doctrine. Thus their religious practice and morality can keep pace with their scientific knowledge and with an ever advancing technology . . ." *(The Church in the Modern World*, 62)

Surely, even the most rabid liberal would find it difficult to believe that such a statement emanated from that "ecclesiastical community" claiming to be the Roman Catholic Church. My God, how can the Church ever hope to guide the world, if it is to blend its morality and doctrine with the latest scientific theories — yes, "theories"?

It is this idea of progress that underlies the modernist's compulsion to "adapt" the faith to the modern world — or as Paul VI put it with regard to the liturgy, "accommodate itself . . . to contemporary mentality". It is as Pius XII said only twenty-five years ago, "these false evolutionary notions with their denial of all that is fixed or abiding in human experience, that have paved the way for a new philosophy of error." The argument runs along these lines: contemporary man is the result of a long and progressive development and is far more intelligent than his predecessors. His insights into the truth are therefore more profound and of greater value than those of men who lived 2000 years ago. The Church must accept these new insights and adapt her earlier conceptions to them. Evolution and Progress are fundamental forces of nature and existence. Therefore truth and the church must evolve along with man and the world. As Avery Dulles S.J. puts it; "The traditional doctrinal formulations were forged in the light of a general world-view that has by now become obsolete; an unconditional allegiance to any single view of the universe, such as the Christian faith seems to demand, impresses the modern mind as fanatical and unscientific . . . The claim that some privileged source . . . contains the totality of saving truth is likewise distasteful . . . The assertion that divine revelation was complete in the first century of our era seems completely antithetical to the modern concept of progress."[20] If modern man has changed, then the Church must change or die.

What after all is a "modernist", but one who would "modernize" the Church, bring her "into the twentieth century" and make her acknowledge "the normative patterns of contemporary thought". He is not interested in her using telephones and other paraphernalia of the current world, but in modernizing her thinking and her teaching. He would delete from her character all "absolutism" and "mediaeval rigorism", and make her "acceptable and lovable" to modern man. Now what is "modern man", and what are his "normative patterns of thought"? If he can be characterized at all, he is an individual who believes in no absolute truths and who holds that he himself is the source and the criteria of all value judgments. He holds that all truths are relative and that one man's opinion is as good as another's. He believes that it is in this world that man finds his meaning and purpose; that morality is necessitated by what he calls "social contract"; and that virtue is "enlightened self-interest". Man *qua* man is the centre of his universe and the most altruistic activity he can engage in is "serving mankind". The Catholic modernist (if such a phrase has any meaning at all) is a man who has lost *the* faith, a man who does not believe in a Divine Revelation from above, a "deposit of the faith", and in a Church whose function it is to preserve this deposit. As George Santayana put it: "Modernism . . . is the love of all Christianity in those who perceive that it is all a fable. It is the historic attachment to his Church of a Catholic who has discovered that he is a pagan . . . It is the last of those concessions to the spirit of the world which half-believers and double-minded prophets have always been found making; but it is a mortal concession. It concedes everything; for it concedes that everything in Christianity, as Christians hold it, is an illusion."

Now in point of fact, these concepts of "progress" and "evolution" are the most pernicious pseudo-dogmas and pseudo-myths that the world has ever produced. This is not to state that they do not exist, but their existence is partial and of quite limited applicability, and never without their antithesis in degradation and degeneration. The Truth, being timeless and immutable, is clearly immune from such "forces"

---

20. *Doctrines Do Grow, op. cit.*

of change. What is however radically false is to suppose that our ancestors were intellectually, spiritually, or morally our inferiors. To propose this is the most childish of delusions, for human weakness may alter its style, in the course of history, but not its nature. Based on these false concepts, man dreams of building a world so perfect that no one will need to be good and believes that all the problems that he faces will be effaced at some time in the future. ("We must build a better world for our children".) These concepts are in fact "the opiate of the people", for they hold out a false hope to modern man — a desperate collectivity deprived of the meaning of life. They are the antithesis of all that is traditional. No wonder that the Church has consistently opposed them.

> "The doctrine of the faith which God has revealed has not been proposed to human intelligences to be perfected by them as if it were a philosophical system, but as a divine deposit entrusted to the Spouse of Christ to be faithfully guarded and infallibly interpreted."

Yet it is on the basis of these false ideas of "progress" and "evolution", of the need to "shore up" Christianity by adapting it to contemporary ways of thinking, that the so-called "Northern Alliance" introduced a whole host of questionable teachings into the seemingly "official" teachings of the Church.[21] They are among those that Pius XI speaks of in his Encyclical *Mortalium Animos* ("On the Death of Souls"):

> "These unfortunate souls who are infected with these errors believe that dogmatic truth is not absolute, but relative, and that it is able to adapt itself to the variable exigencies of time, of place and of the various needs of different souls, that it does not depend upon an unchangeable Revelation, but ought by its nature to accommodate itself to the life of man."

---

21. Archbishop Lefebvre lists some of these: "Since the Council was initiated it has in a more or less general manner, shaken the certitude of many truths taught by the authentic Magisterium of the Church, and which belong most definitely to the treasure of her Tradition . . . (the) question of the jurisdiction of Bishops, of the two sources of Revelation, of the inspiration of the Scriptures, of the necessity of grace for justification, of the necessity of Catholic Baptism, of the life of grace among heretics, schismatics and pagans, of the ends of marriage, of religious liberty, of the last ends, etc . . ." *(J'accuse le Concile")*

They were nevertheless condemned before, and remain condemned today by the traditional Church:

"One must condemn . . . anything that seems to be animated by the unhealthy spirit of novelty; anything that holds up to derision the piety of the faithful or suggests new orientations for the Christian life; anything that suggests new directions for the Church to follow or new hopes and aspirations that are more suitable to the souls of modern day Catholics; anything that implies a new social vocation for the priesthood or for Christian civilization; in fact any ideas that remotely resemble these concepts."

Pius XII *Pleni l'Animo*

"If anyone shall say that, because of scientific progress it may be possible at some time to interpret the Church's dogmas in a different sense from that which the Church understood and understands, let him be anathema!"

Vatican I

It is not the Church that has become "irrelevant", and therefore in need of "adapting" itself to modern man, but rather "modern man", a collectivity that seeks above all to avoid "the one thing necessary", who is in need of adapting himself to religion.[22] As Pius X said in his Encyclical *E Supremi*

---

22. It should be obvious that the traditional Church is not against "progress", if by this term we are referring to the advances of modern science. The designing of "better mouse traps" is clearly of advantage to society, providing of course that justice is not violated, and the true and proper ends of man are not subverted. As Pope Saint Pius X said in his Encyclical *E Supremi Apostolatus*, "It is not progress, but ignorance in knowledge" that "extinguishes the faith". What she is diametrically opposed to is the "mystique of progress" that sees in this concept a "dynamic" force applicable in the natural and supernatural realm to all of reality. It is this mystique that is reflected in the vague pantheism pervading modern religiosity, and underlies the dream of the Post-conciliar Church — "that all may be one". The idea that the world in which we live today is in any way "Christian" is absurd, and any attempt to adapt our religion to this world is inevitably a betrayal of Christ. (Even the historians and sociologists refer to it as the "Post-Christian" world). The *Civitas Dei* and worldly progression as envisioned by modern man cannot converge and those who strive to accommodate the religious message to profane illusions and

Apostolatus, "Who can fail to see that at the present society is suffering more than in any past age from a terrible and radical malady which, while developing every day and gnawing into its very being, is dragging it to destruction? You understand, Venerable Brethren, this disease is apostasy from God . . . We must use every means and bend every effort to bring about the total disappearance of that enormous and detestable wickedness so characteristic of our time — the substitution of man for God." The modernist argument is the exact opposite of this, for it holds that the Father of the "prodigal son" should go and eat swill with the rebellious offspring. What has resulted from Vatican II is not a "rejuvenation of the Faith", but a "theological pigstye". A New Church has been created — to use the words of Cardinal Benelli, "a new ecclesiology"[23] — the self-styled "Post-conciliar Church", a Church which, as Paul VI says:

"Seeks to adapt itself to the languages, to the customs and to the inclinations of the men of our times, men completely engrossed in the rapidity of material evolution and similar necessities of their individual circumstances. This 'openness' is of the very essence of the (new) Church . . . THE RESTRICTIONS OF ORTHODOXY DO NOT COINCIDE WITH PASTORAL CHARITY."

A New Church, a Church with "a different ecclesiology", a Church that fulfills the dreams of the Freemason Eliphas Levi. Let us consider the form of this *Levi-athan* dream as Levi expounded it in the year 1862:

---

agitations are among those whom Christ labeled as "scatterers". Those who look forward to a millennium in which all men of good will are united in a "new humanity" would do well to remember the Scriptural prophecies of Anti-Christ. The faithful will, at the end of time, be a "remnant". Pray God, we may be among that small "remnant".

23. Consider the following taken from an article in *Christian Order,* Oct. 1978: "At the end, Dr. Saventham asked the Prelate (now Cardinal Benelli) whether the traditional liturgy could not be permitted at the side of the new one. The answer was startling: 'Sir, all these reforms go in the same direction, whereas the old Mass represents another ecclesiology'! Dr. Saventham: 'Monseigneur, what you said is an enormity'! Benelli: 'I shall say it again: those who want to have the old Mass have another ecclesiology.'!"

"A day will come when the Pope, inspired by the Holy Spirit, will declare that all the excommunications are lifted, and all the anathemas are retracted, when all Christians will be united within the Church, when the Jews and Moslems will be blessed and called back to her. While keeping the unity and inviolability of her dogmas, she will permit to all sects to approach her by degrees, and will embrace all mankind in the communion of her love and her prayers. Then Protestants will no longer exist. Against what will they be able to protest. The Sovereign Pontiff will then be truly king of the religious world, and he will do whatever he wishes with all the nations of the earth. It is necessary to spread this spirit of universal charity . . ."

Nor, should it be thought that this is the first time such a generalized apostasy has occurred. Consider the following taken from Maccabees:

"In those days went there out of Israel wicked men, who persuaded many, saying, let us go and make a covenant with the heathen that are round about us: for since we departed from them, we have had much sorrow. Then certain people were so forward therein, that they went to the King who gave them licence to do after the ordinances of the heathen . . . (and they) made themselves uncircumcised, and forsook the holy covenant, and joined themselves to the heathen . . ."

Truly, as Cardinal John Fisher said before his martyrdom, "The fort is betrayed even of those who should have defended it."[24]

---

24. To say a "New Church" has been created is not to say that the true Catholic Church, the "Church of All Times", does not continue to exist — that Church against which the Gates of Hell shall not prevail. With regard to this promise consider the words of Leo XIII: "All the world knows that this Divine promise ought to be understood to apply to the Universal Church (that is to say, the Church of All Times, that Church which is as Universal in "time" as it is in "space" — Ed.) and not to any part of the Church taken in isolation, for individual segments may, and in fact, indeed have, been overcome by the forces of evil. *Satis Cognitum.*"

PART V

THE "NOVUS ORDO MISSAE"

One final problem remained. The Reformers feared that "nothing would come out of the Council". Even though they had managed to insert in the "official" Documents of the Council their false ideas, they knew that this alone was insufficient. After all, how many Catholics ever read the Canons of the Council of Trent? (What need was there when the clergy could be trusted?) How many would wade through the tedious and ambiguous statements of the New Council? Change would occur far too slowly for the impatient innovators. The greater majority of the faithful had never asked for the Council (the Curia had opposed it also), and were perfectly content with the way the Church had always been. Even John XXIII had acknowledged and praised it as being "vibrant with vitality". For most people things would have gone on much as before. It was absolutely necessary to introduce into the fabric of the every-day life of the Christian, all these new ideas, the "new economy of the Gospel". How then to achieve this? The answer was obvious. One had to "reform" the Liturgy.

It was only logical that they should — indeed they absolutely had to — attack the liturgy directly. What is extraordinary is the degree to which all this was and had been predicted. Pope Leo XIII had stated in his *Apostolicae Curae* that the modernists and reformers (they had other designations then) "knew only too well the intimate bond which unites faith and worship, *lex credendi* and *lex orandi:* and so, under the pretext of restoring the order of the liturgy to its primitive form, they corrupted it in many respects to bring it into accord with the errors of the innovators." The Abbé Guéranger described what resulted over 100 years ago in an article entitled

"The Anti-Liturgical Heresy".[1] It has also been predicted that the true Mass would be taken away from us. Listen to the words of Saint Alphonse de Liguori, a doctor of the Church:

"The devil has always attempted, by means of the heretics, to deprive the world of the Mass, making them precursors of the Anti-Christ, who, before anything else, will try to abolish and will actually abolish the Holy Sacrament of the altar, as a punishment for the sins of men, according to the prediction of Daniel 'And strength was given him against the continual sacrifice' (*Daniel viii:12*)."

What then are we to think when we find Paul VI thanking the six Protestant "observers" for helping in the creation of the *Novus Ordo Missae* — for assisting in the "re-editing in a new manner liturgical texts tried and tested by long usage, or establishing formulas which are completely new . . . (thus) imparting greater theological value to the liturgical texts so that the *lex orandi* conformed better with the *lex credendi*" (*L'Osservatore Romano*, May 11, 1970).[2] Quite apart from admitting the scandal of non-Catholic involvement in the creation of this new "rite", the statement implies that either the liturgical texts prior to 1969 did not possess that degree of theological value which was desirable, or that the *lex credendi* had changed! Should we have any doubt about which of these two alternatives to choose, the Protestants have resolved them for us. The Superior Consistory of the Church of Augsburg Confession of Alsace and Lorraine (Evangelical Lutheran) publicly acknowledged that Lutherans could take part in the "Catholic eucharistic celebration", because it allowed them to "use these new eucharistic prayers with which they felt at home". And why did they feel at home with them? Because they had "the advantage of giving a different interpretation to the theology of the sacrifice than they were accustomed to attribute to Catholicism". Another Protestant theologian, Dr. Jaroslav Pelikan, has stated that the Vatican II "Constitution on the Liturgy", "does not merely tinker with the formalities

---

1. A translation is available in *Studies in Comparative Religion*, Summer 1975 (Pates Manor, Bedfont, Middlesex, England) and will be available in *The Roman Catholic* (Oyster Bay Cove, N.Y.) soon.
2. *Lex credendi*, literally the law of belief; *lex orandi*, the law of prayer.

of liturgical worship, but seeks to form and to reform the very life of the Church". He states further that this Constitution represents, on the part of the Post-conciliar Church, "the acceptance, however belated, of the liturgical programme set forth by the Reformers". And what was this aim? It was to destroy the Mass, and in so doing, to destroy the Church. *"Tolle Missam, tolle ecclesiam."* Dr. M. G. Siegvalt, a Professor of dogmatic theology in the Protestant faculty at Strasbourg has testified that "nothing in the renewed Mass need really trouble the evangelical Protestant".

Before considering the *Novus Ordo Missae* in detail, it is necessary for the reader to have some idea of the "central" position the traditional Mass has always had in the traditional Catholic Church. As St. Alphonse de Liguori said:

"The Mass is the most beautiful and the best thing in the Church. At the Mass, Jesus Christ giveth Himself to us by means of the Most Holy Sacrament of the altar, which is the end and the purpose of all other Sacraments."

"The celebration of the Mass", says Gihr, "is the most worthy and most perfect divine service, for it procures to the Most High a worship and a veneration which millions of words would be incapable of rendering Him . . . It is a unique Sacrifice (and) infinitely excels in value and dignity, in power and efficacy, all the many prayers of the Church and of the faithful . . . As often as this memorial sacrifice is celebrated, the work of redemption is performed . . . It is the soul and the heart of the liturgy of the Church; it is the mystical chalice which presents to our lips the sweet fruit of the passion of the God-Man — that is grace." Pope Urban VIII said of it:

"If there is anything divine among the possessions of men, which the citizens of Heaven might covet (were covetousness possible for them), it would certainly be the most Holy Sacrifice of the Mass, whose blessing is such that in it man possesses a certain anticipation of Heaven while still on earth, even having before their eyes and taking into their hands the very Maker of both Heaven and earth. How greatly must mortals strive that the most awesome privilege be guarded with due cult and reverence, and take care lest their negligence offend the eyes of the angels, who watch with envious adoration."

Si Quid Est

Not only is the Mass the most sacred and central act of worship in the Church, and, as Faber said, "the most beautiful thing this side of heaven", it is also, as Pius XI said, "the most important organ of the ordinary magisterium of the Church". Having been in greater part established by Christ and the Apostles, "it is a theological *locus* of the first importance in knowing the living Tradition of the Church" (Father Henry, O.P.). If the Christian Revelation comes to us in Scripture and Tradition, then the Mass is that Organ that is the most important vehicle for the passing on of Tradition. Through it we learn how the Apostles taught and acted.

"Christ's example was the norm for the Apostles at the celebration of the Sacrifice. They did, first, only that which Christ had done before. According to His directions and under the inspiration of the Holy Ghost, they observed other things besides, namely, according to circumstances, they added various prayers and observances, in order to celebrate the Holy Mysteries as worthily and as edifying as possible. Those constituent portions of the sacrificial rite, which are found in all the ancient liturgies, have incontestably their origin from Apostolic times and tradition: the essential and fundamental features of the sacrificial rite, introduced and enlarged upon by the Apostles, were preserved with fidelity and reverence in the mystical blessings, the use of lights, incense, vestments and many things of that nature she (the Church) employs by Apostolic prescription and tradition . . ."[3]

Now, there is no question but that throughout the ages, prayers and practices were added to the Apostolic foundation, but the central core or "Canon" (meaning *"rule"*) has been fixed throughout history. As Sir William Palmer, a non-Catholic historian has stated:

---

3. Dr. Nicholas Gihr, *The Holy Sacrifice of the Mass*, Herder: N.Y. 1929.

"There seems nothing unreasonable in thinking that the Roman Liturgy, as used in the time of Gregory the Great may have existed from a period of the most remote antiquity, and perhaps there are nearly as good reasons for referring its original composition to the Apostolic age . . ."

Historical research has instructed us that Pope St. Gregory added to the prayer *Hanc Igitur* of the Canon, the phrase *Diesque nostros in tua pace disponas, atque ab aeterna damnatione nos eripi et in electorum tuorum jubeas grege numerari,* and that Pope St. Leo added the phrase *Sanctum Sacrificium immaculatam hostiam* (440-461). Apart from these minor additions (not deletions), the Canon in use today by the traditional Church is the same as that used in the time of Pope St. Damasus in the year 366-384. Thus it is that Chapter IV, Session XII of the Council of Trent states:

"For it (the Canon) is composed out of the very words of the Lord, the traditions of the Apostles, and the pious institutions of the holy pontiffs."

Finally, Father Louis Bouyer, a convert from Luther's sect prior to Vatican II, and currently "in obedience" to the New and Post-conciliar Church, wrote prior to the Council:

"The Roman Canon, as it is today, goes back to Gregory the Great. There is not, in the East or in the West, a Eucharistic prayer remaining in use to this day, that can boast of such antiquity. In the eyes not only of the Orthodox, but of Anglicans and even those Protestants who have still to some extent, a feeling for tradition. TO JETTISON IT WOULD BE A REJECTION OF ANY CLAIM ON THE PART OF THE ROMAN CHURCH TO REPRESENT THE TRUE CATHOLIC CHURCH."

Historical evidence prior to St. Damasus is sparse. After all, before the reign of Constantine (who died in 337), the Church was under constant persecution. Any claim to "return to primitive practice" other than that which retains in toto this Canon is patently false. But what of additions to the Canon —

that is to say, the prayers used before and after it? There are also of ancient origin.

Consider for example the reading of Scripture. The first Gospel was written as best we know, eight years after the Crucifixion, and the Apocalypse many years later. We know that it was the custom to read from Scripture and other Sacred writings (such as the "Shepherd of Hermes") before the Canon, because St. Procop who was martyred in the year 303 had the function of translating these readings into the vernacular. Scripture was "canonized" in the year 317, and the Scriptural readings used in the Mass of the traditional Church today were fixed by St. Damasus I in the Fourth Century. In the Fifth Century St. Celestine I introduced the Introit and the Gradual — and what are these? They are selected readings from the Psalms appropriate to the season and the Feast. In the Sixth Century St. Gregory added the *Kyrie Eleison* though in point of fact the phrase is Biblical and its use goes back to the time of Christ — "Lord have mercy upon me." In the Seventh, St. Sergius "introduced" the *Agnus Dei*. Over the centuries then, various additions were made, both in liturgical prayers used, as well as in customs. The practice of the priest saying *"Corpus Domini nostri Jesu Christi custodiat . . ."* (May the Body of Our Lord Jesus Christ preserve . . .) when he gives out Communion is said to date from the time of the Albigensian heretics who denied the "Real Presence". Also, the various great religious orders often inserted special prayers of their own. But throughout all this the Canon (which incidentally includes the Words of Consecration) remained intact. Finally, at the time of the Reformation when the authority of tradition was being questioned, and when innovations and novelties of all sorts were being introduced, it became necessary to codify and "fix" for all time the most Holy Mass so as to protect it from any possible corruption. This was achieved over the course of several pontificates; scholars went back to all the original documents available; any errors that had crept in were eliminated, and the Roman Missal and Breviary were published by Saint Pope Pius V in accordance with the wish expressed by the Fathers of the Council of Trent. This publication of the Roman Missal was accompanied by the proclamation of the Apostolic Constitution *Quo Primum*. [4] From henceforth this Missal was to be used throughout the Roman Church by all her members, though exceptions were made in favour of certain religious orders like the Dominicans who had said essentially the same Mass with slightly different ceremonies for at least 200 years prior to that time. Thus, even today, should one have the privilege of hearing a traditional Dominican Mass, one would recognize certain minor variations, but would be easily able to follow it with the standard Roman Missal. This *Quo Primum* is to be found in the front of every Missal published since 1570 and has been re-published and re-proclaimed by every Pope — some 42 in all — from Pius V to John XXIII. Of course, this is no longer true of the Post-conciliar Church which without officially abrogating it (can it be abrogated?), has disobeyed this law. Not only has the new Church disobeyed this Apostolic Constitution, it has ordered that all the tra-

---

4. A "Constitution" is defined as "an irreformable statement of what the Church's belief is" (Louis Bouyer, *The Liturgy Revived),* and "the binding force of pontifical constitutions is . . . beyond question" *(Catholic Encyclopedia).* We quote from this Constitution:

"We specifically command each and every patriarch, administrator, and all other persons of whatever ecclesiastical dignity they may be, be they even cardinals of the Holy Roman Church, or possessed of any other rank of pre-eminence, and *We order them in virtue of holy obedience* to chant or to read the Mass according to the rite and manner and norm herewith laid down by Us and, hereafter to discontinue and completely discard all other rubrics. They must not in celebrating Mass presume to introduce any ceremonies or recite any prayers other than those contained in this Missal . . . Furthermore, by these presents (this law), *in virtue of Our Apostolic authority,* We grant and concede *in perpetuity* that for the chanting or reading of this Mass in any church whatsoever, *this Missal is hereafter to be followed absolutely, without any scruple of conscience or fear of incurring any penalty, judgment or censure, and may freely and lawfully be used.* Nor are superiors, administrators, canons, chaplains, and other secular priests, or religious of whatever order or by whatever title designated, obliged to celebrate the Mass otherwise than as enjoined by Us. We likewise declare and ordain that no one whatsoever is to be forced or coerced to alter this Missal, and that *this present document cannot be revoked or modified, but remains always valid and retains its full force* . . . Therefore, no one whosoever is permitted to alter this letter, or heedlessly to venture to go contrary to this notice of Our Permission, statute, ordinance, command, precept, grant, indult, declaration, will, decree, and prohibition. Would anyone however presume to commit such an act, he should know that he will incur the wrath of Almighty God and of the Blessed Apostles Peter and Paul." (italics mine).

ditional Roman Missals in stock be burnt and destroyed, and *forbidden* the use of this Missal — the traditional Mass — to those it is responsible for guiding![5]

In providing the reader with this background material, we have clearly shown that, as the great liturgical scholar Abbé Guéranger said:

> "It is to the Apostles that those ceremonies go back that accompany the administration of the sacraments, the establishment of the sacramentals, the principal feasts . . . The Apostolic liturgy is found entirely outside of Scripture; it belongs to the domain of Tradition . . ."

and we have further exposed the lie promulgated by the "Pope and the Bishops in union with him" in claiming — as has been done time after time — that in forcing the *Novus Ordo Missae* down the throats of the laity, they have done exactly what Pius V did in his *Quo Primum* following the Council of Trent. To quote Paul VI, the perpetrator of this act:

> "Let us clearly understand the reasons why this serious change has been introduced . . . (it is) an obedience to the Council (*La Croix*, Sept. 4, 1970) . . . In no different way did our holy predecessor Pius V make obligatory the Missal reformed under his authority, following the Council of Trent *(Custos, Quid de Nocte)*."

*   *   *

It is our contention, despite appearances to the contrary,

---

5. Many authorities can be called upon to prove this contention. To quote but a few, The late Archbishop Hallinan of Atlanta (USA) noted that "We have come to the end of an era". Father Gelineau, S.J., a liturgical "peritus" from the Council said of the *Novus Ordo*, "It is a different liturgy of the Mass. This needs to be said without ambiguity: the Roman rite as we knew it no longer exists. It has been destroyed." Father Henri Denis states: "To claim that everything has changed is quite simply to be honest about what has happened." Father Louis Bouyer has said, "There is practically no liturgy worthy of the name today in the Catholic Church." More recently he has stated "The Catholic liturgy has been overthrown under the pretext of rendering it more compatible with the contemporary outlook — but in reality to conform it with the buffooneries that the religious orders were induced to impose, whether they liked it or not, upon the other clergy." I am indebted to Michael Davies' *The Roman Rite Destroyed* for these quotations. Many others could be cited.

and one that can easily be proved, that the *Novus Ordo Missae,* or "mass" of the Post-conciliar Church is a radical departure from the traditional Mass of the Church of All Times. It cannot be said of this new "service" that "it is composed out of the very words of the Lord, the traditions of the Apostles, and the pious institutions also of holy pontiffs". True, it uses many Scriptural passages and phrases taken from the words of Christ or the Apostles, but these are of an innocuous nature, inoffensive to the Reformed Churches, and are fundamentally similar to those found in the most liberal of the various Protestant services. Just as we know who wrote the Anglican and the Lutheran forms of worship, so also do we know who wrote the New "mass". The *Novus Ordo* has in no instance returned to "primitive practice". True that it uses a "eucharistic prayer" *similar* to that of Hippolytus and written in the third century — but it has significantly altered this prayer, and Hippolytus was in "schism" at the time that he wrote it down. The *Novus Ordo Missae* is a skilful blending of the Anglican and Lutheran services, and in many places follows them verbatim — this is particularly true of those phrases used by the Reformers specifically to deny the Real Presence and the Sacrificial nature of the rite. It is a study in *ambiguity* which allows of its meaning to be taken in different ways. It has dropped approximately 80 per cent of the traditional Mass, and only retained those portions that are least likely to give offence to the Protestants. "Its chief innovation", that is to say, its chief departure from tradition, according to Paul VI, is in "the eucharistic prayer", the central core or "Canon" of the Mass. It has changed the Words of Consecration from those traditionally used by the Church since time immemorial, words fixed by the decrees of Ecumenical Councils, thus changing the "form" of the Sacrament. In the vernacular it has mistranslated these words so as to change their meaning (or "substance", as the theologians say), and thus brought into the most serious doubt their ability to effect the Transubstantiation. The Words of Consecration, even in the Latin version, are said in a manner that allows them to be understood as part of a historical narrative, which makes their efficacy dubious and entirely dependent upon the priest's personal beliefs and "intention". In the vernacular version portions of the service teach overt heresy. The definition or description of the Mass in the *Novus Ordo Missae* is false.

The New "mass" was substantially rejected by the Episcopal Synod consisting of over 160 theologians whose function it was to approve it. As Cardinal Ottaviani stated, it "represents, both as a whole and in its details, a striking departure from the Catholic theology of the Mass as it was formulated in Session XXII of the Council of Trent", and as the Episcopal Synod said, "it teems with insinuations or manifest errors against the purity of the Catholic religion and dismantles all defences of the deposit of Faith." In summary, the *Novus Ordo Missae* is a *"parody"*[6] intentionally foisted upon the faithful to deprive them of the true Mass without their being aware of it. And yet, despite all this (which we will consider in detail), Paul VI assured us:

> "Let everyone understand well that nothing has been changed in the essence of our traditional Mass . . . There is nothing in this idea, absolutely . . . The new rite, the Mass, is the same as always. If anything, its identity has been made more recognizable in certain of its aspects." (*Allocution,* Nov. 26 1969), and "It is in the name of tradition that we ask all our sons and daughters, all the Catholic communities, to celebrate with dignity and fervour the renewed liturgy. The adoption of the New *Ordo Missae* is certainly not left to the free choice of priests or faithful . . . The New *Ordo* was promulgated to take the place of the old . . ." (*Custos, Quid de Nocte,* May 24, 1976).

*   *   *

It is well known that the Reformers hated the traditional Mass. Listen to the words of Luther. He called it an "abomination", a "false blasphemous cult", and instructed the rulers under his influence to "attack the idolators" and to suppress their worship as much as possible. He repeatedly denied its true sacrificial nature and hated the "abominable Canon in which the Mass is made a sacrifice". As he put it, "the Mass is not a Sacrifice . . . Call it benediction, eucharist, the Lord's table, the Lord's supper, memory of the Lord, or whatever you like, just so long as you do not dirty it with the name of a sacrifice or an action." Indeed, he went so far as to

---

6. A "Parody", according to Webster's dictionary, is "a writing in which the language and style of the author is imitated or mimicked; a burlesque; a feeble or ridiculous imitation of an action".

say "I affirm that all brothels, murderers, robberies, crimes, adulteries are less wicked than this abomination of the Popish Mass." As to the Canon or core of the Mass, he stated:

> "That abominable Canon is a confluence of puddles of slimy water, which have made of the Mass a sacrifice. The Mass is not a sacrifice. It is not the act of a sacrificing priest. Together with the Canon, we discard all that implies an oblation."

In words that are almost prophetic he noted that "when the Mass has been overthrown, I think we shall have overthrown the Papacy. I think it is in the Mass, as on a rock, that the Papacy wholly rests . . . everything will of necessity collapse when their sacrilegious and abominable Mass collapses."

When we come to the Anglicans we fare little better. While their phraseology was more restrained (one of the finer English traits), it is quite clear that they also denied the "Real Presence". Texts current during the time of the Reformation describe the Blessed Sacrament as "a vile cake to be made God and man", and the Mass itself as "the worshiping of God made of fine flour". The Anglican theology denied that the Mass was a "sacrifice" as Catholics understood it, and allowed only for three ways of using the term: the sacrifice of thanksgiving; benevolence and liberality to the poor, and the mortifying of our own bodies. None of these requires an altar. As Cranmer said, "the form of a table shall more move the simple from the superstitious opinions of the Popish Mass into the right use of the Lord's supper. For the use of an altar is to make a sacrifice upon it: the use of a table is to serve for men to eat upon".[7] Cranmer and the reformers specifically denied the doctrine of Transubstantiation, and if the First Book of Common Prayer, due to the ambiguous use of language, was capable of a Catholic interpretation, changes were made in the Second Book of Prayer specifically to exclude this possibility. Should any doubt remain as to their attitude, the reader is refered to the "Thirty-nine Articles" that every Anglican clergyman must adhere to, and which "no man

---

7. Altars were destroyed and replaced by wooden tables throughout England. Altar stones were incorporated into Church steps in order to force the faithful to walk on them when entering the Church. (*The Church under Queen Elizabeth,* F. G. Lee, Thomas Baker: London, 1896).

hereafter shall either print, or preach, to draw the Article aside in any way, but shall submit to it in the plain and full meaning thereof . . ." The list of articles which are *de fide* for the Anglicans includes one — number thirty-one — that states that the Mass as understood by the Council of Trent is a "blasphemous fable and a dangerous deceit".

Under these circumstances, it is a remarkable thing that both Lutherans and Anglicans — to say nothing of the other "separated brethren", find absolutely no objection to parricipating in the *Novus Ordo Massae,* and indeed, in using it themselves as an alternative form of worship. Do they find the New "mass" to be a "blasphemous fable" and "more wicked than all brothels, murderers, robberies, crimes and adulteries"? The answer is a resounding NO! They can almost be said to love· it. They have even made changes in their own "rites" to conform to it. Let us listen to the statement of the Superior Consistory of the Church of the Augsburg Confession of Alsace and Lorraine again. Dated December 8, 1973, in it, the Protestants publicly acknowledge their willingness to take part in the "Catholic eucharistic celebration", because it allowed them to "use these new eucharistic prayers with which they felt at home". And again, why did they feel at home with them? Because they had "the advantage of giving a DIFFERENT INTERPRETATION to the theology of the sacrifice than they were acustomed to attribute to Catholicism". Perhaps the Holy Spirit has guided them to see a change where Paul VI and the Bishops in union with him cannot see one. Yet we are repeatedly told — to quote this same individual — "nothing has been changed in our traditional Mass".

Those who wish to follow this discussion with care would do well to obtain a "People's Mass Book" from the pews of the New Church, and to search for an old Roman Missal such as their parents — yea, their great grand-parents used. We shall however attempt to present the facts in such a manner as not to require this effort.

The changes made, we are told, are "minor". Minor though they may be (and the reader can judge their "minority" for himself), they are precisely those changes that bring the *Novus Ordo* into line with Lutheran and Anglican "theology". I shall only in passing call attention to the deletion of such phrases as "breaking the bonds of sin and crushing the power of hell", so offensive to those who cannot accept the doctrine of "original sin". What is particularly offensive is the addition to the Roman Canon, in Anaphora I[8] (Purporting to be the same as the traditional Canon) of the New Mass, the words *for us* in a totally ambiguous context. In Cranmer's first edition of the Book of Prayer, he prefaced the words of Institution (the Words of Consecration) with this phrase: "Hear us, O merciful Father, we beseech thee; and with Thy Holy Spirit and Word vouchsafe to bless and sanctify these thy gifts and creation of bread and wine that they may be made *unto us* the body and blood of thy most dearly beloved son, Jesus Christ." This formula was attacked on the grounds that it was capable of being construed as effecting transubstantiation! To this Cranmer indignantly replied: "We do not pray absolutely that the bread and wine may be made the body and blood of Christ, but that *unto us* in that holy mystery they may be made so; that is to say, that we may so worthily receive the same that we may be partakers of Christ's body and blood, and that therefore *in spirit and in truth* we may be *spiritually* nourished." It is of course true that in the traditional Roman Canon the phrase *nobis* (for us) is to be found. The *Quam Oblationem* states: "Be pleased to make this same offering wholly blessed, to consecrate it and approve it, making it reasonable and acceptable, so that it may become *for us* the Body and Blood . . ." But here the sense is unequivocal, for the transubstantiation has been prepared for by the magnificent *Te Igitur, Memento Domine* and *Hanc Igitur.* In Cranmer's Second Book of Common Prayer however, and in the *Novus Ordo's* "Anaphora II", these preliminary prayers are omitted. Thus we follow in the New "mass", Cranmer's sense with exactitude. For the consecration there is no preparation whatsoever. After the *Benedictus,* the celebrant merely says "You are truly holy, Lord, the fount of holiness" and then immediately prays that "these gifts may be made *for us* (words not in the original Hippolytus prayer — and why in

---

8. The *Novus Ordo* has four exchangeable "Canons", or "eucharistic prayers". They are also called "Anaphoras". The first is a parody of the traditional Roman Canon in which the above changes are made to bring it into line with Reformation theology. The second is taken from Hippolytus' Canon though similar alterations are made. The others are entirely new creations. There is a move abroad to introduce 100 new alternative ersatz Canons and many of these are already being used by the "up-to-date" clergy on an "experimental" basis.

the world would anyone insert them but to make the prayer conform to Anglican theology) the Body and Blood." In the Traditional Roman Canon, it is quite impossible to understand *"nobis"* in the Cranmerian sense; In Anaphora I, it is at best equivocal; in Anaphora II it is almost impossible to understand "for us" in any other way than as the Reformers do. What makes it even more offensive is that the instruction of the Concilium orders us to make this ersatz Canon, Anaphora II, the one in ordinary use, and further, indicates that it is to be the one utilized for the catechetical instruction of the youth in the nature of the Eucharistic prayer.

Now, the *Novus Ordo Missae* is replete with this pattern of using Protestant phraseology, especially in the "official 'ICEL'" translation.[9] Thus the *Quam Oblationem* which immediately preceeds the Consecration in two (of the four) ersatz Canons, should read "do thou, O God, deign to bless what we offer, and make it approved, effective, right and wholly pleasing in every way . . ." is now translated as "make it *truly spiritual* and acceptable", or as "make it acceptable to you, an offering *in spirit and in truth*". Apart from the fact that these are mistranslations (by scholars yet!), there is nothing *per se* wrong with such phrases as *"truly spiritual"*, or *"in spirit and in truth"*, except that in the historical context of the Reformation they become a serious affront to the Divine Majesty. Wycliffe, Ridley, Coverdale, Cranmer, Latimer, Grindall, Jewell, Beacon and the Book of Common Prayer all use this phrase "spiritual" precisely to deny, and with the full intent of denying, the Transubstantiation. To quote Cranmer directly: "Therefore . . . we do not pray absolutely that the bread and wine may be made the body and blood of Christ, but . . . that therewith *in spirit and in truth* we may be *spiritually* nourished." Similarly, in the New "canon", the phrase *"and praise"* is gratuitously added to the statement *giving thanks*. There is no such phrase in the original Latin, and it is derived from the statement of Luther

---

9. "ICEL", or International Committee for English in the Liturgy is one of the most powerful organizations within the New Church, capable of "over-ruling" even National Bishop's Conferences. Its complex and far reaching organization is described in Gary Potter's "The Liturgy Club", *Triumph*, May 1968.

that "the Mass may be called a sacrifice, if it be understood as a sacrifice of *praise and thanksgiving*, not a work, nor propitiatory" *(De Use. Sacram Euch. Salut.)* No wonder then that the Episcopal Synod responsible for passing judgment on the New "mass" stated:

> "The three ends of the Mass are altered; no distinction is allowed to remain between Divine and human sacrifice; bread and wine are only "spiritually" (not substantially) changed."

Now, any single one of these "innovations" might pass unnoticed or be "innocent", but all of them taken together force on us the conclusion that someone is intentionally attempting (or more exactly, succeeding), in Protestantizing the Mass.

What we see in all this misuse of language is a pattern of intentional "ambiguity". We have already called attention to the modernist technique of using the equivocal phrase in order to insinuate their (mis-)understanding of the truth into orthodox minds. Bugnini and the others responsible for writing the *Novus Ordo* again followed the lead of Luther and Cranmer. The First Prayer Book of Edward VI could not be convicted of overt heresy, for it was adroitly framed and contained no express denial of Catholic doctrine; it was as Richard Cheyney, Lord Bishop of Gloucester said, "expressly designed to suit persons of various and even contradictory religious views: Catholic; not-so-very Catholic; ex-Catholic; non-Catholic; and anti-Catholic!"[10] This would, in the Latin version, also seem to be true of the *Novus Ordo*. As T. M. Parker, an Anglican theologian said, it was "an ingenious essay in ambiguity, purposely worded in such a manner that the more conservative could place their own construction on it, while the Reformers would interpret it in their own sense and would recognize it as an instrument for furthering the next stage of the religious revolution". Many points of Catholic

---

10. Louise I. Guiney, *Blessed Edmund Campion,* Benzinger: N.Y., 1910. Even the Reformers admitted the ambiguity of their work. Dryander wrote to Zurich (concerning the First Book of Common Prayer) that it harbored "every kind of deception by ambiguity or trickery of language" (*Liturgies of the Western Church,* Bard Thompson, New Amer. Lib.: N.Y. 1974).

doctrine are not specifically denied, but only omitted. Others are stated in such a manner — and this is especially true in the "ICEL" translation — that multiple interpretations can be placed upon them. As the Protestant writer A. G. Dickens said of Cranmer's service:

> "Though wholly in the English language, this Prayer Book remained a masterpiece of compromise, even of studied ambiguity. While it did not specifically deny Catholic doctrine, its ambiguous phrases were understood by its author in a Protestant sense and were intended to enable Protestants to use it with good conscience."

It is *ambiguity* that allows both Catholics and Protestants to utilize the *Novus Ordo Missae*. It was the same ambiguity that encouraged Richard Cheyney to attempt the impossible reconciliation between the Reformers and the Papists — "to smooth matters over . . . to escape the terribly severe penalties, and in the end become able to leaven the lump of English error, by the mere preliminary of attendance at the service of Common Prayer according to law". This poor individual was used by the Reformers until he was no longer necessary.

Other techniques were brought into play in order gently to insinuate the *Novus Ordo* into the hearts and minds of the faithful. As with Cranmer's several "Prayer Books", so also with the *Novus Ordo* introduced in stages. As Cardinal Heenan said in a pastoral letter:

> "It would have been foolhardy to introduce all the changes at once. It was obviously wise to change gradually and gently. If all the changes had been introduced at once, you would have been shocked."

It was important to keep appearance intact. The outer ceremonies were the last to be changed. As Comrade Lenin said, "Keep the shell, but empty it of its substance." Luther had already used this technique with great success. To quote Grisar's famous study on Luther, "One who entered the parish church at Wittenberg after Luther's victory, discovered that the same vestments were used for divine service as of yore, and heard the same old Latin hymns. The Host was elevated and exhibited at the Consecration. In the eyes of the people it was the same Mass as before, despite the fact that Luther omitted all prayers which represented the sacred function as a Sacrifice. The people were intentionally kept in the dark on this point. 'We cannot draw the common people away from the Sacrament, and it will probably be thus until the gospel is well understood', said Luther. The rite of celebration of the Mass he explained as 'a purely external thing', and said further that 'the damnable words referring to the Sacrifice could be omitted all the more readily, since the ordinary Christian would not notice the omission and hence there was no danger of scandal. The words in question, especially those of the Canon, are pronounced almost inaudibly in the Popish Church'." The actual Lutheran service used today is based on Luther's prayer book published in 1523 and 1526. The first part of the Mass is retained, but the Offertory, Canon and references to the sacrificial nature of the rite are dropped. The Collect, Epistle and Gospel, as in the traditional Mass, vary according to the Sunday of the year. The Creed is followed by a sermon which is the principal part of the service. Ordinarily, the "Lord's supper" is administered only a few times during the year; the Latin and the elevation of the Host have been deleted; Vestments and lighted candles are still retained.

When we come to the Anglican service, we find it a cross between the Lutheran service and the *Novus Ordo Missae*. As is well known, Luther was in touch by correspondence with the English reformers. The service is begun with the *Introit* (the whole Psalm being sung). The *Judica me* (the priest going to the altar of God — also taken from the Psalms). and the *Confiteor* are both omitted. The confession of sins to Our Lady, the angels and the saints, and the request for their intercession is hardly compatible with the Protestant doctrine of Justification. In the *Novus Ordo Missae* we also do not confess to them, though we do still ask for their intercession. The *Kyrie* and *Gloria* follow as with Luther. Then they have the Credo and two exhortations taken from the 1548 Order of Communion. The sermon becomes a central issue. It is however, after the sermon that the greatest changes occur, for it is the Canon that most explicitly expresses Catholic belief. As Luther said, "all that abomination called the Offertory, and from this point almost everything stinks of

oblation". Luther did away with it entirely. The Anglicans
solved the problem by radically altering it. As Cardinal
Gasquet explains, Cranmer "substituted a new prayer of
about the same length as the old Canon, leaving in it a few
shreds of the ancient one, but divesting if of its character of
sacrifice and oblation". It was this pattern that those responsible for writing the *Novus Ordo* followed.

For both Luther and the Anglicans the service was "a
sacrifice of praise and thanksgiving". (Note how often this
phrase occurs in the "People's Mass Book".) In no place in
either service is the Transubstantiation specifically denied.
Luther added the phrase to the Words of Consecration *"quod
pro vobis traditur"* and dropped both the *Mysterium fidei* and
the words *pro multis*. He specifically considered that what
remained was part of a "narrative" of the Lord's Supper. He
further designated the service as being divided into two parts,
the "Liturgy of the Word", and the "Liturgy of the Eucharist".
(The identification of the "Word" with God as in *John* i:2 was
by implication denied, as was indeed the meaning of the
phrase *"and the Word was made flesh"* as in *John* i:14. The
"Word" is now to be identified with Scripture only. The word
"Eucharist" is acceptable for it means literally "thanksgiving".)
He also instituted communion in both species,[11] the distribution
of communion by lay men and women, the use of ordinary
bread for the service, the use of vessels made of any substance,
the suppression of the altar stone and the use of a table
covered with a single piece of cloth, the need for the "priest"
to face the people (no longer an "intercessor" between man
and God who performs a sacrifice upon an altar, but one who
is a "leader of his community", and who gathers together the
"people of God" around the table to partake of the "Lord's
supper"), and the leaving of the host on the Paten instead of
placing it after consecration on the Corporal. Now almost all
these "customs" which Luther and the *Novus Ordo* disregard,
are of either Apostolic or ecclesiastical Tradition. Thus it is
with reason that the Episcopal Synod already referred to in
rejecting the *Novus Ordo* said that:

11. Communion under both species was practised in the primitive Church,
and is still practised in the Eastern Uniate rites. The issue is discussed in
detail in Session XXI of the Council of Trent. See *Dogmatic Canons and
Decrees of the Council of Trent*, TAN:Rockford III, 1977.

"The position of both priest and people is falsified and the celebrant appears as nothing more than a Protestant minister, while the true nature of the Church is intolerably misrepresented . . . By a series of equivocations the emphasis (in the *Novus Ordo*) is obsessively placed upon the "supper" and the "memorial" instead of on the unbloody renewal of the Sacrifice of Calvary . . . The Real Presence of Christ is never alluded to and belief in it is implicitly repudiated . . . It (the New "mass") has every possibility of satisfying the most modernist of Protestants."

And yet we are told: "Nothing has been changed in the essence of our traditional Mass . . ." and even more, it is "in the name of tradition that we ask all our sons and daughters, all the Catholic communities, to celebrate with dignity and fervour the renewed liturgy". Yes, in the "name of Tradition" we are asked to destroy the Tradition.

*   *   *

It is often said, by those who would defend the New Church that "a few external movements and words added or cut off do not touch the Mass or change it". Let us for a moment examine just what these few changes are.

The *Novus Ordo* has abolished the Offertory, one of the principal parts of the traditional Mass. The *Suscipe Sancte Pater*, the *Deus qui Humanae*, the *Offerimus Tibi*, the *Veni Sanctificator*, the *Lavabo* (*Ps.* xxv), and the *Suscipe Sancta* are all gone. Turn to the old missal and read these prayers. Note how many concepts that the New Church finds objectionable are clearly proclaimed within them. Only the *Orate Fratres* with the *Suscipiat* have been retained. Of course, all the prayers said at the foot of the altar (not a table), the *Aufer a Nobis*, the *Oramus Te*, the *Munda Cor Meum* and the *Dominus Sit* are gone. As to the Canon, if the "president"[12] chooses not to use the "Eucharistic Prayer Number One" (which is falsely claimed to be the old Roman Canon, and

---

12. The term "president" is taken from Justin Martyr where it is used in the sense of one "presiding" over the gifts. Obviously, in the present context it is impossible to divorce the meaning of this word from its political connotations. This ambiguity is most satisfying to those who in line with Protestant theology, consider the "minister" not as one called ("vocation") by God, but as a person chosen by the congregation.

which being the longest Anaphora, is rarely in fact used), the following six prayers before the questionable Consecration are dropped: *Te Igitur, Memento Domine, Communicantes, Hanc Igitur, Quam Oblationem* and the *Qui Pridie*. After the consecration, the following seven prayers are dropped, the *Unde et Memores, Supra quae Propitio, Supplices Te Rogamus, Memento Etiam, Nobis quoque Peccatoribus,* the *Per Quem haec Omnia* and the *Per Ipsum*. As if this was not enough, the following prayers that used to fullow the *Pater Noster* are also dropped, the *Libera Nos, Panem Coelestem, Quid Retribuam,* the second *Confiteor* and its *Absolutionem* (which absolution was also dropped at the start of "mass" so that the post-conciliar Catholic is not reminded of the need to approach the "sacrament" in a reasonable state of "purity"). the *Domine Non sum Dignus,* the *Quod Ore,* the *Corpus Tuum,* the *Placeat Tibi* and the Last Gospel, all of which call specific attention to the Real Presence.

Not mentioned in this list are the changes made in the prayers that are retained (such as we have discussed above), and the changes made in the Words of Consecration (to be discussed below). Nor do I include the many genuflections, the many signs of the cross and the numerous versicles that have been deleted. Clearly, if only on the basis of the above list, somewhere between 70 and 80 percent of the traditional Mass has been "sacrificed" on the "altar" of "unity with the Protestants". Yet Paul VI and the Bishops in union with him repeatedly assure us that — "Let everyone understand well that nothing has been changed in the essence of our traditional Mass . . ."

*   *   *

It is claimed, by the modernists who have "captured" the Church, that the *Novus Ordo Missae* is in many places a "return to primitive practice". As Paul VI said in his Apostolic Constitution, since the time of Pius V and the Council of Trent

> "Other ancient sources (of the liturgy) have been dis-
> covered, and liturgical formulas of the Eastern Church
> have been studied. Many wish that these doctrinal and
> spiritual riches be not hidden in libraries, but be brought
> to light to illuminate and nourish the minds and spirits
> of Christians."

Several points must be made. First of all, it is a typical Protestant ploy to claim to be returning to "primitive simplicity". The Church has always been accused of adding a whole host of prescriptions to the pure Christianity of Love that Christ founded. Where did Christ ever forbid abortion (is it not murder?). Where did he ask us to fast during Lent? Where did he tell us about the sign of the Cross? This is nowhere to be found in Scripture. Of course not, such things come to us through the medium of tradition. It is a typical example of sawing off the branches, yea even the trunk, in an attempt to expose the "roots", as if the trunk and branches were not a legitimate and even an essential aspect of the growth and manifestation of the tradition throughout time. Hypocrisy this clearly is, for if man has "progressed" and "evolved" since the primitive times of the Apostles, surely going back to "primitive practice" is the last thing that is necessary. Actually both these techniques of attacking the Tradition leave very little behind in the middle that is not innocuous and innocent. But let us at least give some consideration to the argument.

First of all, we are never told just what these "ancient sources" are that have been discovered. It is true that Hippolytus's writings came to light during the last century, but in them nothing is to be found that changes the conclusions of previous scholars. The Dead Sea scrolls have done nothing but affirm the accuracy of the texts that have come down to us, and despite their historical value, have in no way changed our understanding of the times in which they were hidden away to protect them from the Roman hordes. As to the Eastern liturgies, they have always been available to us, they have always been recognized by the Church as valid liturgies going back to Apostolic times. They have always been so similar to our own that apart from linguistic differences, one can find parallels to all the essential parts of our traditional Mass. Indeed, the Roman Church has accepted them intact and without change in the various "Uniate" Churches that have returned to communion with Rome. Finally, unless one wishes to point to such prayers as the Our Father, not one prayer in the *Novus Ordo* has been taken from the Eastern Liturgies. What then of the claim to return to "primitive practice"?

There are in the *Novus Ordo* only two prayers that have any claim to be a return to "primitive practice". These are the words from the new Offertory: *"Benedictus tu Deus noster, Rex universi . . .* Blessed are you, our God, ruler of the universe, who brings forth bread from the earth . . ."* and the "Anaphora" or "Eucharistic Prayer Number Two" which is said to be taken from Hippolytus. We shall consider each of them in turn.

As to the first, as Jungmann states in his last book on the Mass, this is a "reconstructed" prayer, and is "probably the very words used at the blessing of bread and wine in a Jewish meal at the time of Christ". Anyone who has had the privilege of being invited to participate at a formal Jewish dinner will recognize them. Before starting to eat, the Rabbi says these words as he slices the bread and drinks the wine. This prayer is the Jewish "grace before meals" and nothing more. And how appropriate for the Protestants in Rome to have their new "service", the "memorial to the Lord's Supper", introduced with "grace before meals". No one has ever denied their consistency.

As for Hippolytus' "Anaphora", Father John Barry Ryan, a liturgical modernist in "obedience" to the Post-conciliar Church, frankly calls its author a "schismatic", and has stated that his prayer was a "model" on which "Anaphora II", an entirely "new creation", was based. He further tells us that it was the heresiarch Hans Küng who first suggested its use — though in a modified form of course.[13] Finally, while it has nothing to do with the authenticity or the validity of the prayer, it should be noted that, as Josef Jungmann states, Hippolytus "allowed himself to be chosen as an anti-Pope, though because he was subsequently martyred for the faith, we may rightly conclude that before his death, he returned to the unity of the Church" *(The Early Liturgy)*. Those who are interested in comparing the original form of Hippolytus' prayer with that used by the *Novus Ordo* will find it in Cipriano Vagaggini's book[14] — another interesting individual, as he was the author in greater part of Anaphora IV, the "Arian" Canon. *(Notitiae,* 1974, p. 249-52) From what healthy roots this "vine" has sprung!

As to returning to the "primitive practice" of the Church, this is but another way of "picking and choosing" just what

---

13. John Barry Ryan, *The Eucharistic Prayer*, Paulist Press: N.Y., 1974.
14. Cipriano Vagaggini, *The Canon of the Mass and Liturgical Reform*, Alba House: N.Y., 1966.

the modernists think Christianity should be. It is true that
there were certain Churches in which the priest had to face
the people — occasionally architectural restrictions imposed
by the desire to have the altar face the east, forced this
alternative on those responsible for the decision. On other
occasions, a Church was enlarged and the sacredness of an
altar led to the decision not to move it (many of the early
altars were sepulchres built over the graves of saints). During
the time of persecution the laity, with appropriate reverence,
were allowed to transport the Eucharist. But what about the
all night vigils? What about the practice of the laity saying
the office? We hear of no return to "primitive practice" where
it involves intensifying the spiritual life of the faithful — only
when it allows the reformers to destroy what has been accepted
practice for hundreds of years. Surely this is one of the most
hypocritical ploys that the Reformers have come up with!

*   *   *

In the *Novus Ordo Missae,* and particularly in the
vernacular, the context in which the Words of Consecration
are said can with the greatest ease be understood as being
"historical". That is to say, as the priest repeats the words
ascribed to Christ, and without in any way "abusing" his
privilege, the context is such that he can understand them as
part of the "Narration of the Institution", as a re-telling of
the story of what happened some two thousand years ago. In
the "Missal" on the "table" from which the minister reads,
the words in question are still capitalized, but in the "People's
Mass Book" (which is often used by the priest, and is the only
one used by the laity), there is no way to tell which words are
those ascribed to Christ and which are part of the narration.
No capitals are used. Indeed, the words are not even found in
a separate paragraph. Now it is these words that perfect the
sacrament. Listen to the teaching of St. Thomas Aquinas:

> "The consecration is accomplished by the words and
> expressions of the Lord Jesus. Because, by all the other
> words spoken, praise is rendered to God, prayer is put
> up for the people, for kings, and others; but when the
> time comes for perfecting the Sacrament, the priest uses
> no longer his own words, but the words of Christ. There-
> fore, it is Christ's words that perfect the sacrament."

To say the Words of Consecration as part of a narrative clearly invalidates the Mass (both the traditional and any other).

> "The words of Consecration have to be said, not merely as a historical narrative of words used once by our Lord — as the Celebrant recites them, e.g., in the accounts of the Last Supper, which are read in the Mass in Holy Week, or on the Feast of Corpus Christi — but as a present affirmation by the priest speaking in the person of Christ, and intending to effect something, here and now, by the pronouncing of these words . . ."
>
> Rev. J. O'Connell, *The Celebration of Mass*

It is important that this doctrine be understood, even by those who may not accept it, for we are not expounding here any personal views, but only the teaching of Holy Mother Church.

> "The Form of Consecration is not considered to be a prayer of the priest. Rather, it is the evocation of a direct and most glorious act from God Himself. Through his pronunciation of the Consecration Form, the priest's humanity and individuality become identified with the infinite power and redemptive intention of Christ on the Cross. At this point the priest speaks as if he were Christ Himself, and Christ acts through the priest's will both as the Consecrator and the Oblation, the Eternal High-Priest and the saving Victim, the supreme Mediator and the mutual gift."

I repeat, in the *Novus Ordo Missae,* all the Words of Consecration (if such they be) are part of the "Narration of the Institution".[15] Not only are most of Luther's changes

___

15. The term "Institution" refers to the Institution of the Sacrament by Christ, and is a perfectly legitimate theological term. The idea that the Mass is a "narrative" however, is patently false. Despite this, official French Catechisms make such statements as that "At the heart of the Mass lies a story . . ." The Official French Missal published with the approval of the hierarchy states that the Mass "is simply the memorial of the unique sacrifice accomplished once! *("Il s'agit simplement de faire mémoire de*

incorporated — changes he made to stress the narrative aspect — but the entire setting is one in which, unless the "president" makes a positive intention to the contrary — a narrative is clearly implied. Without the proper "intention", no sacrament is confected.

*   *   *

This leads us to consider another very important aspect of the problem. As Father Howard Morrison and the editorial staff of *The Wanderer* admit, even when said according to the wishes of Paul VI, no consecration occurs in the *Novus Ordo* if the proper intention is lacking on the part of the "president". Of course, in the traditional Mass, it was also possible for the priest positively to intend *not* to consecrate, and thus to invalidate the confection of the Sacred Species. However, in saying the rite correctly, he assumed the proper intention automatically, and as long as he intended to do what the Church intends, the validity of the Mass could be presumed. As long as the priest did not specifically *intend not to consecrate*, no problem arose, and should such have been his intention, he committed a clear act of sacrilege.

In the *Novus Ordo Missae,* the wording of the rite no longer automatically supplies this intention. Indeed, it is necessary for the "president" specifically to intend to consecrate for the Sacred Species to be effected. It follows then, as *The Wanderer* admits, that one must positively ascertain in each and every individual case that the priest has a truly Catholic intention if one is to consider his action as "valid". If the priest is a modernist, or an atheist, or if he himself does not believe in the "Real Presence", one must presume that consecration has not occurred.[16] Hence the warning of the Episcopal Synod previously refered to:

"The words of consecration, as they appear in the

---

l'unique sacrifice déjà accompli"). This statement has been repeated in more than one edition, and despite the protest of the faithful. It is overtly heretical. It would however appear to be the "official" teaching of the Conciliar Church — another accommodation to Protestant "theology".

16. *The Wanderer,* St. Paul, Minn., June 16, 1977. This is perhaps the most "conservative" publication of the Post-conciliar Church in North America. It is unwittingly one of the most valuable sources of documentation of "The Destruction of the Christian Tradition" available today. In future years, its pages will provide a "historical document" of the greatest importance.

context of the *Novus Ordo* (in Latin) may be valid according to the intention of the ministering priest. But they may not be, for they are so no longer *ex vi verborum* (by the force of the words used) or more precisely, in virtue of the *modus significandi* (way of signifying) which they have had till now in the Mass."

A further warning is added which if one knows anything about the way priests are being trained in the Post-conciliar seminaries, is truly pertinent:[17]

"Will priests who, in the near future, have not had the traditional training and who rely on the *Novus Ordo* in order to "do what the Church does", make a valid consecration? One may be permitted to doubt it."

*   *   *

Let us pause in the narration of this dastardly subterfuge to make certain points. All that we have said is true of the *Novus Ordo*, whether it be said in Latin or the vernacular. Unquestionably, in the vernacular it is more offensive than in the Latin, and unquestionably the use of Latin prevents the priest from introducing still further changes in accordance with his personal judgment — not only by adding a prayer here and there, but by changing further the prayers that are supposedly "fixed". We are not talking of *abuses*, but of the text as it officially stands, and as each Post-conciliar priest is supposed to adhere to it. Now the reader will ask two questions. How can this be? Why has no one done anything

---

17. To quote Father Robert Burns, C.S.P., editorial writer for *The Wanderer* (Aug. 10, 1978): "Many newly ordained priests are either formal or material heretics on the day of their ordination. This is so, because their teachers embraced modernist errors and passed them along to their students. The students, after ordination, in turn propagated these errors, either in catechetical teaching or in pulpit preaching. The same situation is also true in the cases of many older priests who return to schools of theology for updating courses or 'retooling in theology'." Further witness to this sad state of affairs is drawn from the *Homiletic and Pastoral Review*, (January 1975). To quote its editor: "I have a confession to make to our readers. Often I have been asked to print some good articles in the field of moral theology. The sad fact is that I have had to reject over 90% of the material sent to me on the subject. The principal reason for the rejections has been that the articles either espoused or assumed the relativism and subjectivism which are the basis of situational ethics. Moreover, most of those articles were written by professors in Catholic colleges and seminaries."

about it? With regard to the first question, it is truly hard to understand how it can be, but it is. All that I have said is true and cannot be controverted. The situation is prefigured in Scripture. Consider Daniel ix:27 *"The Victim and the Sacrifice shall fail: and there shall be in the Temple, the abomination of desolation",* and in *Daniel* xi:31, *"and they shall defile the sanctuary of strength and shall take away the continual sacrifice".* Listen to *Malachi* i:7: *"You offered polluted bread upon My altars, and you say, wherein have we polluted Thee?"* And *Jeremias* speaks in God's name when he says *"My tabernacle is laid waste, all My cords are broken: My children are gone out from Me, and they are not . . . Because the pastors have done foolishly, and have not sought the Lord: therefore have they not understood, and all their flock is. scattered."* And further, we find *Ezechiel* saying *"Her priests have despised my law, and have defiled my sanctuaries: they have put no difference between holy and profane."* Consider the words of St. Cyril:

> "Let no one at that day say in his heart . . . 'unless God willed it, He would not have permitted it'. No: The Apostle forewarns you, saying beforehand, 'God shall send them a strong delusion', not that they may be excused, but condemned."

Nor is it true that there have been no protests. Thousands upon thousands of signatures have been sent to Rome in petitions asking for the old Mass to be given back. They have been ignored. When over 400 pilgrims walked (yes, walked) from France to Rome to petition Paul VI for the old Mass, he refused to see them. He was too busy. He was entertaining a soccer team. He could not claim that there was insufficient time to schedule an appointment for the pilgrims. They had requested it months before and their journey was carried in many of the newspapers. They were simply ignored. Books have been written and open challenges laid down to debate the issue. They have been ignored. The New Church dares not debate the issues and only cries out again and again to the mournful faithful, "you must obey". It is a false obedience that is asked. The Episcopal Synod appointed by Paul VI to review the *Novus Ordo Missae* substantially rejected it. They gave their reasons in a brief but accurate summary. The

Church has never published this report. One is to this day
unsure how it was "smuggled" out of the Vatican. However,
we have this report and have quoted from it. It is added as an
appendix to this book. When the Latin Mass Society in
England sent a copy of it to every priest in Britain, the English
hierarchy instructed their clergy under obedience not to read
it, but to throw it in the waste-paper basket. This report is an
unequivocal condemnation of the New "mass". It has never
been answered by the New Church, just ignored. Imagine an
attack on the old and traditional Mass made during the years
of the English Reformation. By God, dozens of books were
published and smuggled into England to defend it. And yet
this report which has been abroad some ten years has never
been answered. But we have not told the whole story.

It is quite clear that the entire Mass centres on the "Words
of Consecration", and it is with this topic that we shall next
deal. Let the reader remember that without these few words,
the Roman Mass is nothing — not entirely nothing, for the
prayers are beautiful and the doctrine they teach sublime,
but relatively speaking, nothing.

*   *   *

It is admitted by many conservative Post-conciliar Catholics
that much of what we have said is true. They argue however
that despite all this, "Consecration" still occurs, and that they
go to the New "mass" for the Sacrament, and simply ignore
what the priest has to say. Such a statement assumes that the
act of Consecration is valid — and valid under almost any
circumstance. It is however, only valid providing the "matter",
"form", "minister" and "intention" are all valid. Let us assume
for the moment that the "form" of the Sacrament in the
Novus Ordo has not been changed, and that a validly
ordained priest intended to confect the Sacred Species with
the new ersatz Canon of his choice. Consecration *might* occur
under such circumstances.

> "Accordingly, it must be held that if the priest were to
> pronounce only the aforesaid words (the Words of
> Consecration) with the intention of consecrating the
> sacrament, this sacrament would be valid because the
> intention would cause these words to be understood as
> spoken in the person of Christ, even though the words

were pronounced without those that preceded (i.e. the Canon in its entirety). *The priest however, would sin gravely in consecrating thus,* as he would not be observing the rite of the Church."

St. Thomas, *Summa., III, 78, 1.*

To place the contention in a proper context, consider the possibility of a priest saying the proper Words of Consecration during a "Black" or "Satanic" Mass. Would consecration occur? According to St. Thomas, absolutely not, for the priest would not be intending to do what the Church intends. Further, there would be a conflict of intention involved in doing what is holy and what is sacrilegious. Now consider the possibility of a priest confecting the Sacred Species using the proper formula within a Lutheran or an Anglican service.[18] Here again, almost any priest before the Council would have said that he was committing a sacrilege and that the consecration was invalid because of the sacrilegious context and the improper intention incorporated into the rite. But what, pray, is the difference between using the proper words in an Anglican or a Lutheran service, and using them in the *Novus Ordo Missae?* I challenge anyone, in the light of the definition and description of the Mass as originally given in Paragraph 7 of the General Instructions on the New "mass", and in the light of the historical parallels that we have clearly demonstrated, to show me a difference.[19]

---

18. Some Anglican "priests" have had their "orders" validated by going to the Old Catholic Church and the Greek Orthodox Church. The Words of Consecration as originally chosen for the Anglican service are: "Hear us (O merciful Father) we beseech thee: and with thy holy spirit and worde, vouchsafe to blesse and sanctify these thy gyfts, and creatures of bread and wyne, that they maie be unto us the bodye and bloude of thy moste derely beloued sonne Jesus Christe. Who in the same nyght that he was betrayed: tooke breade, and when he had blessed, and geuen thankes: ne brake it, and gaue it to his disciples, saying: Take, eate, this is my bodye which is giuen for you, do this in remembraunce of me. Likewise after supper he toke the cuppe, and when he had geuen thankes, he gaue it to them, saiying: drynk ye all of this, for this is my bloude of the newe Testament, whyche is shed for you and for many, for the remission of synnes: do this as oft as you shall drinke it in remembraunce of me." Surely these words have an equal validity to those used in the *Novus Ordo* — and perhaps, an even greater validity, as the phrase "for all men" instead of "for many" is not used.

19. The "definition" or "Description" of the New "mass" given in Paragraph 7 of Paul VI's Apostolic Constitution is discussed below.

Sacrilege is defined by St. Thomas as "the irreverent treatment of sacred things". In his discussion on the topic, St. Thomas makes several distinctions, and notes that since the Eucharist is the most sacred possession of the Church, sacrilege with regard to the Sacrament is a "most heinous sin" (*Summa* III Q. 80, Ar. 5). Unfortunately, despite the fact that in all likelihood no consecration occurs in the *Novus Ordo,* objective sacrilege is still committed. And if the priest is aware of all that we have so far said, and that the New "mass" is a *parody,* this sacrilege becomes subjective in character. But what of the Words of Consecration?

*   *   *

The Words of Consecration used in the Roman Catholic Church derive from Tradition. They are said by the theologians to be given us *in specie:*[20]

> "Christ determined what special graces were to be conferred by means of external rites: for some sacraments (e.g. Baptism, the Eucharist) He determined minutely *(in specie)* the matter and form: for others He determined only in a general way *(in genere)* that there should be an external ceremony, by which special graces were to be conferred, leaving to the Apostles or to the Church the power to determine whatever He had not determined — e.g. to prescribe the matter and form of the Sacraments of Confirmation and of Holy Orders."

Further, the "form" of the Sacrament has been fixed by tradition since Apostolic times. It has been "canonically" fixed since the so-called "Armenian Decree" of the Council of Florence (1438-1445). The Council of Trent in a solemn decree guaranteed the authenticity of the sacramental forms laid down in the then-to-be written Catechism — as it says in Session XXIV, Chapter 7: "The form will be prescribed for each of the Sacraments by the Holy Council in a Catechism, which the Bishops shall have faithfully translated into the language of the people." This Catechism in turn states:

---

20. "The form of this Sacrament is pronounced as if Christ were speaking in person, so that it is given to be understood that the minister does nothing in perfecting this Sacrament, except to pronounce the words of Christ". (*Summa,* III, Q. 78, Art. 1).

with regard to the consecration of the wine it is necessary . . . that the priest know and understand well its form. We are, then, firmly to believe that it consists in the following words:

(the "Form" is Capitalized)

Who the day before He suffered took bread into His holy and venerable hands, and with His eyes lifted up to heaven, to You, God, His almighty Father, giving thanks to You, He blessed broke and gave it to His disciples, saying: Take and eat you all of this

FOR THIS IS MY BODY

In like manner, after He had supped, taking also this glorious chalice into His holy and venerable hands, again giving thanks to You, He blessed and gave it to His disciples saying: Take and drink you all of this,

FOR THIS IS THE CHALICE OF MY BLOOD, OF THE NEW AND ETERNAL TESTAMENT: THE MYSTERY OF FAITH: WHICH SHALL BE SHED FOR YOU AND FOR MANY UNTO THE REMISSION OF SINS. As often as you shall do these things, you shall do them in memory of Me.

As the Catechism continues, "of this form no one can doubt". Taken from the "People's Mass Book", the following is the "form" used in the *Novus Ordo Missae:* No words are capitalized and they are given in a running fashion so that they form part of the "narration of the institution" without any distinction. However, in the Latin original the italicized words appear in capitals:

"Before he was given up to death, a death he freely accepted, he took bread and gave you thanks. He broke the bread, gave it to his disciples, and said: *this is my body which will be given up for you.* When supper was ended, he took the cup. Again he gave you thanks and praise, gave the cup to his disciples, and said: Take this, all of you, and drink from it: *this is the cup of my blood, the blood of the new and everlasting covenant. It will be shed for you and for all men so that sins may be forgiven.* Do this in memory of me."

We have said that the Form of the Words of Consecration come to us from Tradition. The innovators who created the *Novus Ordo* argue that in changing the form, they are "bringing it into line with Scripture". Now, there is absolutely no reason why this should be done. Scripture is not a greater source of Revelation than Tradition. Imagine the hue and cry that would be raised if we were to change Scripture to bring it into line with Tradition! It is from Tradition that we receive the form, and not from Scripture. Listen to the words of Cardinal Manning:

> "We neither derive our religion from the Scriptures, nor does it depend upon them. Our faith was in the world before the New Testament was written."

As Joseph Jungmann states:

> "In all the known liturgies, the core of the *eucharistia*, and therefore of the Mass, is formed by the narrative of the institution and the words of consecration. Our very first observation in this regard is the remarkable fact that the texts of the account of institution, among them in particular the most ancient (whether as handed down or as reconstructed by comparative studies), are never simply a Scripture text restated. They go back to pre-Biblical Tradition. Here we face an outgrowth of the fact that the Eucharist was celebrated long before the evangelists and St. Paul set out to record the Gospel story."

Indeed, one could suspect that the Scriptural accounts intentionally avoided giving the correct form lest it be profaned. Listen to St. Thomas Aquinas again:

> "The Evangelists did not intend to hand down the forms of the Sacraments which in the primitive Church had to be kept concealed, as Dionysius observes at the close of

his book on the ecclesiastical hierarchy: their object was to write the story of Christ." (*Summa,* III, 78, Art. 3)[21]

No one can doubt but that the New Church has gone against tradition as well as the decrees of the Ecumenical Councils and the Catechism of the Council of Trent in changing the form of the sacrament. It is *not* a matter of debate as to whether she has the right to do so:

> "The Church is forbidden to change, or even touch, the matter or form of any sacrament. She may indeed change or abolish or introduce something in the non-essential rites or 'ceremonial' parts used in the administration of the sacraments, such as processions, prayers or hymns before or after the actual words of the form are recited . . ."

> Pope Leo XIII, *Apostolicae Curae*

Defenders of the New Church will of course argue that such is only an opinion, and like the form itself, is not part of what is termed *de fide*. Whether this is true or not, when we come to the "substance" of the form, no debate is possible. The "Substance" of a Sacrament is said to consist of those elements which are absolutely necessary in order for the Sacrament to be effective. Quite clearly the statement "This is My Body; This is My Blood" are substantial and cannot be deleted. Now the Church has never absolutely defined what words are essential to the form of the Sacrament, and theologians have debated the issue throughout the ages.[22] St. Thomas Aquinas and the great majority of the theologians before the 20th Century claim that all the words belong to the "substance of the Sacrament".

---

21. The fact that modern scholars have re-dated the writings of Dionysius changes nothing. Such scholars appear to be more interested in dating works than in understanding their content.
22. The difference between what is "essential" and what is "substantial" is not pertinent to the issue, but will be discussed in later paragraphs briefly.

"It is well known that to the Church there belongs no right whatsoever to innovate anything on the substance of the Sacraments."

Pope Saint Pius X *Ex quo nono*.

"It (the Council of Trent) declares furthermore that this power has always been in the Church, that in the administration of the sacraments, *without violating their substance*, she may determine or change whatever she may judge to be more expedient for the benefit of those who receive them . . ."

Session XXI, Chapter 2

The crux of the debate about "substance" resolves around the issue of "meaning". In the *Novus Ordo Missae*, when said in Latin, no one can absolutely state that the substance of the formula has been altered. The phrases that have been added or removed do not clearly or necessarily change the meaning of the words. In the vernacular however, (and in all the various languages used), as we shall show, the meaning, and thence the "substance" has been altered. Now

"It is clear, if any substantial part of the sacramental form is suppressed, that the essential sense of the words is destroyed; and consequently the sacrament is invalid."

St. Thomas, *Summa* III, Q. 60, Art. 8

"If anyone omits or changes anything in the form of the consecration of the Body and Blood, and in this change of words, does not mean the same thing, then he does not effect the Sacrament."

De Defectibus, Missa Rom.

Another argument put forth by the modernists is that in the various rites that exist, (some 76 in all), and that the Church has always recognized as valid, the consecratory form varies greatly. This is of course a half-truth. There are minor variations. Some have the phrase "which will be given up for you", and others omit the *Mysterium fidei*, the "Mystery of the Faith". (This phrase is said by tradition to have been inserted by the Apostles, an insertion that was entirely within their function to make — and this fact perhaps explains why it is not to be found in all the 76 known "forms"). It was after all, the Apostles that established these different forms in various parts of the world, and not Bugnini and his cohorts. We list some of these below.[23]

In any event, within the Roman rite, and it is within this framework that we in the West "live and breathe", the traditional "form" of the Sacrament has been fixed since time immemorial; it has been "codified" in the Canons of the Ecumenical Councils and proclaimed in the Catechism of the Council of Trent. To change it is a grave sin.

> "Thus in the form of the Eucharist, *-for this is My Body* . . . the omission of the word *for* . . . does not cause the sacrament to be invalid; although perhaps he who makes the omission may sin from negligence or contempt." (Summa III, Q, 60. Art. 8).

> "If anyone omits or changes anything in the form of the Consecration of the Body and Blood, and in this change of words the words do not mean the same thing, then he does not effect the Sacrament. If words are added which do not alter the meaning, then the Sacrament is valid, but the celebrant commits a mortal sin in making such an addition."

> *Missale Romanum, De Defectibus*

---

23. Byzantine: "This is My blood of the New Testament, which is shed for you and for many for the forgiveness of sins."

Armenian: "This is My blood of the new testament which is shed for you and for many for the expiation and forgiveness of sins."

Coptic: "For this is My blood of the New covenant, which shall be shed for you and for many unto the forgiveness of sins."

Ethiopic: "This is My blood of the new covenant which is shed for you and for many for the forgiveness of sin."

Syrian: "This is My Blood, of the new covenant, which shall be poured out and offered for the forgiveness of the sins and eternal life of you and of many."

Maronite: As in the Latin Rite.

Chaldean: "This is My blood of the New covenant, the mystery of faith, which is shed for you and for many for the forgiveness of sins."

Malabar: "For this is the chalice of my blood of the New and Eternal Testament, the Mystery of Faith, which is shed for you and for many for the remission of sins."

It will of course be argued that all this insistence upon the correct words being used is a sort of "legalism", and has little to do with that "love" which Christ bore witness to. After all, what are a few words here and there? If we accept this position however, we must admit that the entire Counter-Reformation was absurd. Surely we must also admit that the various Lutheran and Anglican "rites" have been valid from the day they were instituted. We must also admit that the Anglican orders are valid — and indeed, as Bernard Haring has claimed, that the Lutheran ministers (at least those in Europe, for this sect has no "Bishops" in America) are also validly ordained. And surely then, we can also change around a few — or for that matter many — of the words of Scripture. Let us leave out a few of the "nots" in the Ten Commandments. Let us "pick and choose" to our heart's content. The important thing to realize is that the Reformers made these changes precisely to deny the Sacrificial nature of the Mass. The *Novus Ordo* follows these significant changes almost verbatim. The Mass is, after all, one of our most sacred possessions. As Pope Innocent I said in the year 416:

> "Who does not know and consider that what was delivered to the Roman Church by St. Peter, the Prince of the Apostles, and is to this day kept (by it), ought to be observed by all, and that no practice should be substituted or added . . ."

And, how can what is a mortal sin one day be other than a mortal sin the next? How can the "constant" Church become so "fickle"? Regardless of how we view the issues, one thing is clear from what has been so far said. The New and Post-conciliar Church has changed the form of the sacrament. This in itself is a most dastardly act, even apart from considerations of validity. In thus attacking the heart of the Mass, the New Church both declares herself and exposes herself to be a "despoiler" of all that is most sacred. In this one act she has presumed to alter the very words of Christ; she has gone against Tradition and Apostolic custom; she has altered the customs and disciplines adhered to by the Fathers of the Church and innumerable saints; she has disregarded the teachings of the Ecumenical Councils and gone against the Council of Trent; She has disobeyed numerous laws and statements to be found in the various organs of the teaching Magisterium. When she is reprimanded, she loudly protests that "It is valid; it is more Scriptural; it is adapted to the needs of modern man, and it helps to promote unity!" Unity with whom? But we have yet to consider in more detail the issue of "substantia". If the changes are minor and "accidental", no matter how offensive, the formula may still be valid. If the changes are "substantial", if the meaning of the formula has been changed, then clearly the Sacred Species is not confected.

According to St. Thomas:

> "Some have maintained that the words 'This is the Chalice of My Blood' alone belong to the substance of the form, but not those words which follow. Now this seems incorrect, because the words that follow them are determinations of the predicate, that is, of Christ's blood; consequently they belong to the integrity of the expression. And on this account others say more accurately that all the words which follow are of the substance of the form down to the words 'As often as ye shall do this'. (Not including these words, for the priest puts down the Chalice when he comes to them — Ed.) hence it is that the priest pronounces all the words, under the same rite and manner, holding the chalice in his hands." (*Summa*, III, Q. 78, Art. 3)

Most theologians of the Church agree with this position, namely that the form of the Sacrament has been fixed since time immemorial, and that the "substance" includes all of the above specified words. Admittedly there are some, such as St. Bonaventura and Cajetan who hold that "This is the Chalice of My Blood" would suffice for Validity (these words being essential), though it should be noted in passing that when Pope Saint Pius V ordered the works of Cajetan to be published, he also ordered that this opinion (and only this opinion) should be struck from them. Furthermore, even the Cajetan Thomists admit that these latter words (i.e. "which shall be shed for you and for many . . .") do indeed belong to the substance of the form, even though they deny their necessity for validity. That is to say, they distinguish between what is of the "substance" and what is of the "essence". Hence they assert that while these latter words are not essential for the validity of the Sacrament, they are nevertheless necessary for the integrity or completeness of the form, and therefore belong to the substance. It would appear, then, that the New Church has not only attacked and changed the form of the Sacrament; it has also — in the various vernacular usages — altered the Substance! The mistranslating of *"multis"* as to make it read *"for all men"* changes the meaning of the formula, as we shall clearly demonstrate. In doing so the Conciliar Church adds injury to insult. Such an act is clearly illicit, for it goes against the laws of the Church and as such is contrary to the will of God. As Father Joseph Pohle says in his Dogmatic Treatise on "The Sacraments": "Had the Church received from her Divine Founder the power to institute Sacraments, she would also have the power of changing the substance of the sacrament . . . But this is not so . . ."

It is of course theoretically conceivable that the "form" can be altered without changing the *meaning* of the formula. Should such be the case, consecration might still occur. It is a change in meaning that invalidates all possibility of confecting the Species — it is this that characterizes a "substantial" change. The New Church holds that she still retains the essential words "This is My Body . . . This is My Blood". These words are also retained in the Reformation services. But it is important to remember that, as St. Thomas says, "the words which follow 'This is My Blood' are determinations of the predicate." Thus, if the priest were to say, "This is My Blood and by this statement I mean a symbol and not the reality", clearly he would not consecrate because the second phrase would alter the meaning of the predicate. In the *Novus Ordo Missae,* in the vernacular the substitution of the words *"for all men"* in place of *"for many"* clearly alters the meaning of the predicate and thus "the essential sense of the words is destroyed". This being so, according to the opinion of St. Thomas, it follows that "THE SACRAMENT IS CLEARLY RENDERED INVALID".

The New Church of course argues that "many" means "all", or something along these lines. (In passing, it is worth noting that the Post-conciliar "Popes" have used "all" — *tutti* — when saying the *Novus Ordo* in the vernacular). She argues that there was no such word as "all" in the Aramaic, or that when Christ said "many", He really meant "all". She will quote for you all sorts of philological studies to prove it. To all this I say "nonsense". The first person to come up with this silly idea was a Protestant theologian named Joachim Jeremias (recently deceased) who personally denied the doctrine of Transubstantiation. Even a child knows the difference between "all" and "many". As for the argument that no such word as "all" exists in Aramaic, this is proved false by referring to the *Porta Linguarum Orientalium*. None of the 76 forms of Consecration in a wide variety of languages uses "all" in place of "many", and above all, the Greek form established by the Apostles does not.[24] And are we to change all the "manys" in the Bible to "alls"? — it would be insanity.

Now, superficially, it may seem that changing "many" to "all" is not a very important issue. After all, what is in a word? The problem is, this is a very important word:

"Nothing is more dangerous than the heretics who, while conserving almost all the remainder of the Church's teaching intact, corrupt WITH A SINGLE WORD, like a drop of poison, the purity and the simplicity of the faith which we have received through tradition from God and through the Apostles."

Leo XIII, *Satis Cognitum*

In order to understand how *all men* alters the sense of the words, one must turn to the Church's teaching on the difference between *efficacy* and *sufficiency*. It is a truth of our Faith that Christ died for all men without exception. *"And He is the propitiation of our sins: and not for ours only, but also for those of the whole world"* (1 John ii:2). Thus His act of Sacrifice has sufficiency. It is also a truth of our faith that not all men are saved, but some indeed suffer eternal damnation. *"The wicked shall be turned into hell, all the nations that forget God"* (Ps. ix:18). Hence it follows that the *efficacy* or effectiveness of Christ's act is not communicated to all men, but only unto those who are actually saved. This is why St. Thomas states in *Summa* III, Q. 78, Art. 3 and elsewhere that *for all men* was NOT used, and *for many* was.

---

24. As St. Thomas informs us, "James the brother of the Lord according to the flesh, and Basil, Bishop of Caesarea, edited the rite of celebrating the Mass". *Summa* III, Q. 83, Art. 4.

Such was hardly a "slip of the tongue" or a casual opinion, for the same point is made by the Catechism of the Council of Trent:

> "The additional words *for you and for many,* are taken, some from *Matthew* (xxvi:28), some from *Luke* (xxii:20), but were joined together by the Catholic Church under the guidance of the Spirit of God. They serve to declare the fruit and advantage of His Passion. For if we look to its value, we must confess that the Redeemer shed His blood for the salvation of all: but if we look to the fruit which mankind have received from it, we shall easily find that it pertains not unto all, but to many of the human race. When therefore Our Lord said: *For you,* He meant either those who were present, or those chosen from among the Jewish disciples with whom He was speaking. When He added *and for many,* He wished to be understood to mean the remainder of the elect from among the Jews and Gentiles. With reason, therefore, were the words *for all* not used, as in this place the fruits of the Passion are alone spoken of, and to the elect only did His Passion bring the fruit of salvation."

This opinion is further confirmed by St. Alphonsus Liguori:

> "The words *Pro vobis et pro multis* ('For you and for many') are used to distinguish the virtue of the Blood of Christ from its fruits: for the blood of Our Saviour is of sufficient value to save all men, but its fruits are applicable only to a certain number and not to all, and this is their own fault. Or, as the theologians say, this precious Blood is (in itself) sufficiently *(sufficienter)* able to save all men, but (on our part) effectually *(efficaciter)* it does not save all — it saves only those who cooperate with grace."

Treatise on the Holy Eucharist

This then is the teaching of the Church. It has always been the teaching of the Church, and as the great scholar Pope Benedict XIV said, St. Thomas' opinion "explains correctly" Christ's use of "for many" as opposed to "for all men". *(De*

Sacrasanctae Missae Sacrificio ii:XIV). Now, when one sees the care with which those responsible for writing the *Novus Ordo Missae* changed the many minute details of even those prayers that were retained, one cannot assume that they were ignorant men. And certainly this error has been repeatedly pointed out to those responsible, and complaint upon complaint has been totally ignored. Why then the persistence of the "innovators" in the use of this offensive distortion? The answer is to be found in the new concept of "unity" which will be discussed in the next section. Suffice it to say for the present that it is a reflection of the heresy called *apocatastasis*, the false doctrine which teaches that a time will come when all free creatures will attain to salvation: that is to say, a final restoration for all mankind. Now this belief in *universal salvation* is to be found among the Anabaptists, the Moravian Brethren, the Christadelphians, among rationalistic Protestants and among the Universalists. It is also a concept that is fully Teilhardian. While not openly expressed in the Documents of Vatican II, the concepts of "salvation history", the "birth of a new humanism" and the idea that man is saved as a member of the community rather than as an individual are all highly suggestive of this error. Also conductive to the acceptance of this heresy is the ecumenical idea that those outside the Church, no matter what they believe (and how they behave) have "access to the community of salvation". Whether or not we can prove that the "innovators" intended either to teach false doctrine or to invalidate the consecration, the fact remains that, under the circumstances which we have pointed out, a false doctrine is implied, the laws of the Church are ignored, the teaching of the Church is contradicted and the consecration is rendered extremely doubtful.

In practice, THE VERY RAISING OF QUESTIONS OR DOUBTS ABOUT THE VALIDITY OF A GIVEN MANNER OF CONFECTING A SACRAMENT — IF THIS QUESTION IS BASED ON AN APPARENT DEFECT OF MATTER OR OF FORM — WOULD NECESSITATE THE STRICT ABSTENTION FROM USE OF THAT DOUBTFUL MANNER OF PERFORMING THE SACRAMENTAL ACT, UNTIL THE DOUBTS ARE RESOLVED. This same statement would apply pari passu to the laity receiving the doubtful Sacrament. IN CONFECTING THE SACRA-

MENTS, ALL PRIESTS ARE OBLIGED TO FOLLOW THE "MEDIUM CERTUM".[25] As traditional Catholic theology teaches, "Matter and Form must be *certainly valid.* Hence, one may not follow a probable opinion and use either doubtful matter or form. Acting otherwise, one commits a sacrilege."[26]

No wonder then that traditional theologians like J. M. Herve, instruct the priest to

> "Omit nothing of the form, add nothing, change nothing; Beware of transmuting, corrupting, or interrupting the words."

Yes indeed, beware of all the New Church has done!

*   *   *

Who then was responsible for writing this new "mass"? Clearly, not the Apostles, or even the Church Fathers, for it was created after the Second Vatican Council. It was in fact written by a committee of individuals gathered together in a "concilium" under the direction of a certain Archbishop Annibale Bugnini. This individual was the instigator and persistent advocate of the so-called "youth Masses", and the person who insisted on continuing the "yea, yea Masses" in Rome, and who got his way despite the protest of Rome's Vicar General, Cardinal Dell'Acqua. During the reign of John XXIII before the modernists had consolidated their gains, he was dismissed from the Lateran University where he was a teacher of liturgy precisely because he held such ideas — only to become, later, secretary of the Congregation dealing with liturgical reform. Now, according to Michael Davies, a most careful scholar, this individual was and is a FREE-MASON![27] It is of course well known that the Freemasons

---

25. Quoted by Patrick Henry Omlor in his book *Questioning the Validity of the Masses using the New All-English Canon*, Athanasius Press, Reno, Nevada, 1969.

26. Rev. Herbert Jone, *Moral Theology*, Newman: Westminster, Md., 1962.

27. Michael Davies, *Pope John's Council*, Augustine Publ. Co., Devon, England, 1977. "A priest placed what he claimed was documentary evidence proving that Mgr. Bugnini was a Mason into the hands of the Pope himself and warned that if drastic action was not taken, he would be bound in conscience to make the facts public." What followed was the "exiling" of Bugnini and the dissolving of the Congregation. Michael Davies, having investigated the facts, is willing to stand warrant for their truth.

have always dreamed of destroying the traditional Church, both by attacking it from without and by infiltrating it from within. This organization has been condemned by every Pope since Clement XII (1730-1740) to Pius XII, and in the traditional Church, to be a Freemason is to be automatically EXCOMMUNICATED.[28] Further, this strange individual was

---

28. To those who are familiar with the centuries of conflict between the Catholic Church and the Freemasons, such a fact is indeed shocking. Even on the lowest level, entry into Freemasonry involves a rite in which the applicant "enters into light from darkness". He then swears to obey and keep secret things he is totally unaware of. Such acts are simply not possible to the Catholic. Freemasonry, according to authorized spokesman F. Limousin (writing under the pen-name of Hiram) is a Religion. To quote him:

> "Freemasonry is an association . . . an institution . . . so it is said . . . but it is not that at all. Let us lift up the veils risking even to evoke numberless protestations. FREEmasonry IS A CHURCH: It is the Counter-Church, Counter-Catholicism: It is the Other Church — the Church of HERESY AND FREE-THOUGHT". It is opposed to "the Catholic Church . . . the first Church . . . the Church of dogmatism and of orthodoxy."

Those interested in further information are referred to *The Mystery of Freemasonry Unveiled,* by the Cardinal of Chile, Christian Book Club of America, Hawthorne, Calif. 1971.

Now consider the following statements of Yves Marsaudon, State Minister, Supreme Council of France (Scottish Rite of Freemasonry):

> "The sense of universalism that is rampant in Rome these days is very close to our purpose for existence. Thus, we are unable to ignore the Second Vatican Council and its consequences . . . With all our hearts we support the 'Revolution of John XXIII' . . . This courageous concept of the Freedom of Thought that lies at the core of our Freemasonic lodges, has spread in a truly magnificent manner right under the Dome of Saint Peter's . . ."

Again, he states elsewhere:

> "Born in our Masonic Lodges, freedom of expression has now spread beautifully over the Dome of St. Peter's . . . this is the Revolution of Paul VI. It is clear that Paul VI, not content merely to follow the policy of his predecessor, does in fact intend to go much further . . ."

Both "over" and "under" the Dome of St. Peter's! Needless to say, the New Church has officially lifted the ban on Catholics being Freemasons, and "Catholics" may freely join Masonic lodges as long as they do not plot against the Church. Of course, the Freemasons have no intention of plotting against the Post-conciliar Church — it is a tool in their hands, whether witting or unwitting.

assisted by six non-Catholic "observers". We know their names because Paul VI has publicly thanked them for their help *(L'Osservatore Romano,* May 11, 1970).[29] Of course, the New Church has persistently claimed that their presence at the meeting of the Concilium was strictly restricted to their capacity as "observers", and that they had no active function in the creation of the parody that is called the *Novus Ordo Missae.* (*Notitiae,* 1974, p. 249-252 presents this "defence" in ambiguous form). Unfortunately for the innovators, this has been contradicted by both the "observers", and the other "Catholics" present. Mgr. Baum has stated that the observers "were not simply observers, but also consultants as well, and fully participated in the discussions on renewing the Catholic liturgy. Their presence would have been meaningless if they were only listeners; they also contributed". As Canon Jasper, one of the non-Catholic observers said in a letter to Michael Davies dated February 10, 1977:

"However, after lunch, we always gathered together informally with the periti (experts) who had prepared the agenda, and at these meetings we were most certainly authorized to make comments, suggestions and criticisms. It was of course up to the periti to decide whether some of our observations should be brought into the general discussions of the Concilium. But these informal meetings were carried on in perfect freedom — a complete free-for-all — and the exchanges of opinion were very open . . ."[30]

And so we have a "mass" that could well be called "Bugnini's mass", a service that is truly "ecumenical" and fully approved by the World Council of Churches, whose representative was also present at its creation, a form of worship that can be described as a "FREEMASONIC MEAL", a "mass" created

---

29. Paul VI's photograph with the six heretics is published in this source, as well as his famous statement that the New "mass" re-edited "in a new manner liturgical texts tried and tested by long usage, or   established formulas which are completely new . . . (thus) imparting greater theological value to the liturgical texts so that the *lex orandi* conformed better with the *lex credendi.*" Either the texts prior to 1969 did not possess that degree of theological value which was desirable, or the *lex credendi* was changed.
30. *Itinéraires* (Paris), April 1977

with the assistance of excommunicated apostates and other individuals who not only did not believe in the Real Presence, but who also denied many of the other teachings of Holy Mother Church. Bugnini has said that "the liturgical reform is a major conquest of the Catholic Church" (*Notitiae* April 1974, p. 126). One wonders just who the conqueror is. No wonder then that it is in fact a monstrosity.

Let us be quite clear. Scandalous as all this is, our criticism of the *Novus Ordo Missae* is made on theological grounds alone. It would be a dissipation to argue that its authors were not even Catholic, for theoretically it is even possible for satan to come up with something that is valid despite himself.

*   *   *

Now, in the face of the facts so far presented, one must legitimately ask what Paul VI had to say about all this. Let us quote him directly:

> "It would be well to understand the motives for such a great change introduced (into the Mass) . . . It is the will of Christ. It is the breath of the Spirit calling the Church to this mutation . . ." (*General audience*, Nov. 26, 1969)

Paul VI, in using the term "mutation", quite apart from the scientific implications of abnormality, has used a term familiar to anyone trained in theology. It is the term used in discussing just these issues that can invalidate the sacrament. To quote Father Felix Cappello, S.J. of the Gregorian University in his text *De Sacramentis: Mutatio substantialis materiae aut formae semper reddit invalidum sacramentum*. ("A substantial mutation in the matter or form of the Sacrament, always renders it invalid . . .") He continues: *Accidentalis contra, nunquam officit valori sacramenti; set culpam inducit, gravem vel modo voluntaria sit, pro mutationis gravitate aut parvitate*. ("Accidental changes however do not affect the validity of the Sacrament, but are sinful, the gravity of the sin being dependent upon the seriousness of the change, and on the basis of whether or not it is voluntary . . .").

Paul VI is of course fully responsible for introducing the *Novus Ordo Missae*, whether he personally wrote it or not. As Cardinal Heenan stated in the foreword to the English translation of the text:

"It is important to realize that the revision has been carried out under the Holy Father's personal supervision."

What then is Paul VI's concept of the Mass? Let us turn to his description or definition as given in Section 7 of his Apostolic Constitution:

"The Lord's Supper is an assembly or gathering together of the people of God, with a priest presiding, to celebrate the memorial of the Lord. For this reason the promise of Christ is particularly true of a local congregation of the Church: 'where two or three are gathered in my name, there am I in their midst'."[31]

How similar this definition is to that of Cranmer:

"Christ is present whensoever the Church prayeth unto Him, and is gathered together in His name. And the bread and wine be made unto us the body and blood of Christ (as it is in the Book of Common Prayer), but not by changing the substance of the bread and wine into the natural substance of Christ's natural body and blood, but that in the godly using of them they may be unto the receivers Christ's body and blood . . ."

The Works of T. Cranmer, Vol I

Returning to the Apostolic Constitution on the *Novus Ordo* again, this document of Paul VI contains other statements such as: "the Mass is the culminating action by which God in Christ sanctifies the world and men adore the Father . . .", or "the Eucharistic celebration, in which the priest acts for the salvation of the people . . .", neither of which statements helps us understand Paul VI's definition of the Mass in any other sense than that signified by the words he uses in Paragraph 7. Reading still further, we find that "the eucharistic prayer, a prayer of thanksgiving and sanctification is the center of the entire celebration", and Paragraph 48 states: "when he instit-

---

31. This is the definition given in the first edition of the Apostolic Constitution. It has since been "revised", but those responsible for the revision have made it quite clear that the change does not alter the essential theological meaning or intent.

uted the paschal sacrifice and meal, he handed it over to his disciples for them to do it in his memory". Now, while there are still some allusions to the nature of the Sacrifice as a Catholic *must* understand it, they are only allusions. The word "Transubstantiation" is conspicuously absent and the only reference to the Real Presence is in a footnote — number 63 — which in turn refers without quotation to the Council of Trent. One is reminded of Luther's words: "call it benediction, eucharist (which means 'thanksgiving'), the Lord's Supper, the Lord's table, memory of the Lord, or whatever you like, just so long as you do not dirty it with the name of a sacrifice or an action". As the members of the Episcopal Synod stated:

> "By a series of equivocations the emphasis is obsessively placed upon the 'supper' and the 'memorial' instead of on the unbloody renewal of the Sacrifice of Calvary."

As to the statement that Our Lord is present in the Mass because "two or three are gathered together in His name", this would certainly imply that He is just as present — and in the same sense — in any Protestant service — or for that matter in my home during evening prayers. And if this is so, then what is the purpose of the Mass? Here again the *Novus Ordo* suggests a heretical answer — note, I do not say *gives,* but only *suggests* — "a common posture, as a sign which both expresses and fosters the inner spirit and purpose of the community . . ." (Paragraph 20).

Paul VI has stated that the "New Mass" was "Mandated" by the Second Vatican Council:

> "The reform which is about to be brought into being is therefore a response to an authoritative mandate from the Church. It is an act of obedience. It is an act of coherence of the Church with itself. It is a step forward for her authentic tradition. It is a demonstration of fidelity and vitality, to which we must all give prompt assent."
>
> *Allocution,* Nov. 26, 1969

Now there is no evidence that the Council Fathers ever

envisaged anything like the *Novus Ordo Missae* when they signed the Constitution on the Sacred Liturgy. Apart from certain individuals like Cardinal Leinart and his côterie, the majority would doubtless have been shocked at what was happening. Listen to the words of Archbishop R. J. Dwyer:

> "Who dreamed on that day (when the Council Fathers voted for the Liturgy Constitution) that within a few years, far less than a decade, the Latin past of the Church would be all but expunged, that it would be reduced to a memory fading in the middle distance? The thought of it would have horrified us, but it seemed so far beyond the realm of the possible as to be ridiculous. So we laughed it off."
>
> *Twin Circle,* Oct. 26, 1973

The Constitution states that "the liturgy is made up of unchangeable elements divinely instituted and of elements subject to change. Surely the "unchangeable elements" referred to the Canon and above all to the form and substance of the Sacrament. As one reads the *Novus Ordo,* one finds that the only unchangeable elements are such words as "alleluia" (why not in the vernacular?) and certain prayers such as the Our Father and the Gloria[32] that have always been acceptable to the Protestants. Indeed, such an opinion is strengthened if one reads the *Council Daybook* (a sort of running log) for Nov. 5, 1962 where it states that "it was insisted that the Canon of the Mass especially should remain intact . . ."

Returning to Paul VI's statement quoted above, we note that if we are "faithful" and "vital" we will give our "prompt assent". I am not sure just what it means to be "vital" but I am sure that if we are faithful, we can never give anything but our prompt rejection. As for the changes having anything to do with "authentic tradition", that is patently absurd. Since when has it been traditional to fool around with the Canon and to change the very words of Christ.

*   *   *

What then is left of the traditional Mass after all these changes? What elements remain to give the "parody" some semblance of the real thing? After the "president" enters the sanctuary and says "good morning" (the Sign of the Cross is

---

32. In Latin the *Gloria* is retained intact. In the vernacular, it is mistranslated and large segments are deleted.

a rarity), we start out with a truncated confession that is made to "our brothers and sisters". Like the Anglicans, we no longer confess to the Blessed Virgin, the angels and the saints. We have dropped, or rather, we are denied, the traditional formula of sacramental absolution which starts *"Indulgentiam . . ."* (Must we come to the "supper" with unwashed hands?) We proceed then to the "Liturgy of the Word" (another Reformation concept as we have already pointed out) or "Scriptural readings" taken from the new and false translations, interspaced with a "Responsorial Psalm" such as Luther introduced into his Worship service. (The use of three Scriptural readings instead of two is also a Lutheran innovation.) We are still allowed the *Gloria* (falsely and incompletely rendered — with the emphasis that peace is given to *all men,* and not to *"men of good will".* We say the *Credo* (as do Lutherans and Anglicans) but with the "communitarian" "We believe . . ." and not the correct "I believe . . ." We then have a few "bidding" prayers in which the priest or selected members of the "community" suggest or ask us to pray for certain purposes (often quite profane).[33] After this we have a sermon. In an "ecumenical" community, this may even be given by a visiting Protestant clergyman; otherwise it consists of a lecture in the "new theology". Orthodoxy and spiritual content is an almost unbelievable rarity. Then one or two laymen are selected at random to bring the sacred vessels to the "table". We used to be taught that only those in Holy Orders or "Sacristans" could handle these so sacred vessels. These "gifts" are brought forward with the money from the weekly collection and you now have the "offertory" as conceived in the *Novus Ordo.*

Next comes the "Liturgy of the Eucharist". Please note a subtle (or is it really such a subtle?) point. The "mass" is divided into the "Liturgy of the Word", and the "Liturgy of the Eucharist". What a lovely word Eucharist is, and how the modernists love it. It means *thanksgiving* and can be used to disguise their absence of belief. This in effect teaches us that

---

33. "Bidding prayers" were introduced by King Henry VIII with the intention of using carefully-phrased petitions in the vernacular by means of which the people's thoughts should be directed in correct political and theological channels. For a full discussion see Hugh Ross Williamson, *A Revision to the Reforms of Cranmer, the Modern Mass,* TAN Rockford, III., 1971.

the Sacred Species is *not* the "Word made Flesh", and that it is in Scripture only that the Word of God is to be found. Of course, we have already been "softened up" for the change in emphasis. After all, the tabernacle has been replaced by the Bible.

The Liturgy of the Eucharist is initiated with the prayer *"Benedictus Tu Deus* . . . (Blessed are you O Lord, ruler of the universe), which is as we have pointed out above, the Jewish "grace before meals". From this we go into one of the ersatz "canons" followed by the *Narratio institutionis* (or the "Narration of the Institution"). The dubious consecration is followed by the "Proclamation of the Mystery of the Faith": "Christ has died, Christ has risen. Christ will come again!" And what has such a statement to do with the fact that Christ is presumably at that very moment present upon the "table"? Is this acclamation a denial that transubstantiation has occured? But then, alas, ambiguity is what the New Church feeds on.

Communion follows. Kneeling is no longer permitted (the Anglicans also forbade it). When the priest distributes the "host", he no longer says the traditional *Corpus Domini nostri Jesu Christi* . . . "May the Body of Our Lord Jesus Christ . . ." He frequently uses the word "Eucharist". Further, we are "encouraged" to take communion in the hand as Luther also advocated, and distribution is given by "extraordinary administrators of the Eucharist", who are in fact laymen and women without consecrated hands. In some of the more "advanced" parishes, where ordinary bread (another Lutheran innovation) has been "consecrated", we can pick our piece out of a basket, and let the "crumbs" fall where they will. During and after Communion we are regaled with the latest "folk-tunes" ("Gumbaya" being a favorite — though I am told this statement "dates" me) accompanied by badly played guitars.

Now, I have left out only two items. The *Our Father* with its "Doxology", ("For Thine is the Kingdom, the power and the glory . . ." a perfectly legitimate phrase, but one always insisted upon by the Protestants),[34] and the "Kiss of Peace",

---

34. Those of us who went to "public" school in America, at a time when prayer in the classroom was still allowed, will remember that the Our Father was said in common with the Protestants, but that this doxology was said by them alone. Catholic students kept quiet. This "silly" practice was one of the first things that aroused my interest in the Catholic Church.

where we are encouraged to greet our neighbours and to exchange with them such worldly amenities as phone numbers. (Some Churches have had to place a time limit on this communitarian activity!) We conclude with a final blessing (also received standing) and exit to the accompaniment of guitars and tambourines.

Please understand, I am nowhere in all this refering to the so-called "abuses" that the *Novus Ordo* is subjected to. Of course, according to the *Constitution on the Sacred Liturgy*, "competent territorial ecclesiastical authority" can allow for "even more radical adaptions of the liturgy". This same power — the local ordinary in practice — can grant permission for "the necessary preliminary experiments over a determined period". When bewildered Catholics protest at a "dance mass" or a "yoga mass", they are informed that it is done with the permission of appropriate authority on an experimental basis. "Abuses" carried on with Episcopal permission (or neglect) and under "obedience" however is not what we have been discussing in the above paragraphs, but the new parody of a mass as performed by conservative priests with "decorum and dignity".

Provision was of course made for those priests who could not accept the changes. They were free to say the old Mass *sine populo* — that is, alone and in retirement (needless to say, another innovation, as Cardinal Ottaviani has pointed out). It is unfortunate that many older priests — and many, not so old— took advantage of this option; instead of being foci of resistance to these stupid changes, they retired into obscurity (with full financial support by the New Church). As for the laity, no such charity was extended to them. The traditional Mass was and is forbidden. "The New *Ordo* was promulgated to take the place of the old . . ." as Paul VI instructed us. One is reminded of the words of Thomas Cromwell, the ravisher of Ireland:

"I had rather that Mahometanism were permitted amongst us than that one of God's children should be persecuted . . . I meddle not with any man's conscience. But if by liberty of conscience you mean a liberty to exercise the Mass, I judge it best to use plain dealing, and to let you know . . . that will not be allowed of".

English liberty, 1650

And yet, despite this, Paul VI assures us:

> "Let everyone understand well that nothing has been changed in the essence of our traditional Mass . . . There is nothing, absolutely nothing to this idea . . . The New rite, the Mass is the same as always . . . If anything, its identity has been made more recognizable in certain of its aspects . . . It is in the name of tradition that we ask all our sons and daughters, all the Catholic communities, to celebrate with dignity and fervour the renewed liturgy . . ."
>
> *Allocution*, Nov. 26, 1969 and
> *Custos, Quid de Nocte.*

Enough has been said of the *Novus Ordo Missae* to show that it is indeed a PARODY created as a substitution intended to replace our traditional Mass. But it is only an imitation or a mimickry. It is in fact a burlesque, created by those who have usurped the magisterial function; it is a "sop" and a "Christmas Game" to befuddle the faithful. Much more could be said. Its ugliness is proverbial; it is boring and dull; it has introduced the language and the customs of the marketplace into the sanctuary; it has "turned off" thousands of the young, but all this to what effect, if by now the reader is not convinced. One last point requires mentioning. Would traditional Catholics ever accept some form of accommodation with the New "mass"? Would they accept a situation where one could choose which service one went to — a sort of situation that exists in the Anglican Church where some are "high" and some are of "low" persuasion? (This is not to imply that "high" Anglicans have a valid Mass.) The answer must be NO! One cannot mix oil and water. Such an *aggiornamento* would be as false as one made with the Lutherans or the Unitarians. The reason is simple. It is not a matter of intolerance. The new "mass" is not Catholic and never can be Catholic and we "cannot bear the yoke with unbelievers".[25]

---

35. At the risk of "overkill", and for the sake of completing our intention of proving all the contentions we made at the start of this section, we must show that the *Novus Ordo* in translation teaches overt heresy. This is to be seen in "Anaphora IV" where the Latin is itself innocuous, but where the "ICEL" translation is heretical. Consider the following passage:

One can do no better than to conclude this section with a quotation from the Angelic Doctor:

> "Falsehood in outward worship occurs on the part of the worshipper, and especially, in common worship which is offered by ministers impersonating the whole Church. For even as he would be guilty of falsehood who would, in the name of another person, proffer things that are not committed to him, so too does a man incur the guilt of falsehood who, on the part of the Church, gives worship to God contrary to the manner established by the Church or divine authority, and according to the ecclesiastical custom. Hence St. Ambrose says: 'He is *unworthy who celebrates the mystery otherwise than Christ delivered it'*."

Summa II-II Q. 93, a. 1

Novus Ordo	Traditional Canon
Father in heaven, it is right that we should give you thanks and glory; You alone are God, living and true . . ."	It is truly meet and just, right and profitable unto salvation, that we should at all times and in all places give thanks unto Thee, O holy Lord, Father Almighty, everlasting God. Who with the only begotten Son and the Holy Ghost, art One God, One Lord: not in the oneness of a single person, but in the trinity of One substance . . ."

Considering the fact that as Jungmann says "the entire teaching of the Church is contained in the liturgy", *(Handing on the Faith)*, this is a most instructive piece of skulduggery. In the Latin version of the *Novus Ordo* the words *"Unus Deus",* or "One God . . . living and true", are to be found, and no explicit heresy is taught. However, even in the Latin, the faithful are not clearly taught the doctrine of the Trinity. True, this doctrine is alluded to in the Creed, but it is certainly not expressed there with the same precision and clarity of thought (what a striking economy of language is used in our traditional Canon!). When Anaphora IV is used, this doctrine is nowhere else taught. When we come to the vernacular, the translating of *Unus Deus* as "You alone are God" is a clear and explicit teaching of heresy. Look up the meaning of "alone". The statement is a denial of the doctrine of the Trinity. It is for this reason that some theologians refer to this Canon as the "Arian Canon". Another example of a "return to primitive practice!"

As St. Basil said at the time of the Arian heresy:

"Religious people keep silence, but every blaspheming tongue is let loose. Sacred things are profaned; those of the laity who are sound in faith avoid the places of worship as schools of impiety, and raise their hands in solitude with groans and tears to the Lord of Heaven." (*Ep.* 92) . . . "Matters have come to this pass; the people have left their houses of prayer and assemble in deserts. To this they submit, because they will have no part in the wicked Arian leaven." (*Ep.* 242) . . . "Only one offence is now vigorously punished, an accurate observance of our fathers' traditions . . . Joy and spiritual cheerfulness are no more; our feasts are turned into mourning; our houses of prayer are shut up, our altars deprived of the spiritual worship." (*Ep.* 243).

THE OTHER SACRAMENTS

We have, to this point, discussed in some detail the issue of the Mass, and the changes imposed by or in the name of Vatican II.[1] It would be surprising if the "attack on tradition" was limited to this sacrament alone. The other sacraments are similarly undermined, if indeed, not nullified. In marriage,

1. In view of the fact that the conciliar Church may at some time allow for her "priests" to say the traditional Mass in an attempt to win back or retain the "conservative" element, the following comment by a theologian and seminary professor of the Society of Pius X is pertinent. It is in the form of an answer to a query.

Dear Father,
    A priest in our area has just begun to say the traditional Latin Mass. The only problem is that he was ordained in the early 1970's. Can I attend his Masses if he was ordained in the new way? T.D., Maryland.
Dear T.D.,
    Since the new rite of ordination was imposed in 1968, we must assume that the priest was ordained according to the new rite rather than with the traditional Catholic ceremony. In any case, you could ask him — for his sake as well as your own. If he understands enough to reject the new Mass, he should certainly be concerned about the validity of his priestly orders.
    If he was indeed ordained in the new way, then no true Catholic may attend the Masses he offers, even though they are traditional. The reason is that there are very serious doubts about the validity of the new ordination ceremony.
    The first difficulty is found in the new rite itself. Although the new rite keeps the necessary words of ordination (decreed by Pope Pius XII in 1947), nevertheless, in the context of the new rite, these words cannot be understood in the Catholic sense. The priesthood exists for the sacrifice. Thus the Catholic priesthood exists for the true Catholic Mass, which is the unbloody sacrifice of Calvary. But the new priesthood exists for the new Mass, which is not the unbloody sacrifice of Calvary.
    According to the new rite of ordination, a priest is ordained to offer only a sacrifice of "praise and thanksgiving", which is the new Mass; the

new ceremony has suppressed all mention of the sacrifice in reparation for sin. The sacrifice of Calvary, however, was offered to God the Father in adoration, reparation, thanksgiving and supplication. A "mass" which purposely excludes any one of these four ends cannot be the same as the sacrifice of Calvary, and thus is no Catholic Mass at all. And a priest ordained for such a mere "sacrifice of praise and thanksgiving" is very doubtfully a Catholic priest at all. It is of interest to refer to the Council of Trent in this regard, for the Council explicitly condemned any attempt to make of the Mass nothing but a sacrifice of praise and thanksgiving by denying its reparatory value: "If anyone says that the Sacrifice of the Mass is merely an offering of praise and thanksgiving, or that it is a simple memorial of the sacrifice offered on the cross, not propitiatory . . . let him be anathema!" (session 22, canon 3 on the Holy Eucharist). Because the new rites of ordination and the Mass do just this, they are not Catholic rites at all.

A further reason to question the validity of orders given by the new rite involves the intention of the man to be ordained. Did he really want to become a Catholic priest? Did he even understand what the Catholic priesthood is? These are fair questions today, when the instructions given in nominally Catholic seminaries are both anti-Catholic and anti-clerical. Even if the ordained had the necessary intention, what of the ordaining bishop? Did the bishop intend to ordain a true Catholic priest or merely a "president of the assembly"? In his encyclical *Apostolicae curae*, Pope Leo XIII explains that the intention of the bishop in such cases must be interpreted according to the ceremony which he uses. If he uses a Catholic ceremony, then the presumption is always in favour of validity. In the case of the new ordinations, however, the presumption is always against validity, since a non-Catholic rite was used in place of the Catholic ceremony.

Another difficulty concerns not only the bishop's intention, but whether he is a bishop at all. It is uncertain that bishops consecrated under the new rite of episcopal consecration are really bishops, since the necessary words of episcopal consecration have been changed altogether. Adding to the confusion is the Second Vatican Council's decree on the episcopacy, which implicitly re-defined the sacrament of Holy Orders contrary to the traditional teaching of the Church. Vatican II upheld the sacramental character of the episcopacy on the grounds that *it is directed to governing and teaching the faithful* who are the Mystical Body of Christ. This doctrine that a sacrament, as a sacrament, is directed primarily to the faithful is precisely the teaching of Martin Luther. The Catholic teaching, rather, is that a sacrament is a sacrament only in that it is directed to the *Real* Body of Christ in the Holy Eucharist. Thus, the problem of the new ordination rite involves much more than the tampering with one single sacrament; it is the fruit springing from a whole new concept of "sacrament" in itself, and so the perversion of all the sacraments.

Finally there is, again, the intention of the man to be consecrated and the intention of those consecrating him. Did the bishop-elect want to be a Catholic bishop? Did he even know the true nature of the Catholic episcopacy? And did the consecrating bishops really want to consecrate a true Successor of the Apostles? Again, the presumption must be against

the vow of obedience has been deleted despite the fact that it is Scriptural in preceptal origin. In fact, the individuals contracting the marriage are now allowed to create their own service. An excellent example of this is described in Malachy Martin's book, *Hostage to the Devil* (Reader's Digest Books, 1977). In many instances this leads to invalid marriages and sacrilegious ceremonies. As to divorce, the post-conciliar Church has gotten around Christ's injunction by allowing "annulments" practically for the asking. During the last year, of 640 requests before the Brooklyn Marriage Court, 640 were granted. One of the grounds for granting annulments is "psychological immaturity". Now, I ask you, who cannot claim to have been psychologically immature at the time of his (her) marriage? And who but a saint is psychologically completely mature?

As to the other Sacraments, let me quote Michael Davies. "The modifications made in the rite of ordination are, if anything, more serious than those made in the Mass". Archbishop Lefebvre has stated that the Sacrament of Confirmation in the Post-conciliar Church is "of doubtful validity". We cannot discuss in detail all these changes, but will present those made in the Sacrament of "Extreme Unction" as a brief study of "anti-traditional methodology". This Sacrament, given to those in danger of death, has certain specific functions. Like all the Sacraments, it was instituted by Christ as a "visible" sign and vehicle of grace. Let us consider its purpose.

The effects of Extreme Unction are as varied as they are potent. As to its "end" or "purpose", it is "the perfect healing of the soul" — and it surely has the inherent power to attain its end in those who pose no obstacle to the grace it conveys.

---

validity, since their intentions must be interpreted according to the rite which they used, and the new rite is simply not Catholic.

So we see that there are many difficulties involved with the new rite of ordination of a new priest for the Conciliar Church. Any single one of the factors mentioned above would serve to render the ordination totally null and void.

On the practical level, I might also mention the decision of Archbishop Lefebvre with regard to the new ordination rite. When I spoke with him last June, Monseigneur said that if a priest ordained with the new rite wished to help the Society of Saint Pius X in the administration of the Sacraments, such a priest would have to be ordained conditionally according to the traditional Catholic rite of priestly ordination.

As the Council of Trent explains it, "this effect is the grace of the Holy Ghost, Whose unction blots out sins,[2] if any remain to be expiated, and the consequences of sin, and alleviates and strengthens the soul of the sick person, by exciting in him a great confidence in the divine mercy, sustained by which he bears more lightly the troubles and sufferings of disease, and more easily resists the temptations of the demon lying in wait for his heel;[3] and sometimes, when it is expedient for the soul's salvation, recovers bodily health". These effects are usually grouped under four headings.

Its first effect is the *Remission of Sins* which follows from the passage in St. James: "If anyone be in a state of sin, his sins are forgiven him", and such is indeed confirmed by the very "form" of the Sacrament *Indulgeat tibi Dominus . . . quidquid . . . deliquisti . . .* ("May God pardon thee whatever sins thou has committed . . .") Of course, it is true that mortal sins are forgiven by Confession, Absolution and Penance — but it is not unusual that a sick man cannot confess; yet providing he places no obstacle to the infusion of Grace into his soul through this Sacrament, even if he cannot confess, he is still washed clean of sin and regains his Baptismal purity. To such an individual Extreme Unction becomes the pillar of salvation. It can be argued that conditional Absolution obviates the need for this final Sacrament, but it has yet other effects.

Secondly, this Sacrament remits temporal punishment due to us for our sins. It was, as Father Kilker says, "instituted for the perfect healing of the soul with a view to its immediate entrance into glory, unless indeed the all-knowing Master of Life and Death should deem the restoration of bodily health more expedient. Consequently, it must accomplish the removal of all disabilities, it must render us fit to enter our heavenly home without delay. Were this not so, it would be absurd to say that the Sacrament is *consummativum spiritualis curationis*".[4] This doctrine must not however be construed to mean that infallibly the remission of the entire temporal debt occurs when Extreme Unction is received. Often the subject blocks the completeness of the effect by defective and

---

2. This Sacrament is traditionally preceded by Confession and Absolution.
3. The reference is to Genesis III:15.
4. Taken from Rev. Adrian Kilker's text *Extreme Unction, A Canonical Treatise*, B. Herder: St. Louis, Mo., 1927. The Latin is from St. Thomas' *Summa Contra Gent., lib. 4., c. 73, de Ext. Unct.*

impeding dispositions. But, if the subject has in every way the correct disposition and devotion, it must be conceded that he receives the *plenissimam poenarum relaxationem* — the complete remission of temporal punishment.

A third and terribly important effect is what is called the *confortatio animae:* or the "Comforting of the Soul". The approach of death with its distressing pains, its physical prostration and the associated mental disquietude, can truly be a most appalling experience. Man dreads few things as much as this "moment of truth". He reviews his past actions, and, as it says in the Book of Wisdom, *"They shall come with fear at the thought of their sins, and their iniquities shall stand against them to convict them."* At the same time he recognizes that soon he must stand before the judgment seat of God. It is precisely at this time that the Devil uses all his powers to attack the soul. As the Catechism of the Council of Trent puts it: "Although the enemy of the human race never ceases, while we live, to meditate our ruin and destruction, yet at no time does he more violently use every effort utterly to destroy us, and if possible, to deprive us of all hope of divine mercy, than when he sees the last day of life approach." Now the third effect of this Sacrament is "to free the minds of the faithful from this solicitude, and to fill the soul with pious and holy joy". It further provides "arms and strength . . . to the faithful . . . to enable them to break the violence and impetuosity of the adversary, and to fight bravely against him . . ." Who of us can be so presumptuous as not ardently to desire such assistance?

Fourthly, it is a doctrine of our faith that one of the effects of the Extreme Unction is the restoration of bodily health, if recovery is expedient for the soul's welfare.

Lastly, though not strictly speaking a theological effect, the administration of the Sacrament under traditional circumstances, made it perfectly plain to the individual concerned that he was facing death. He could no longer hide from himself the reality of his situation. He was forced, as it were, to the battlefield, and not allowed to drift away in some gentle morphinized dream that "everything was going to be all right".[5] And how often did physicians and relatives see the

---

5. A Catholic should fear the American dream of dying on the golfcourse "suddenly" (i.e. with no preparation), away from the sacraments and family.

wonderful effects this Sacrament worked upon the souls of those who received it — turning as it were, their last moments on earth into a foretaste of that heavenly peace and glory that is potentially offered to every soul.

It is a teaching of the Church that for a Sacrament to be valid, several pre-requisites are necessary. These are usually listed as Matter, Form, Minister, Subject and Intention. Since the subject here is obviously the (Catholic) individual who is in danger of death, and the minister is presumably a valid priest with the appropriate intention, it behoves us to consider in turn both the "matter" and the "form". If the changes introduced by the New and Post-conciliar Church, in their so-called "Sacrament of the Anointing of the Sick", attack the integrity of the "matter", and the substance of the "form", then the Sacrament is rendered invalid and none of the important effects mentioned above can occur. Let us first of all consider "matter".

According to Kilker, "The remote matter of Extreme Unction is oil of olives. This the Council of Trent definitely defined: *Intellexit enim Ecclesia materiam esse oleum ab episcopo benedictum*. There has been no doubt that the oil meant by St. James is the oil of olives". In the Latin Church it has ever been the custom to employ pure unadulterated olive oil. In some Eastern rites the practice of adding a little water as a symbol of Baptism, or of a little wine in memory of the Good Samaritan, or even of the dust of the sepulchre of some saint, has long been in vogue.

Now this oil is blessed by the Bishop at the magnificent Mass of Maundy Thursday in Holy Week — a Mass so sacred that the Bishop is attended by twelve priests and seven Deacons and seven Subdeacons in order to say it properly. It is then distributed to all the pastors in his diocese for administration by the clergy. In the Latin Church this has been an episcopal prerogative since at least the second Council of Carthage (390 A.D.). Such has always been the tradition of the Church, though it is to be admitted that the privilege is "jurisdictional", and not "episcopal" in nature, and that some Popes (very few) have allowed priests the "faculty" for giving the blessing (according to the same ritual), and that in the Eastern Church, priests routinely have this privilege. Be this as it may, according to the Council of Florence, and most specifically, according to the Catechism of the Council of

Trent, it is *oleum olivae per episcopum benedictum* ("olive oil blessed by the Bishop"). The rite to be observed in this blessing is to be found in the *Pontificale* under the title *De officio in Feria V Coenae Domini*. While too lengthy to give in full, it starts out with the following phrase: *Emitte, quaesumus, Spiritum tuum sanctum Paraclitum de caelis in hanc pinguidinem olei* . . . ("Send forth, we pray, your Holy Spirit, the Paraclete from heaven into this rich substance of oil . . ."). For Catholics the remote matter of Extreme Unction is oil of olives; the proximate matter is "the anointing with oil". Should a parish priest ever be given the faculty of blessing the oil, it would be with the understanding that he used the traditional rites for doing it.

What then is this "matter" in the New Church? According to the "Rite of Anointing and Pastoral Care of the Sick" promulgated by Paul VI's Apostolic Constitution of November 30, 1972, olive oil need no longer be used. Any oil of plant origin can be blessed — and pray — what oil is ultimately not of plant origin? Axle-grease, vaseline and Mazola oil can satisfy the requirement. Further, the oil can be blessed by any priest who has the "faculty", and this faculty has been extended by the "Bishop's Committee on the Liturgy" to any priest "where didactic or catechetical reasons prompt it". The blessing has of course been changed. No longer is the Holy Spirit invoked, but rather, it now reads: "May your blessing come upon all who are anointed with this oil, that they may be freed from pain and illness and made well again in body and mind and soul." Notice that the emphasis is now entirely upon the healing of illness, and not on the forgiveness of sins. Chrism is now an ersatz oil with an ersatz blessing.

Let us now consider the "Form" of the Sacrament, or the words the priest uses when anointing the patient "in danger of death". The traditional words are: *Per istam sanctam unctionem et suam piissimam misericordiam, indulgeat tibi Dominus quidquid per . . . deliquisti* ("Through this Holy Unction (oil), and through the great goodness of His mercy, may God pardon thee whatever sins thou hast committed [by the evil use of sight — smell, touch etc. — depending on the organ anointed".]) Needless to say, this also has been changed by the Post-conciliar Church to *Per istam sanctam unctionem et suam piissimam misericordiam adiuvet te Dominus gratia*

Spiritus Sancti, ut a peccatis liberatum te salvat atque propitius alleviat. The semi-official translation given out through the Holy See Press Office is: "Through this holy anointing and his most loving mercy, may the Lord assist you by the grace of the Holy Spirit, so that when you have been freed from your sins, he may save you and in his goodness raise you up." Another translation taken from Father C. J. Keating's article is closer to the original: "Through this holy anointing and his great love for you, may the Lord who freed you from sin, heal you and extend his saving grace to you . . ."[6] No where are the "essential" words *indulgeat tibi Dominus* used.

Has the Church the right to change the matter and the form of her Sacraments? The answer is given by Pope Leo XIII's *Apostolicae Curae* from which we take the following quotes:

> "The Church is forbidden to change, or even touch, the matter or form of any sacrament. She may indeed change or abolish or introduce something in the non-essential rites or 'ceremonial' parts used in the administration of the sacraments, such as processions, prayers or hymns before or after the actual words of the form are recited . . . All know that the sacraments of the New Law, as sensible and efficient signs of invisible grace, ought both to signify the grace which they effect, and effect the grace which they signify . . ."

There is no question but that the New and Post-conciliar "form" violates the canons of the ecumenical councils, the ecclesiastical traditions, the teaching of the Catechism of the Council of Trent, and the constant teachings of the Popes as enshrined in the above quotation. What however must be questioned is whether this New form is rendered invalid by the changes. Is the change, as the theologians would say, "substantial"? To answer this question, we must know what in the traditional form was considered "essential" for efficacy. The answer is almost unanimous among the theologians — the phrase *indulgeat tibi Dominus* ("may God pardon thee") is the very minimum that must be present. Most insist upon *quidquid deliquisti* and *sanctum unctionem*. After all, as Leo

6. Charles J. Keating, "The Sacrament of Anointing the Sick" *Homiletic and Pastoral Review*, June, 1974.

XIII said, "the sacraments . . . ought . . . to signify the grace which they effect", and in the present situation, this is the health of the soul which is effected by strengthening of the soul through grace and by the remission of sin and the punishment due to sin. As St. Thomas Aquinas says, "Extreme Unction is a Spiritual remedy, since it avails for the remission of sins . . ." (*Summa*, III, Suppl 29, 1). Now, the New Form OMITS these critical words, and only asks that God "heal" one. While it is to be admitted that throughout history several valid forms have been in use — since the Council of Florence the form has been fixed. If some of these forms have used the word *"parcat"*, *"remittat"*, or even *"sanat"* in place of *"indulgeat"*, this does not interfere with validity. (In the traditional form, replacing the word "pardon" by "spare", "remit" or "heal" — but always with regard to "whatever sins thou has committed".) To OMIT this phrase entirely is to remove from the "form" its ability to absolve — to change its "meaning", and hence to make a change of such a *substantial* nature as almost certainly to render it totally invalid. Even if the "blessing" is preceded by a valid absolution — which in many cases is questionable, one is deprived of the other sacramental effects that are so important.[7]

Clearly then, if the Post-conciliar "blessing" (and it is nothing more) is upon the sick, the ersatz sacrament should no longer be limited to those in "danger of death". Twice during the Second Vatican Council the Fathers rejected suggestions that the requirement of "danger of death" for the reception of the Anointing be omitted. As Father Keating points out, however, "the new rite does what the Council was not able to do". In contrast to the negative wording of Canon 940 which states "Extreme Unction is not able to be offered except to the faithful who, having attained the use of reason, fall into the danger of death from illness or old age", the new rite can be administered to those who are ill, but in no danger of death whatsoever. Further, it states in the Constitution on the Liturgy (Vatican II) that "it is to be stressed that whenever rites, according to their specific nature, make provision for communal celebration involving the presence and active participation of the faithful, this way of

---

7. Incidentally, the Post-conciliar priest is "forbidden" to use the traditional "form" by Paul VI's Apostolic Constitution.

celebrating them is preferred, as far as possible, to a celebration that is individual and quasi-private". Thus we see that officially, this new ersatz sacrament can be given communally. Indeed, in my erstwhile parish, it was the custom to gather all the mildly infirm and aged together — the arthritics, the elderly and the infirm — and to bestow this "blessing" upon them (with no preceeding "Penance" or "absolution") — to be followed by coffee and cake in the rectory!

Now any Catholic who still believes in Sacramental "efficacy", must surely hold that certain pre-requisites are also necessary for "validity". (If not, then any words can be used, and any individual can say them). Validity in turn demands a certain integrity in "matter" and "form", and hence it is our right to have this integrity retained by any Church that claims to be founded by Christ and the Apostles. No traditional Catholic admitted "in extremis" to the emergency room of a Hospital, and asking for a priest, would settle for a Baptist minister — even if he should say the proper words of the form. Yet in fact, of what more use is a priest who uses an incorrect and invalid form? One must further express great wonderment at the new breed of priest who feels at home with this kind of "playing fast and free" with what is so sacred. The bestowal of Extreme Unction must be one of the paramount and most satisfying features of a priest's career, and something further that he is bound both in charity and *ex justitia* to do. What is one to say of a Church that would foist such a "parody" upon its faithful at the time of death.

The Sacraments relate to one of the essential functions of the Church. Without them, one aspect of her holiness is attacked. If we are to remove the Sacraments and to destroy the validity of the priesthood, then what is the function of the Church? Even a Moslem can validly baptize us (if he uses the correct "form" and "matter", and has the proper intention). As for the New Church, if her doctrine is defective, and her sacraments invalid, then what function does she serve? In what way does she differ from, say, the Presbyterians, or, "The Ethical Culture Society"? In all honesty, the answer is none!

THE ROAD TO HELL IS PAVED
WITH "GOOD INTENTIONS"

"In the Gospel also we read that it was foretold that our foes should rather be of our own household, and that they who have first been associated in the sacrament of unity shall be they who shall betray one another."

Epistles of St. Cyprian LIV

Why have all these changes been instituted? One must remember that, as William Blake said of a former pontiff:

"And Caiaph was, in his own mind,
A benefactor to mankind."

What led men who presumably are "sincere" and of "good will" to break with the traditions established by the Apostles and the teachings held by the Church throughout the ages? What has induced those responsible to follow the suggestions of the Modernist Tyrrell to the effect that they believed that what the Church needed was "a liberal infusion of Protestant ideas"? Why has the "fort" been abandoned "by those even of whom it should be guarded"?

Either those responsible had a defective faith, or they were not even Christian! For all their "sincerity" and "good will", they, like the Protestant Reformers of an earlier age, could not abide and accept Holy Mother Church as she had always been. It was perfectly obvious to those brought up in the traditional Church that her mind and thinking was diametrically opposed to that of so-called "contemporary man". The innovators felt that if "the Church did not speak to modern man" (they themselves being modern man), it was clearly the Church that was at fault. Imbued with the false ideas of progress and evolution, they forgot that it was "modern man who would not listen to the Church". Despite their decrying of the title, they were themselves "modernists" and "liberals" who sought to bring the Church — essentially a "timeless" structure — into the modern world: not as something inimical to the modern world, not as an entity whose function it was to instruct and guide the modern world in God's ways, but as part and parcel of that world — in the "avant-garde" and "forefront" of its deviations from the norm that Christ established. It is precisely in this sense that the Conciliar Church has abandoned its role of "master" *(magister)* and declared itself to be the "servant" of the world.[1] They wished to make the Church "relevant" in a world that itself had lost all relevance and was *entleert* of meaning, a world that was "alienated" and had lost sight of "the one thing necessary". What is all this talk of "serving" the "world", but the rendering unto Caesar of what is God's?

Now, if the Church was to be "changed", what guidelines and what authority was to be appealed to? The only alternative to "tradition" is in the last analysis, "private judgment" — the "collective" private judgment of those whose souls had been corrupted by the "collective" errors of our times. What resulted has been described by Malcolm Muggeridge as "suicide".[2] It was both predictable and inevitable.

Aggiornamento is the battle cry of the innovators. With

---

1. Those who so loudly proclaim that the function of the Church is to *serve* would do well to consider the words of Chesterton: "What is the matter with the cult of Service is that, like so many modern notions, it is the idolatry of the intermediate, to the oblivion of the ultimate. It is like the jargon of the idiots who talk about Efficiency without any criticism of Effect. The sin of Service is the sin of satan: that of trying to be first where it can only be second. A word like Service has stolen the sacred capital letter from the thing which it was once supposed to serve. There is a sense in serving God, and even more disputed, a sense in serving man; but there is no sense in serving Service . . . The man who rushes down the street waving his arms and wanting something or somebody to serve will probably fall into the first bucket-shop or den of thieves and userers, and be found industriously serving *them*".

2. "In my opinion", says Malcolm Muggeridge, "if men were to be stationed at the doors of the Church with whips to drive worshippers away, or inside the religious orders specifically to discourage vocations, or amongst the clergy to spread alarm and despondency, they could not hope to be as effective in achieving these ends as are the trends and policies seemingly now dominant within the Church." *(Something Beautiful For God)*.

what is this *aggiornamento* to take place? What are some of the main themes that run through the thinking of the Post-conciliar Church? Let us try to come to terms with this entity.

Paramount and basic is the modernist concept of "LIBERTY".[3] This is in its extreme form what can be described as the absolute sovereignty of the individual in his entire independence of God and God's authority. Rejecting the principle of absolute authority in religion, modern man holds that every individual (or sect) may reject part, or all, of the deposit of Revelation, and may interpret whatever he chooses to retain according to the dictates of his private judgment. For man to submit to any authority that is higher than himself is for him to lose his "dignity" as man. (Anyone who does so is described as "rigid", "old-fashioned", "super-stitious", "unwilling to be a responsible person", and above all, a person who is "opposed to progress".) Now, this "liberal" principle, impelled by the law of its own impotence, inevitably gives birth to endless differences and contradictions. In the last analysis, it is forced to recognize as valid, any belief that springs from the exercise of private judgment — dogma is replaced by mere opinion. Therefore does it finally arrive, by the force of its own premises, at the conclusion that one creed is as good as another; it then seeks to shelter its inconsistency under the false plea of "liberty of conscience".

Stemming from this false idea of liberty that makes each man his own highest authority for the determination of the Truth, is the contention that all religious points of view are equally good (or bad). Surely, it is clear that a man, who under the plea of rational liberty has the right to repudiate any part of Revelation that may displease him, cannot logically quarrel with another man who, on the same grounds, repudiates the

---

3. Satan has always promised to his followers a false "liberty". As the serpent said to Eve, *"Ye shall be as gods"*. St. Paul warns us against those who would *"promise men liberty, while themselves the servants of corruption"* (2 Pet. 2:19). St. Thomas Aquinas teaches us that "the end at which the devil aims is the revolt of the rational creature from God . . . This revolt from God is conceived as an end, inasmuch as it is desired under the pretext of liberty (or autonomy)" (*Summa* IIIa P., Q. 8, a.1). Christ promised us that the Truth — His Truth — would make us free. Nowhere in scripture does it say that Freedom, as modern man understands the term, would bring us to the Truth. As Jean-Paul Sartre and the anarchist Bakunin have both said: "If God exists, I am not free. But I am free, therefore God does not exist!"

whole! Not only is one creed as good as another; no creed is as good as any. Modern man is tired of all the individualistic and subjective religious controversy that has resulted, and being totally unfamiliar with traditional concepts, cannot understand religious exclusivity. For him the supernatural is vaguely identified with the superstitious, faith with credulity, firmness with fanaticism, the uncompromising with the intolerant, and consistency with narrowness of outlook. The very idea that a religion should have the "fullness of the truth" appears to him both incongruous and offensive. Hence he not only holds that one religion is as good as another, but that all religions should be relegated to the "private sector" of our lives. All he asks of his fellow man is a modicum of "sincerity" and "good will", and that he keep his religious views to himself. The very topic is not to be discussed "in polite society". And these are precisely the ideas that are fundamental to the "Ecumenical Movement", a phenomena so patently anti-Christian that the Greek Orthodox Church in North America has been led to promulgate a document advising its followers to avoid any involvement in this form of "secularized Christianity".

It further follows, once the above propositions are accepted, that no religion should hold a position of prominence in the state. Civil authority should treat all denominations equally, whether they be good or bad. Since the possibility of objective truth is denied, religion becomes at best "tolerated", — when it competes with the state for the "control" of mankind's mind, it is decried as being "against progress", and labelled as "the opiate of the people". The basis for the authority of the civil state resides, not in God, but in the rights of the people ("self-determination") to make their own laws in entire independence and utter disregard of any other criteria than the popular will expressed at the polls. These in turn are often controlled and manipulated by anti-Christian forces. Not infrequently what results is that Barabbas is released while Christ is crucified![4]

---

4. History is replete with examples of how small pressure groups can manipulate the "popular will". The New Church itself is a perfect example. Modernists have infiltrated and captured its "organs" while proclaiming that the Church has been "democratized", and vociferously proclaiming that they themselves are fulfilling "the will of the People of God". All protests are ignored and every psychological method short of physical force known to man is used to make the faithful comply.

The idea of a "Catholic state" is not only rejected, it is seen as an "evil" to be destroyed. What is shocking is that such an attitude has been embraced by Vatican II! Listen to the documents:

> "The Christian faithful, like other men, should enjoy on the level of the state, the right of in no way being hindered from leading their lives according to their conscience. It is entirely in accord with the liberty of the Church and the freedom of religion that all men and all communities should have this right accorded to them as a civil and legal right."

This is why the hierarchy in such Catholic countries as Spain and Portugal have actively interfered with the political structure to favour its "liberalization" and "democratization". And it naturally follows from such attitudes that there should be absolute freedom of worship, the supremacy of the state, the separation of Church and God from civil authority, secular education[5] and civil marriage. The New Church with a "mandate from Vatican II" is actively campaigning to promote the secularization of Catholic countries such as Italy and Ireland. In the practical order what results is that Communists, Freemasons and satan worshipers are treated on an "equal footing" with Divine Revelation.[6]

---

5. The assumption that "secular education" is in any sense of the word "neutral" is absurd. Children are inculcated from infancy with the pseudo-religious ideas of the liberal philosophers, and prepared in every way to accept a world that is inane and even stupid. "Success", not "Sanctity" becomes the "ideal". By the time they complete a college education, they either join the "system", or are spewed forth as "misfits". Few escape the devastating effects of a secular education whose avowed aim is to teach men to "think for themselves", rather than to "think correctly". The end result is that the great majority do not think at all. (The average American is said to watch television 60 hours a week!) By traditional standards, modern man is probably the most uneducated man that has ever lived upon the face of the earth. He may be "literate", but he is "ignorant". In passing, one would like to call attention to the almost total destruction of Catholic educational institutes that has followed in the wake of the Second Vatican Council.
6. The idea that the Church, with its "mandate from heaven", and its well defined teachings applicable to the economic, social and political order, should take such a "liberal" position is truly extraordinary and an insult to her founder, "Christ the King". To what form of civil government then, is the Catholic Church committed? It should be clearly understood that the

traditional Church does not consider any specific political form of govern-ment in and of itself *(ex se)* as "evil". The various forms of government may be perfectly and integrally Catholic (assuming of course that they are not based on principles which are contrary to the natural and divine law). Providing they accept beyond their own sovereignty, the sovereignty of God; providing they confess that they derive their authority from Him; providing they acknowledge as the basis of public right the supreme morality of the Church and her absolute right in all things within her own competency, they are truly Catholic governments, whatever be their actual and "accidental" form. A government, whatever be its form, is Catholic, providing its constitution, its legislation and its policies are based on Catholic principles.

It is to be admitted that every form of government is subject to abuses by individuals who are in a position of power. However, it is only in a govern-ment that recognizes the principles embodied in a Catholic outlook that one can hope to find Justice and Truth prevailing. The leaders of such a government are "leading", not in the name of "the People", not in the name of certain economic or political "power cliques", but in God's name. They are God's representatives in the civil order rather than the repre-sentatives of any private group (be it aristocratic or democratic). They can be judged by an absolute standard in all that they do. They govern by "divine right" — and not by human authority. As Plato taught, the King who subverts this "divine right" — the basis of his authority — to his personal desires or "rights" becomes a "despot" and a dictator. This is in fact what King Henry VIII became. The same is true by reflection in the sacred order. When false rites are imposed on us by those holding the seat of Peter, they are ruling, not by "divine right", but in their own private rights — they are in fact guilty of the most despicable form of despotism.

Finally, the concept that "liberty of conscience and worship is the proper right of every man, and should be proclaimed and asserted by law in every correctly established society . . ." was specifically condemned by Pope Pius in his *Quanto Cura,* and was quite appropriately referred to by Pope Gregory XVI as "insanity". Neither the Anglicans in their heyday, nor the communists today, would afford the Church such guarantees. This does not mean that the Church is "intolerant" of those who disagree with her to the point of forcing them to accept her faith (such is forbidden by Canon law). It does however mean that she is intolerant of error and is obliged to do everything reasonable to prevent its spread among the faithful. It is an offence to the divine Kingship of Christ to guarantee to the enemies of the Church, as does Vatican II, the right to "freely organize, create educational and cultural, charitable and social associations", when the avowed purpose of such is to attack and destroy the true Church. To tolerate error is one thing: to encourage its existence and guarantee its permanent existence is of quite another order. Furthermore, the Church is in existence to guarantee the possibility of "freedom from error", and not to guarantee our right and "freedom to be in error".

This doctrine is plainly taught in Leo XIII's Encyclical *Immortale Dei,* "On The Christian Constitution of States". Another excellent source of information on the social and political teachings of the Church is *The Mystical Body of Christ and the Reorganization of Society,* by Rev. Denis Fahey, Regina: Dublin, Ireland, 1978.

Other consequences also result. In the realm of morality, no absolute values are to be embraced. What is considered to be for the greatest convenience of the most people (often a well organized minority in practice) is legislated by the state, a process that allows for such abominations as abortion and euthanasia to become the "law of the land". Apart from this, private morality is limited only by the need to protect others from the ravages of any one individual's passions. This new moral outlook is propagandized under the title of "situation ethics", and we find the Catholic Theological Society of America stating without any official contradiction that homosexuality and adultery can be considered acceptable, so long as they are, in the pseudo-scientific terms of modern psychology, "self-liberating, other-enriching, honest, faithful, socially responsible, life-serving and joyous".[7] Those who will rapidly cry that such a statement is an "abuse", should consider the teaching of Vatican II in which the faithful are instructed to:

"blend modern science and its theories and the understanding of the most recent discoveries with Christian morality and doctrine. Thus their religious practice and morality can keep pace with their scientific knowledge and with an ever advancing technology . . ."

(Pastoral Constitution on the Church in the Modern World — Gaudium et Spes)

There can never be "Joy and Hope" in such a teaching as anyone who is a victim of modern technology well knows.

Beyond this, all hierarchy in values, in persons and in function is to be eliminated. (In Practice, those established by God and based on the "natural law" are eliminated in favor of those established by a monied society or the state). Just as in the intellectual order, the "shackles" of Revelation were

---

7. Morality that is advocated with no other end than that of "not doing unto others what one doesn't want done to oneself", or of maintaining the *status quo* of what is termed a "social contract", is bound to fall flat on its face. For a Catholic, morality not only involves submitting to the eminently reasonable laws established by God (as incorporated in the Decalogue), it is also predispositive to the spiritual life. Thus it is that mortal sin deprives one of sanctifying grace. Morality is not an end in itself; nor is it merely an effective means of maintaining peace in the social order. Rather, it is a most important means of achieving the proper ends of man.

rejected in the name of "free thought" and "untrammeled reason", which has resulted in some of the basest ideas known to the history of mankind being accepted as "normal", so also in the political realm, the Kings, having rejected any control by the legitimate "spiritual authority", were in turn destroyed by the monied interests — powers which in turn are again threatened by still lower forces. A false "egalitarianism" (all souls are indeed of equal value in the eyes of God) that would make the "lowest common denominators" in all realms the criteria on which we base our value judgments is foisted upon society.[8] Thus for example, the fact that a priest is a man set apart with special privileges and even greater responsibilities is decried. Under the cry of "collegiality", the Bishops encroach upon Papal authority. Priest's "senates" are created to vie with the authority of the Bishops. The laity have preached to them a false concept of "the priesthood of the People of God" (a favourite theme of Luther) which allows

---

8. It is true that all men are equal in *essence,* that all will be judged by God, and that each and every soul is precious to its Maker. But individuals are not equal in merit and will not be equal in glory; they are not equal in knowledge, intelligence, in common sense and wisdom. As Nesta Webster points out in her excellent book on the French Revolution, "It is doubtful indeed whether liberty and equality can exist together, for whilst liberty consists in allowing every man to live as he likes best, and to do as he will with his own, equality necessitates a perpetual system of repression in order to maintain things at the same dead level." As Leo XIII said, "that ideal equality about which they (the modernists) entertain pleasant dreams, would be, in reality, the levelling down of all to a like condition of misery and degradation". The Church's teaching is well summed up by Pius XII: "In a people worthy of the name, those inequalities which are not based on whims, but on the nature of things . . . do not constitute an obstacle to . . . a true spirit of union and brotherhood. On the contrary, so far are they from impairing civil equality that they show its true meaning, namely that . . . everyone has the right to live in his own personal life honourably in the place and in the conditions in which . . . Providence has placed him" (*Christmas Message,* 1944).

The only possible way for equality to become a reality in the social realm is for men to be subjected to the severest form of despotism. The only way in which the conflicting ideals of liberty and equality can be resolved is on the basis of "justice". Now justice in turn, unless we allow it to be defined by the "private opinion" of individuals or groups (despots or the state), if it is to have any "objective" character at all, brings us back to the teachings of the Church relative to the social order. Either we strive to "build the city of God" on earth, or we submit ourselves to what must eventually become an unmitigated slavery. If we buy the ideologies of the modern world, (as Vatican II does), then we have "nothing to gain but our chains".

them to claim the authority of the clergy, and the "hier-archical" structure of the sanctuaries is at great expense torn down so that instead of kneeling at the altar rail, they are invited to "sit around" the "table", to handle the sacred vessels, and to join the "president" in the "Eucharistic meal" as an equal. Nothing will satisfy the forces of rebellion until the "lumpen-proletariat" rules the world, and the basest concepts of brutalized man (such as Russia's "Gulags", Hitler's death camps, or for that matter the acceptance of abortion and euthanasia) become the statistical norm for proper thinking. Satan's theme song will always be "Release Barabbas and Crucify Christ" — a perfectly "democratic" legalism and a classical example of how a small minority is able to influence the "popular vote" to its own sinister ends.

Now, the hierarchy of the New Church would have an *aggiornamento* with all these concepts. True, they do not embrace them in the extreme form — but the principles are accepted. It is an old dream of mankind that one can play with fire without getting burnt — that Christ and Barabbas can come to terms and "co-exist", and that "one can have one's cake and eat it". The problem is, once the principles are accepted, the consequences must inevitably follow. Those who would "revolutionize" the Church would do well to remember the warning of the Jacobean Illuminato (Free-mason) St.-Just who was a leader of the French Revolution. "Whoever stops half-way in revolution digs his own grave!" And thus we have a modern world that is splintered and chaotic, a world that is, in the phraseology of the historian, "post-Christian"; and in that of the psychologist, "alienated"; a "shark's world" that chases after everything but "the one thing necessary". And what role is left for the New Church to play in such a world? This is the question that poses itself to the modernist who would retain at least the semblance of his Christian roots.[9] The answer lies in "unity", a mankind

9. Liberalism is a philosophy that was created by individuals who were outside the Church, and which, in the practical order, gave birth to modern secular democracy (government "from below", rather than "from above"), and to a system which as Leo XIII said, "laid on the toiling millions a yoke little better than slavery". Modernism arose within the Church (both Loisy and Tyrrell were priests and claimed to be "Catholic"), and can be seen as the applications of these same principles to the Church itself. As John McKee states, "If theology is faith seeking understanding, modernism is disbelief seeking repose. A modernist is a man who has lost it: therefore he

dedicated to the "new humanism", to a "universal culture" acting in consort to build a "better world" in the future.[10]

The function of the New Church is to be a "catalyst" for this unity — "The Church is a kind of sacrament of intimate union with God, and the unity of all mankind, that is, she is a sign and an instrument of such union and unity . . . At the end of time, she will achieve her glorious fulfillment. Then . . . all just men from the time of Adam will be gathered together with the Father in the universal Church". In these statements, taken from Vatican II, note the ambiguity and disguised millennarianism. They continue. Of course, the Church "recognizes that worthy elements are to be found in today's social movements, especially in an evolution towards unity", and hence she must join and encourage all such elements, and she must "wipe out every ground of division so that the whole human race may be brought into the unity of the

---

has to fill the traditional dogmas with new content, changing as he does so, *"plus ça change, plus c'est la même chose" (The Enemy Within The Gate* — Lumen Christi: Houston, Texas, 1974).

Modernist philosophers attempt to justify their liberal beliefs in terms they think the Church will find acceptable — hence they appeal to Immanence (the idea that the foundation of faith must be sought in an internal sense which arises from man's need for God — "welling up from the depth of the unconscious under the impulse of the heart . . ."); to "historical criticism" as a means of understanding the Scriptures, and to the explaining away of dogmas as "symbols", and of the sacraments as "faith-nourishing signs". As M. Loisy said, "the avowed modernists form a fairly definite group of thinking men united in the common desire to adapt Catholicism to the intellectual, moral and social needs of today". To quote *Il Programma dei Modernisti,* "Our religious attitude is ruled by the single wish to be one with Christians and Catholics who live in harmony with the spirit of the age". However much it may dislike the terms, the Post-conciliar Church is clearly a "Reformed", a "Protestant", a "Liberal" and a "Modernist" Church.

10. We have already shown that the French Revolutionary ideas of "liberty" and "equality" have been embraced by the Conciliar Church. The third aspect of this false ideology — "fraternity" — is manifest under the guise of "unity". Now this erroneous trilogy has been unequivocally condemned by a whole series of Popes starting from Saint Pius V and including Pius VII, Gregory XVI, Pius IX, Leo XIII and Pius X. Yet despite this we find Father Avril, in an article attacking Mgr. Lefebvre with great violence, stating that "the slogan 'Liberty, Equality, Fraternity' is itself magnificently Christian" (*L'Express, Paris, Sept. 6, 1976).* Of course, the Freemasons are delighted. See Part V, footnote 28.

family of God". Elsewhere, we are given further insights into this proposed unity. "Recent psychological research explains human activity more profoundly. Historical studies make a signal contribution to bringing man to see things in their changeable and evolutionary aspects. The human race has passed from a rather static concept of reality to a more dynamic, evolutionary one . . . Thus little by little, a more universal form of human culture is developing, one which will promote and express the unity of the human race . . . The Church further recognizes that worthy elements are to be found in today's social movements, especially an evolution towards unity, a process of wholesome socialization and of association in civic and economic realms . . . It is a fact bearing on the very person of man, that he can come to an authentic and full humanity only through culture,[11] that is, through the cultivation of natural goods and values . . . The Church believes she can contribute greatly towards making the family of man and its history more human . . . Thus we are witnesses of the birth of a new humanism, one in which man is defined first of all by his responsibility towards his brothers and towards history." (All quotations here are from Vatican II.) Now all these statements falsify the nature and true ends of man, as well as the function of the Church. Further, they are based on a variety of parochial and theoretical sociological assumptions that have no basis in fact such as man's inevitable "progress", his "dynamic" and "evolutionary" character[12], and the idea that we are in fact "building a better world".[13] Yet it is on just these false bases that the New

---

11. Elsewhere the documents tell us that "man is the author of his own culture", and that it is "through his dealings with others, through reciprocal duties, and through fraternal dialogue", that man "develops" all his gifts and is able to "rise to his destiny". Those who feel these quotations are taken out of context are invited to read the original — especially *The Church in the Modern World.*

12. In *Contra Teilhard de Chardin*, Titus Burckhardt says: "The main objection to the evolutionary doctrine of Teilhard de Chardin is as follows: if the spiritual faculty of man — the "noetic faculty", as Teilhard de Chardin calls it — is merely a phase of a continuing biological evolution — or involution — which, seen as a whole, can be compared to a curve or a spiral, then this phase cannot step out of the whole and say: I am part of a spiral. Anything that such an evolution-bound faculty could ever grasp or express would likewise be subject to evolution, and this leads to the marxist view that there is no truth, but only biological pragmatism and utilitarianism. It is here that Teilhard's theory breaks down completely.   *(Contd. overleaf)*

Church would found its concept of "unity". As Paul VI has said, "The time has come for all mankind to unite together in the establishment of a community that is both fraternal and worldwide . . . The Church, respecting the ability of worldly powers, ought to offer her assistance in order to promote a full humanism, which is to say, the complete development of

---

"The human spirit does, in fact, have the faculty of placing itself outside biological change, of viewing things objectively and essentially, and of making judgements. Teilhard de Chardin confuses the cerebral and noetic faculties. The *Nous* (= Intellect = Spirit) is not the same as the activity of the brain; the latter works over, whereas the former judges and knows. The truly spiritual faculty — that of discriminating between true and false, of distinguishing the relative from the absolute — is related to the biological level, metaphorically speaking, as is the vertical to the horizontal; it belongs to another ontological dimension. And precisely because this dimension occurs in man, he is not an ephemeral biological appearance, but, in this physical and earthly world, and in spite of all his organic limitations, an absolute centre. This is also indicated by the faculty of speech, which belongs to man alone, and which, precisely, presupposes the capacity to objectivize things, to place oneself behind and beyond appearances.

"The terrestrial absolutiy of the human state and of the human form is also confirmed by the doctrine of the incarnation of the Divine Word — a doctrine which, in Teilhard's system, loses all its meaning. If man fundamentally possesses the capacity of knowing God, that is to say, if the fulfilling of the function which is his by definition is a way to God, then on the biological plane there is no occasion for a super-man. He would be a pleonasm.

"The poor saints! They came a million years too soon . . . None of them, however, would ever have accepted the doctrine that God could be reached biologically, or again through collective scientific research . . .

"And so I come back to my main objection: according to Teilhard's system, the "noetic" faculty of man is related to biogenesis not as the eye is related to the other human parts, but rather as a part-process is related to a whole process — and this is something quite different. The eye can view the other limbs and organs, even if only in a mirror, but a part-process can never view the whole process of which it is a part. This has already been said by Aristotle: whoever asserts that everything is in a stream can never prove his assertion, for the simple reason that it can rest on nothing that is not itself in the stream; it is thus self-contradictory."

13. It is the communist belief in "progress', or rather in "futurism" that leads them to kill millions of individuals that they think are standing in the way of this future world. The "enemies of the state" are in fact "enemies of progress". The ineluctable "dynamic forces of history" apparently need to be helped on their way — all "revisionists" and "obstructionists" must be eliminated. Thus Vatican II teaches that the New Church must "wipe out every ground of division so that the whole human race may be brought into the unity of the family of God."

the entire man, and of all men . . . to place herself in the avant-garde of social action. She ought to extend all her efforts to support, encourage and bring about those forces working towards the creation of this integrated man. Such is the end which the (new) Church intends to follow. All (Post-conciliar) Catholics have the obligation of assisting this development of the total person in conjunction with their natural and Christian brothers, and with all men of good will." And why did Montini throw in his lot with such ideas? "Because", as he has said on many occasions, "we have confidence in man, because we believe in that fount of goodness which is in each and every heart."[14] Rousseau could not have said it better!

According to Brian Kaiser, John XXIII saw Christian unity as a necessary precursor to the "unity of all mankind". It is, as it were, the first step to be achieved. Thus the *periti* at the Council, wishing to stress similarities rather than differences, developed the concept of "imperfect communion". The various Christian communities that are "outside full communion" with the Catholic Church must be integrated with her. "All those who believe in Christ (whether as God or as an 'ethical leader' is never specified) and have received baptism, are in a certain communion with the Catholic Church, though not a perfect one." They contain "elements" such as "the written Word of God, the life of grace, the theological virtues and the interior gifts of the Holy Spirit", and hence, with them "the Church is linked for various reasons". It is with these groups that "unity" is first of all to be established.

What is lost sight of is that the reason the Protestants lack "perfect" unity is because they reject the fullness of the faith, and accept, in various degrees, the whole liberal spectrum of false ideas that we have outlined in the preceding paragraphs.[15] In any event, "unity" with the Protestants on the

---

14. *Doc. Cath.* No. 1576 and 77.

15. It is not my intention in this book to deal with Protestantism as such, except in so far as the defence of "sound doctrine and pure faith" demands. On the other hand, to quote Chesterton, I have no intention of using "that peculiar diplomatic and tactful art of saying that Catholicism is true, without suggesting for one moment that anti-Catholicism is false . . ." Saint Peter Julian Eymard expresses well the thought of the Church when he states:

part of the true Church is a pure chimera. Apart from the fact that the "Prodigal son" must return to the "bosom of the Father", and not the other way around, no two Protestants even within a given denomination fully agree — except by accident — on what they should believe. Among them, every shade, degree and variety of belief in the Christian dispensation finds easy lodgment. One can almost speak of a "sliding scale" of disbelief which finds its only "unity" in "protesting" against the fullness of the faith. Yet it is to accomodate such groups that the Post-conciliar Church has changed her doctrines and liturgy. Let us note however that these changes have all been in a one-way direction. What doctrine of the traditional Church have the various "ecclesiastical communities" accepted that they formerly rejected? Absolutely none. What ecclesiastical traditions have our "separated brethren" adopted? Again, absolutely none. Yet look at the

---

"People often say 'It is better to be a good Protestant than a bad Catholic'. This is not true. That would mean at bottom that one can be saved without the true Faith. No, a bad Catholic remains a child of the family, although a prodigal, and however great a sinner he may be, he still has a right to mercy. Through his Faith, a bad Catholic is nearer to God than a Protestant is, for he is a member of the household, whereas the heretic is not. And how hard it is to make him become one!"

Actually, Protestantism is hardly a religion as such apart from the fact that it represents the general tendency of modern man to "protest" against all the true Church stands for. The genuine Protestant creed is now hardly held by anybody — least of all, by the Protestants. It began with "Faith without works" and has ended with "Works without faith". The shibboleth of today is "It does not matter what a man believes, it is what he does that matters. Give me a man who lives for his fellow men! That is Christianity!" So completely have most Protestants lost faith in the creeds of Calvin and Luther, that they have almost forgotten what it was they said. (Both, for instance, denied free will). In practice, included under the term Protestantism would be those who are in fact agnostics, atheists, hedonists, pagans (in the sense of having no religion), independent mystics, psychic investigators, theists, theosophists, followers of eastern cults and jolly good fellows living like beasts that perish. Finally, many Protestants (meaning Lutherans, Calvinists, Presbyterians etc . . .,) live lives that are in fact far finer than their theology or ideals would inculcate, for their lives are manifest with many "good works" that they do for no conceivable reason (if we take their theology seriously). Catholics on the other hand, to use the words of St. Thomas More, see "man's duty to God as so great that very few serve Him as they should do". Only the saints in any way approach in their lives the ideals to which a Catholic aspires (again, if we take his theology seriously).

many that the Neo-Protestant Church of Vatican II has abandoned, or if not positively rejected, at least allowed to fall into disuse. What Protestant "house of worship" resembles the sanctuaries we knew as children, and what Neo-modernist church of the Post-Vatican II era cannot be confused with that of a Reformation sect? As Michael Davies has pointed out with regard to the various "agreed statements" made with the Anglicans: "The agreement on the Eucharist and the Ministry does not affirm the Catholic position in a single instance where it conflicts with Protestantism". And yet, we must concede that a certain kind of "unity" has been achieved between the Post-conciliar Church and the various Reformed "ecclesiastical communities". The reason is clear. The Post-conciliar Church is itself a "Neo-Protestant" Church — indeed, it is "The Church of the latter-day Modernists".

Those who would still doubt the nature of the compromises made in this direction have but to consider the official statements of the New Church. With regard to the liturgy for instance, Paul VI told us the changes were made for two reasons — "to bring it into line with Scripture", and for "pastoral reasons". He never personally specified just what "pastoral reasons" were, but the answer is to be found in other documents.

Thus it states in the *'Letter to the Presidents of National Councils of Bishops concerning Eucharistic Prayers'*, an official document of the "Sacred Congregation for Divine Worship":

> "The reason why such a variety of texts have been offered (in the *Novus Ordo*), and the end result such new form-ularies were meant to achieve, *are pastoral in nature:* namely to reflect the unity and diversity of liturgical prayer. BY USING THE VARIOUS TEXTS CON-TAINED IN THE (new) ROMAN MISSAL, VARIOUS CHRISTIAN COMMUNITIES, AS THEY GATHER TOGETHER TO CELEBRATE THE EUCHARIST, ARE ABLE TO SENSE THAT THEY THEMSELVES FORM THE ONE CHURCH PRAYING WITH THE SAME FAITH, USING THE SAME PRAYER. They furthermore become one in their ability of proclaiming the same mystery of Christ in different ways — especially when the vernacular is used."

Here then is the reason for the changes. It is to promote the "unity" of all Christians "praying with the same faith", and proclaiming "the same mystery of Christ" in different ways. The only problem is that the "faith" involved is not the Catholic faith, and the "mystery" involved is not the "recurring unbloody sacrifice of Calvary". If it were, the "separated brethren" would simply become Catholics.[16]

This cry for a false unity with those who reject the teaching of the traditional Church, and even with the entire corpus of Christianity, this desire to be in the 'avant-garde' of the social forces that are creating the "new humanism", the "wholesome socialization" of mankind, and the "universal culture" of the future is the reason why the traditional Mass had to be discarded and replaced by a parody. This is why the New "mass" never clearly teaches the doctrine of the Real Presence. This is why non-Catholic sects, nay even anti-Catholic sects, have no objection to using it. This is why the liberal press approves it, and this is why the world loves it.

Everything is to be sacrificed to this end — even the Sacred Species Itself. The Eucharist is now to become the "Sacrament of the New Unity". It can be referred to as a benediction, the Lord's Supper, the Lord's table, memory of the Lord — but never by that offensive word "Transubstantiation". Read Paul VI's entire Apostolic Constitution on the New "mass" and you will find that this hallowed word never once appears! Thus it is that Montini says: "The Catholic Church is determined to continue and intensify its contribution to the common effort of all Christians for unity . . ." (Not the efforts of Catholics in love and charity to bring the Protestants back to Unity.) And thus it is that he has expressed the hope that "the day would soon come when the unity of all Christians would be celebrated and sealed in a concelebrated Eucharist". Both the "communitarian vocation" of mankind and "salvation history" demand it.

John XXIII had told us that "certain sacrifices would be

---

16. We have already presented evidence that Archbishop "Freemason" Bugnini was the leading architect of the New "mass". It was he who headed the "Concilium" that was responsible for its creation. Now, he himself tells us in his journal, *Notitiae* that the intent and reason for its creation was to introduce the New "Roman form of the liturgy into the usages and mentalities of each individual Church", which means, to create a service that any "ecclesiastical community" could use.

necessary in order to achieve unity". Paul VI and the Post-conciliar Church have made it clear just what these sacrifices are. They entail the sacrifice of what in essence can be called "the Christian tradition".

COMMUNISM — THE NEW VATICAN
"OSTPOLITIK"

In so far as the post-conciliar Church accepts the modernist idea of "progress", i.e., the concept that man through the manipulation of certain "dynamic forces" and "historical processes" is capable of creating on earth some sort of "perfect society", it accepts three of the fundamental tenets of Marxist theory. On their part Marxists find no difficulty in allowing a certain "religious freedom" if such belief involves faith in a "divinity" that would in no serious way interfere with their plans for world conquest. To concede that God is responsible for "progress", that God is the "power" behind the "dynamic forces", and that God in fact really wants what Russia wants, is to place God in the "service of the State". As for private property, as Metropolitan Nikodim, one of the idols of the New Church, has opined, the Catholic Church finds nothing wrong with accepting "a public form of property such as is exemplified by socialism of the Soviet type".[1] Thus it is that long before the Second

1. With regard to "private property", the Church has always defended this as a "right" essential to the well-being of the individual. She well knows that there can be no political or social freedom — to say nothing of religious freedom — on the part of those who live under a system where the State controls food, clothing and shelter in an absolute manner. On the other hand, she has never failed to promote Justice and Charity — as witness her condemnation of usury and her constant teaching that wealth was "held" in trust, a trust for which the individual was responsible and answerable to God. As R. H. Tawney *(Religion and the Rise of Capitalism)* has said, mediaeval society was one in which men "had not learned to persuade themselves that greed was enterprise and avarice economy . . ." The mediaeval serf who paid to the state (represented by the "Baron") one or two days a week of free labour, was infinitely better off than modern man who pays two to four times this in the form of "taxes". Moreover, the serf could never be taxed on his home and small private holding, and could

Vatican Council, the Communist state had taken steps to infiltrate and control the Russian Orthodox Church as well as various Western religious organizations such as the World Council of Churches. As long ago as 1927 Sergius, the Metropolitan of Moscow, had notably distinguished himself as an instrument of Communist policy by declaring himself to be in "total obedience" to the ruling powers — "the joys and victories of the Soviet Union are also our joys and our victories". Even then the line of "detente" offered to the Church was that there is nothing incompatible between socialism and Christianity . . . indeed, Christ and the Apostles were "the first Communists". The principle involved, to quote from a contemporary Communist document, was to "progressively replace the religious element" in Church teaching "by the Marxist element; we shall gradually transform the false conscience of the Catholics to the true conscience, so that they will eventually come around to destroying, by themselves, and for themselves, the divine images which they had themselves created. This is our line of struggle for victory against the counter-revolutionary Catholic Church".[2] Indeed, it seems that to promote such tactics, agents infiltrated the Church and rose to important positions, thereby producing devastating effects.[3] The faithful pontiffs clearly and repeatedly warned the faithful of the dangers involved.

Pope Pius IX in 1846 called Communism "absolutely

---

never be dispossessed of them. (Modern bankruptcy law which to this day protects the home of the individual from confiscation is a hold-over of this mediaeval principle.) His children were educated at the local monastery and hospitals were well endowed, as caring for the "poor" was considered both a privilege and an obligation. All this is not to state that mediaeval society was a "perfect" society, for even in the Garden of Eden a serpent was to be found. It was however a "Christian" society and one that guaranteed the "freedom" and economic security of its members in areas where it was most important.

2. A document meant for use in South America quoted in *"The Mindszenty Report"*, (St. Louis, Mo.) August 1977.

3. A case in point is Father Aleghiero Tondi, S.J., a Jesuit who during the pontificate of Pope Pius XII handed over to the Russians the names of all priests sent behind the Iron Curtain, all of whom were captured and martyred. This man, still suspected of being a Russian agent, was "forgiven" by Paul VI and is presently working in Rome, one hopes in a less sensitive position. *(L'Espionnage Sovietique en France,* Pierre de Villemarest.) Those interested in a somewhat fictionalized account of the infiltration techniques used can refer to Marie Carre's *AA1025 — Memoirs of an Anti-Apostle,* Editions Saint-Raphael, Quebec, Canada.

contrary to the natural law itself . . ." and added that "once adopted, would utterly destroy the rights, property and possessions of all men, and even of society itself". Leo XIII in 1878 called it "a mortal plague which insinuates itself into the very marrow of human society only to bring about its ruin". Pius XI in 1937 called it "a pseudo-ideal of justice, of equality and of fraternity . . ." and further stated that "Communism is intrinsically evil, and no one who would save Christian civilization may collaborate with it in any undertaking whatsoever". It is in the light of such clear-cut statements that John XXIII's proclamation to the effect that "the Church is not a dam against Communism. The Church cannot and should not be against anything . . ." is a clear-cut rupture with the past. No wonder that Khrushchev was delighted to congratulate Roncalli on the occasion of his eightieth birthday. *Aggornamiento* was off and running.

It is well known that Mgr. (now Cardinal) Willebrands, in engineering on behalf of John XXIII the presence of the Russian Orthodox Church at the Council, promised that Communism would neither be attacked nor condemned — such was openly admitted at the Pan-Orthodox Conference of Rhodes in 1964 where this silence was described as the *sine qua non* for their very presence. Indeed, when the petition of Mgr. Castro Mayer, Bishop of Campos in Brazil, introduced such a condemnation signed by over four-hundred Bishops, it was, contrary to the rules of those who had by then captured the Council, "lost" and ignored. If this Council purported to deal with the problems of the Church in the modern world, such a "silence" was, to say the least, extraordinary.[4]

Subsequent to these initial acts of "treason" with regard to the truth and against the divine Kingship of Christ, the post-conciliar Church has made compromise after compromise to appease the Russians. NKVD (now KGB) agents such as Metropolitan Nikodim, who died in the arms of John-Paul I, have repeatedly been welcomed into the heart of the Vatican — those dripping with the blood of martyrs, being wined and dined at the expense of the faithful. Indeed Paul VI invited Nikodim to say Mass over the tomb of St. Peter ! Of course, such hospitality was reciprocated. When Pimen was enthroned as the "Patriarch" of Moscow, Cardinal Willebrands was

---

4. These facts have been confirmed by several authors, including Father Wiltgen, *op. cit.*

present as the official representative of Paul VI. When during his sermon Pimen proclaimed the total destruction of the Ukrainian Catholic Church, and its "triumphal return to Russian Orthodoxy", Cardinal Willebrands made no objection whatsoever. In matters as grave as this, such silence is equivalent to consent.[5] On the other hand, when Mgr. Velychkovsky, a Bishop of the Ukrainian Uniate Church was released after many years in prison and returned to Rome, he was treated as a simple priest — to recognize his rank and pay him due honor would have been equivalent to recognizing the existence of the Catholic Church behind the Iron Curtain. The very reverse occurred when the false Bishop, Exarch Filaret, superior of the Russian Orthodox Church for the Ukraine and an agent for the KGB arrived. This man who was the person responsible for finding, betraying and arresting Bishop Velychokovsky was treated with the highest honours; he was a guest of honour at the Pontifical Collegium Russicum and of the Secretariat for the Union of Christians. Meanwhile, Father Mailleux S.J. of the Vatican Congregation for Oriental Rites and Rector of the Pontifical Collegium Russicum (and known as the "Red Priest") declared that the Ukrainian Patriarchate should not be instituted because the Soviets would consider it to be a "hostile interference in the internal affairs of the USSR". It was shortly after this that the Italian police discovered and exposed an international network of Russian Communist espionage functioning from within this Pontifical College, a fact which the Vatican hastened to use all its influence to suppress. When the Russian Orthodox Church proceeded to set up a "Vicarate" to "govern" the branches of the Ukrainian Church in Western nations, no protest whatsoever was made. Since that time several examples of the use of this "vicarate" to infiltrate espionage agents into the West have come to light, but then, in the eyes of the New Vatican "Ostpolitik", they have a right "to interfere with the internal affairs of Western nations". Things had become so obvious that by December 6, 1971, *Newsweek Magazine* stated that "the Vatican appears to be ready to sacrifice the union of five million Catholics of the Ukrainian Rite within the Soviet Union!" To this day, despite request after request from the some seven

---

5. I am indebted to "Ukraine: A Tragedy Without Frontiers", in *Crusade for Christian Civilization* (New Rochelle, N.Y.) Jan-Feb., 1977 for documentation of these facts.

million Ukrainain Catholics, and despite the fact that Oriental rites with far fewer adherents have been granted the privilege, Rome has not established a Ukrainian Patriaschate. And not satisfied with this, Rome has made of Cardinal Slipyi, the highest ranking Ukrainian prelate, a virtual prisoner of the Vatican, prohibiting him "under obedience" from leaving Rome to visit Ukrainian communities on several occasions.

Now, it might be argued that all this compromise was done for the sake of alleviating the persecution of the Ukrainian Catholics under Russian political domination. In point of fact, it has allowed for the unrestricted persecution of these faithful Catholics as has been documented again and again; and throughout all of his reign, Paul VI, who never hesitated to criticize the abuses imposed upon minorities in Western nations, has never once publicly spoken on this issue. All this led Cardinal Slipyj finally to speak out — to openly disobey the long silence imposed upon him against his will by the Vatican authorities. He stated at the World Synod in Rome in 1971 that

> A dead hero is a more powerful stimulus for the Church than a living prisoner in the Vatican . . . Catholic Ukrainians who have sacrificed mountains of bodies and shed rivers of blood for the Catholic Faith and for their fidelity to the Holy See, even now are undergoing a very terrible persecution, but what is worse, they are defended by no one . . . Our Catholic faithful are prohibited from celebrating the liturgy and administering the Sacraments, and must descend into the Catacombs. Thousands and thousands of the faithful, priests, and bishops have been thrown into prison and deported to the polar regions of Siberia. Now, however, because of negotiations and diplomacy, Ukrainian Catholics, who as martyrs and confessors suffered so much, are being thrown aside as inconvenient witnesses of past evils . . .

Spoken like a Cardinal Mindszenty, which brings us to consider another facet of the new Vatican "Ostpolitik", one which causes every faithful Catholic to hang his head in shame and sorrow. This heroic prelate, the primate of Hungary, was as the *New York Times* obituary notice stated, "regarded in the West as a symbol of anti-Communism". He had for over thirty-five years refused to submit to the "atheistic and materialistic forces" of Fascism and Communism. Even liberal politicians and clerics recognized the greatness of this man. President Ford said at the time of his death that the Cardinal "stood for courage, integrity, and unfailing faith. There was an heroic quality about him that marked this man as a crusader for liberty". Cardinal Cook of New York praised him as a man who had "endured sufferings far beyond the capacity of most human beings, yet he never ceased to be a symbol of courage, integrity and hope. He was a man of faith and of deep, uncomplicated and unswerving belief". As is well known, he was released from a Communist prison by the abortive Hungarian revolution and because he refused to leave his country became a virtual prisoner in the American Embassy at Budapest. Here his presence proved to be a thorn in the side of the illegitimate Hungarian government and, to quote again the *New York Times,* he was "an embarrassment" to "the church which was seeking a modus vivendi with the Soviet bloc". The post-conciliar Church therefore sought to have this Cardinal released from Hungary and actually entered into negotiations with him in order to commit him quietly to withdraw from public life and to cooperate with their betrayal of the Church in Hungary. These negotiations were carried on between Paul VI's representative Mgr. Zagon and the primate, and were aimed at compromising his heroic stand in defence of both the Catholic faith and his native land. He finally left the American Embassy with the understanding that he was no longer welcome there and with the assurance that he would be free to speak for the truth with the support of Rome. Within two weeks of his departure the Vatican lifted the excommunication of the peace priests (those who had cooperated with the Communist regime in Hungary) and the *L'Osservatore Romano* portrayed his leaving as if this act had "removed an obstacle hampering good relationships between Church and state". His attempts to support the struggles of Hungarian exiles were thwarted, and being refused suffragen Bishops, he started to travel throughout the West, despite his age and ill health, to visit personally the faithful for whom he felt he had a spiritual responsibility. His criticisms of the Communist party in Hungary were not pleasing to this government and Rome demanded that all his public statements, even his sermons, be approved by a "Roman adviser". To this thought-control he refused to submit. Subsequently, without his approval, the Holy See gave the Hungarian Communist government a pledge that Cardinal Mindszenty would not "do or say anything that could possibly displease them". In an attempt to fulfill this promise, his words were misquoted in the Catholic press — often whole paragraphs of his talks being omitted — with official connivance. Paul VI made several attempts to discourage the publication of his *Memoirs*[6] (in which all these facts are documented) and when these were not successful, asked him to resign his office for "pastoral reasons", and went so far as to state that there had been "no working primate in Hungary for twenty-five years"! This among other things would dilute his authority to speak and allow for the appointment of someone else to his office who was more acceptable to the Communist regime. When he refused to abdicate his charge, he was relieved of it — the Vatican publishing the fact as if he had in fact resigned himself — and all this on the twenty-fifth anniversary of the "show-trial" that had originally led to his imprisonment by the Communists. Cardinal Mindszenty was forced publicly to contradict this distortion of the truth and to deny that he had in any way willingly abdicated. Thus passed the waning years of one of the Church's most staunch defenders, a man who had spent decades in prison under both the Nazis and the Communists, a man respected by the entire world, a man whose biography was written by a Jew in gratitude for what he did for the victims of oppression, and a man who was a national hero for the Hungarian peoples. One can do no better than to quote the closing words of his *Memoirs:* "There is nothing more to say. I found waiting to greet me at the end of the road, complete and absolute exile."

There are of course still those that will argue that Paul VI made statements in which he condemned "atheistic totalitarian regimes", and that, if at times he acted in a duplicitous manner, it was in order to ease the lot of those under persecution. The fact remains however that it is not within the bounds of decency, honour and Christian charity to act in such a manner, especially for a man who claims to be the Vicar of Christ. How incredible are the utterences of this man. Consider the following conversation between him and

---

6. Josef Cardinal Mindszenty, *Memoirs*, MacMillan, New York, 1974.

Archbishop Helder Camara of Olinda-Recife, Brazil, as reported in *Le Monde,* a very reputable French newspaper, September 26, 1974.

> Opening his arms to Mgr. Helder Camara who approached him, Paul VI exclaimed: *'Good morning, my Communist Bishop, How are you?'* The Archbishop retorted *'And good morning to you, Our Communist Pope!'*

> The same reportage continued, Archbishop Camara noting that "It is as if one played the piano with four hands, I start the theme and the Pope finishes it."

> *'How come one of your predecessors considered himself to be a King?'* asked Mgr. Camara. Pope Paul VI took up the refrain . . . *'And that he was head of the Pontifical States'.* Helder Camara: *'Why is it that Pius IX believed that it was the devil who relieved him of these states and why did he not see that Garibaldi had been sent by God?'* Pope Paul VI answered: *'If one were to go through the archives of the Vatican one would see that Pius IX himself asked the Bishops to deliver him of all that, but that it was the French Bishops that forced it on him'.*

Quite apart from the fact that Paul VI is here indulging in one of his favourite pastimes — that of re-writing history, this is a most unusual statement. Either Paul VI is serious in greeting Archbishop Camara as "his Communist Bishop", or else he is acting like a buffoon in public. One may be permitted to wonder which alternative puts him in a better light. But, if we have any doubts about his actual thoughts, let us again quote him in a discussion of Communist China:

> The Church recognizes and favours the just expression of the present historical phase of China and the transformation of ancient forms of aesthetic culture into inevitable new forms that rise out of the social and industrial structure of the modern world . . . We would like to enter into contact once again with China in order to show with how much interest and sympathy we look on at their present and enthusiastic efforts for the ideals of a diligent, full, and peaceful life.

> *Congregation for the Evangelization of the Peoples,* 1976.

One may also be permitted to wonder just how much his "interest and sympathy" helped the estimated thirty million murdered victims of Mao's "transformation of ancient forms of aesthetic culture".[7] No wonder that members of the hierarchy openly expressed themselves as being in favour of "liberation theology", and see in those who would "transform" the world, a new religion, termed "Atheistic Christianity". No wonder that the *National Jesuit News* can publish a document entitled "National Planning and the Need for a Revolutionary Social Strategy: A Christian-Maoist Perspective", in which the Society is told that it "must purge itself of its bourgeois social consciousness and identify with the proletariat". No wonder Jesuit Father Juan Alfaro who teaches at the Pontifical Gregorian University of Rome instructs the International Theological Commission that "Christ was a kind of Palestinian Che Guevara". No wonder priests in South America are reported as active participants in guerrilla bands and that *The Wanderer* has given examples of where funds donated by the faithful for the missions have ended up in the hands of Communist organizations. Now, all this is not just "hair-splitting"; nor is it a matter of selecting the statements of a few madmen who falsely claim to represent the hierarchy. Consider the following statement put forth at a meeting held at the Catholic International Centre of Research and Information under the title of *Pro Mundi Vita* — an international conference that occurred in Brussels under the auspices of the University of Louvain — which recognized Mao-Tse-Tung as "a new Moses who took his country out of the oppression of feudalism and capitalism, as formerly the chosen people were taken out of the captivity of 'Egypt'".[8] Admittedly this meeting was an "ecumenical colloquium", but it was a colloquium in which the majority of participants were Catholics of high standing, including such luminaries as Cardinal Josef Suenens, Angelo Hernandez, Archbishop of New Delhi, India, and Bernard Jacqueline, vice-secretary of the Secretariat of Non-Believers of the Vatican (under whose aegis problems dealing with Communism would fall). Read with sorrow what the faithful are being taught:

---

7. The Senate International Securities Affairs Committee of the U.S. Government has published an estimate of between thirty and sixty million. *Time* magazine uses the lower one.

8. Father Barry at Fordham University also teaches this in his course on Comparative Religion.

The rejection of a pseudo-Christianity is not necessarily a rejection of Christ Himself . . . It would appear that China accepted the spirit of Christ from another source . . that is, from Marxism. If the Chinese have, in fact, created a society with more faith, more hope, and more love than the "Christian" Apostles of Christ, we must follow where the spirit blows. The Chinese Society today . . . is I believe, further along than our own on the way to the true human society, the Kingdom of God, if you will. I believe China is the only truly Christian nation in the world in our days . . .

Through Marxism, the Christian ideas have reached China, ideas which were new to her . . . a mystique of dis-interested work and service for others; an aspiration for justice; exaltation of a simple and frugal life; the elevation of the peasant masses and the disappearance of social classes — these are the ideals towards which the China of today is orientated. But are not these the ideals that have been incomparably expressed in the encyclicals *Pacem in Terris* and *Populorum Progressio* and in the Synodal document *Justice in the World?* (Vatican II). Today Chinese children are being taught to have a sense of re-sponsibility for the community, but isn't this exactly what the Second Vatican Council has asked so insistently of the People of God?

Again, one must wonder how the "boat people" from Vietnam felt when Mgr. Nguyen Van Bihn, the Archbishop of Saigon, agreed to "cooperate" with the Communist regime, and what the faithful of South America felt when seventeen Bishops in Brazil published a document entitled "The Church in Vietnam is Disposed to Survive" (April 25, 1976) stating:

What difference does it make if the regime expels foreign missionaries . . . In the final analysis, were not the missionaries and the Churches also the symbol of the misery and the domination of our people? The regime which "liberates" our people can now enslave our Church.

It is ideas like this that led Helder Camara to appoint his personal friend and adviser, Father Joseph Comblin, to be a professor in his seminary. This infamous Belgian priest is the author of the famous "Comblin document", which was published by the Brazilian government to show the blueprint that had been prepared to guide the Communists in taking over the country. To quote a pertinent passage:

> Social reforms will not be made through persuasion, nor through platonic discussions in the Congress. How will these reforms be installed? It is by a process of force . . . the power will have to be authoritarian and dictatorial . . . the power must neutralize the forces that resist: it will neutralize the armed forces if they are conservative; it will have to control radio, TV, the press, and other media of communication and censor the destructive and reactionary criticisms . . . in any case, it will be necessary to organize a system of repression.

And again, to demonstrate the international character of the problem, let us quote the statement of the Bishops of Mozambique voicing support for Samora Machel, the Marxist president of this unfortunate country:

> We pledge ourselves to the revolution which intends radically to transform society in Mozambique into a community for solidarity of all people of good will, whether believers or non-believers . . .

Finally, it is worthy of note that some of the more conservative members of the post-conciliar hierarchy are fully aware of what is happening and have attempted to speak out in warning. Consider the statement of Bishop Basil Losten of Philadelphia:

> It is evident that Communism finds in religion today invaluable allies in its quest for global power and empire. The fantastic plan to turn the Church into an instrument of Communist conquest would be unbelievable if we did not see it all happening before our eyes . . .

Speaking to the Bishop's Meeting in Chicago in 1977, he continued:

There are people on our staff of so-called consultants who take many trips to the Soviet Union or atheistically-dominated countries. They receive a certain amount of indoctrination and then return to poison our minds and the minds of the American Catholic public. Perhaps it is too late to turn the tide.

Needless to say, such statements are rarely if ever reported in the liberal post-conciliar Catholic press.[9]

And what of the present situation? It is in the light of this background that one must examine with great care the attitude of John-Paul II — committed as he claims to be to the carrying out of the programs established by Paul VI — towards Communism. Why is an ideology that could not tolerate a Mindszenty able to tolerate a Wojtyla? Has a *modus vivendi* been achieved in Poland that will be the guide to future relations between the Vatican and Communism? Or has in fact, the post-conciliar Church departed from the stance of the traditional Church with regard to this "intrinsically evil . . . plague" that has "insinuated itself into the very marrow of human society"? A careful review of John-Paul II's statements shows that while he is critical of some of the Communist's *methods of ruling*, he has never questioned their *very right to rule*.[10] When at the age of seventy-five Cardinal Wyszynski, the

---

9. I am indebted for this and several quotes to *The Mindszenty Report*, June 1977.

10. Peter Hebblethwaite, in his article on John-Paul II in *Esquire*, May 1979, states:

"First reports from Puebla were most confusing. The pope was — depending on the paper you read — said to have attacked or defended liberation theology. Until one had the complete text, it was impossible to say. When it became available, the reason for the misunderstanding was clear: John-Paul II had recognized the validity of the aspirations of liberation theology while criticizing some of its methods. At the same time, his energetic statements against the abuse of human rights would have brought no comfort to generals Videla and Pinochet".

Similarly, Alan Riding, writing in the *New York Times Magazine* (May 6,1979), stated "the final documents approved in Puebla, however, reflected all the long hours of negotiation that they consumed. Traditional evangelism was stressed for the conservatives and social activism for the liberals. Specific endorsement of the 'theology of liberation' was avoided, yet the word 'liberation' appeared hundreds of times in the text. On balance, Puebla was probably a step forward from Medelin, warning as it did that to preach the gospel without considering its economic, social,

primate of Poland and former superior and close friend of Wojtyla submitted his resignation to the Vatican, the Communist government informed Paul VI that they would be happy to have him make an exception and retain Wyszynski in his present position.[10a] Now, it must be remembered that Poland is a predominently Catholic country, and its government must accept the reality of the Church whether it likes it or not. Why however does it tolerate some prelates and not others? The answer can be found by quoting Cardinal Mindszenty. In a talk given in America shortly before he died, he stated: "Of all the Hungarian Bishops, I am the only one who did not take the oath of fidelity to the Godless State." A careful perusal of John-Paul II's Encyclical *Redemptor Hominis*, as well as of his Puebla speech will show that while he is highly critical of certain aspects of the methods used by the Communists, he has never once clearly condemned Communism or denied their right to control the destiny of millions of his countrymen. He has criticized "social activism" on the part of priests, but not their adherence to Marxist principles.[11] Nor

---

cultural and political implications 'is equivalent to a certain collision with the established order'. But in this religious war, the main weapons are isolated phrases and both sides returned home with their armories well stocked".

It is of interest that John Paul II has named Agostino Casaroli as his acting Secretary of State to replace the recently deceased Jean Villot. *Time* Magazine describes this individual as "loyal, highly skilled, and completely committed to the Second Vatican Council reforms . . . (He) has been the Vatican's top emissary to Communist regimes ever since Pope John XXIII launched negotiations to help East block churches survive. Though the appointment is regarded as John-Paul's endorsement of this policy, Casaroli modestly shuns his common designation as the Architect of *Ostpolitik*".

10a. According to Mary Craig *(Man From a Far Country)*, Cardinal Wyszynski "was a pragmatist . . . in 1950 he concluded an agreement with the (Communist) Government in which he accepted the loss of Church property, (except for actual churches and priests' houses), agreeing that in a Socialist country, the Church must renounce its rights to private property. This agreement incurred the grave displeasure of Pope Pius, and in any case was soon broken by the Government." This same source notes that Father Wojtyla — John-Paul II — "steered clear of politics" in his sermons. ". . . even to mention 'Good' and 'Evil' could bring down the wrath of the authorities . . ."

11. The fact that John-Paul II has spoken out against the "political activism" of priests in South America is a double-edged sword. Clearly, the communist rulers in Eastern Europe would be delighted to have such a prohibition on the books. Cardinal Mindszenty could then have been silenced "under obedience" for "political activism", since this term can mean almost

can such a stance be excused on the basis of the necessity for "diplomatic neutrality", for one cannot be "neutral" in the face of evil.

Now, a Catholic, despite what John XXIII has said, by his very nature must be anti-Communist. Such follows from the fact that the Church teaches that all authority and all rights come from God Himself, and must be exercised according to his will.[12] What does this mean in the practical order? It means that although a ruler may enact certain laws against the will of God, these laws in themselves have no morally binding force. A ruler (or a government) does not necessarily lose authority because it makes mistakes in some of its legislation, but a Communist regime is intrinsically unjust and essentially opposed in principle to the will of God. It presumes to impose a fraudulent authority by force and terror in order to eradicate from mankind the Faith, Hope and Charity which our Lord lived and died to give us. It believes, as we have pointed out elsewhere, that the future will prove its principles correct, and feels free to force those who will not join in the "dynamic forces of history" that are working towards its particular vision of "point Omega" to do so against their will. By controlling all access to food, clothing and shelter, it reduces its citizens to an actual state of slavery — as long as they do the bidding of the state, they are rewarded materially, but if they oppose the state they are either murdered, enslaved in "corrective labor camps", or incarcerated in psychiatric institutions. Above all, even as in Poland, they attempt to control the education of the children and by a variety of overt and covert techniques, subvert their religious belief, replacing it with the false tenets of Marxist-Leninism. Those who claim that in Poland, the Communists have come to accept the Church as more than a temporary necessity are unbelievably naïve. Now, how can anyone say that a band of atheistic murdering revolutionaries dedicated to the destruction of the Church, the dethronement of Christ, the spread of the Kingdom of Satan on earth, and

---

anything from speaking the truth to carrying a gun.

12. This principle is enunciated in the following Papal Encyclicals. *Diurturnum illud, Immortale Dei, Libertas praestantissimum* and *Quod apostolici muneris* of Leo XIII; *Vehementer* of Pope Saint Pius X, and *Quas primas* of Pius XI. I am indebted to Father W. Jenkins "Catholic Doctrine and Anti-Communism", in *For You and For Many*, (Soc. Pius X, Oyster Bay, New York), Jan. 1979 for sections of this paragraph.

indeed to the eradication of all belief in God, could ever be given by God authority to carry out such a program? How can a man who claims to be Peter's successor ever act, as did Paul VI, to persuade the American government to return the crown of Saint Stephen (and against the manifest will of those to whom it extended political asylum) to those who have enslaved and tortured the true descendants of this royal prince? To admit that Communist governments rule legitimately is to claim that they derive their right to do so from God and to proclaim that God is therefore "divided against Himself". It is nothing else than to offer to Caesar (or rather to a false Caesar) that which belongs to God. This is why Pius XI called Communism "a pseudo-ideal" and said that "no one who would save Christian civilization may collaborate with it in any undertaking whatsoever". One can do no better than to conclude this section with the words of Pope Pius XII:

> "One cannot deny today what the anti-religious totalitarian state claims to demand from the Church, which it indeed expects to obtain as the price of tolerance and also of precarious recognition. Now, let us see what is the object of its claims:
>
> A mute Church, when its duty is to speak;
>
> A Church which consents to change the law of God, when its mission is to proclaim and defend it;
>
> A Church which discards its intangible doctrinal foundations on which Christ has established it, in order to submit itself willingly to the caprices of the opinion and instability of the crowds.
>
> A Church without energy to resist the oppression of consciences, to defend the legitimate rights of the people and their liberty;
>
> A cowardly and servile Church to the point of locking itself up in the temples of Christ by betraying the mission entrusted to it: 'Go to all the thoroughfares and preach . . go and teach all the nations . . .'
>
> May the Pope remain mute when the right of teaching the children is denied to their parents, according to the orders of a minority regime which wishes to move them away from Christ? And when this state over-stepping the limits

of its competence, assumes the power of suppressing the dioceses, deposing the bishops, ransacking the ecclesiastical organization and removing from the latter the means indispensable for the well-being of souls."

Speech to the Romans concerning the sacred rights
of the Church, February 20, 1949

All that this saintly pontiff feared has come to be reality in the post-conciliar Church!

CONCLUSIONS

CONCLUSIONS[1]

"It is clear that the Church is facing a grave crisis. Under the name of the New Church, the Post-conciliar Church, a different Church from that of Jesus Christ is now trying to establish itself: an anthropomorphic society allowing itself to be swept along in a movement of general abdication under the pretext of renewal, ecumenism or adaption."

Father Henri de Lubac, S.J., 1967

It should be abundantly clear, even to those who (pardon the expression!) are "outside the faith", that the "New" and "Post-conciliar" Church is both strikingly *new* and strikingly *different* from the Church as it has existed throughout the ages. The old Church was and is unabashedly "triumphant", felt it had the totality of the truth, and proclaimed it with a "militarism" that to modern relativistic man could only seem a great arrogance. The New Church is, as Paul VI has said, more "open", "gentle", and "accommodating", and one that "makes no demands". The Christianity it advocates, is, as he has said, more "acceptable", "lovable", and is "free of mediaeval rigorism". The traditional Church forbade active *communicatio in sacris* or common worship with those who

---

1. Some will suggest that this book should have been submitted to the Post-conciliar hierarchy for rebuttal and/or approval. To do so would be to recognize as having "spiritual authority" those who are trying by every means to destroy all spiritual authority. However, there has been a long correspondence with Mother Theresa in which most of these issues have been raised. She quite appropriately requested the assistance of a Cardinal in Rome who in turn assigned a theologian to discuss the issues. He was not able to refute any of the principal contentions made. It is hoped that this correspondence will be published separately.

rejected her teachings and her liturgy. She saw this as disobedience to the First Commandment — "Thou shalt not
worship false gods." The New Church not only officially
approves of *communicatio in sacris* "because of the grace that
can be derived from it" (Vatican II); she has even created a
liturgy which reflects this belief in the necessity of such a
common worship. The true Church called those who disagreed
with her teachings even on a single point "heretics" while the
New Church sees them, even if they be agnostics and
atheists, as "separated brethren" with whom she should deal
in theological matters on an "equal footing", and with whom
she should labour for the creation of a "universal culture" and
a "new humanity". She sees in various sects and "communities"
that reject her teachings and sacraments "actions" that "can
truly engender a life of grace", and "provide access to the
community of salvation". The old Church regarded "change"
in doctrinal and liturgical matters with nothing less than
horror — as St. Theresa of Avila said, she "would shed her
last drop of blood for the least of the Church's ceremonies".
It took pride in being the "unchanging" Church, for it would
not cast away the "pearl of great price" for "husks fit only for
the swine to eat". The New Church sees itself as "dynamic"
and "evolving", and sees "renewal" as accepting any conceivable innovation as a "gift of the Holy Spirit". The
traditional Church saw the Mass as a "perpetual sacrifice" —
the recurring unbloody sacrifice of Calvary. The New Church
sees it as a "memorial", and at most, as a "sacrifice of
praise and thanksgiving". As a current Protestant quip puts
it: "In the old Church the only thing that changed was the
bread and wine; in the New Church, the only thing that
doesn't change is the bread and wine." If the old Church
had problems, it was never in crisis. The New Church, like
the modern world to which it would accomodate itself,
seems to go from one crisis to another.

What becomes clear from all this is that the New Church is
a vastly different Church. For all its talk of "unity", it is not
one with the Church of All Times. It does not teach all the
Apostolic doctrines, and it does not follow the Divine and
Apostolic "rites". Whatever "unity" it may achieve with itself,
between its "Pope" and the "Bishops in union with him", and
even with the Protestants, it cannot claim "unity" with the
Church that Christ founded. This being so, the New and Post-

conciliar Church is plainly and simply in SCHISM, to say nothing of HERESY. The concept of "unity" is not dependent upon members, but upon adherence to the teaching Magisterium of the true Church. As the Holy Office said (*Osservatore Romano*, Feb. 9, 1942), "The proper grace assured to the magisterium is by no means the grace of substituting a new revelation for what has been once and for all revealed, but, quite on the contrary, the grace of never wandering or allowing the faithful to wander from its true meaning . . ." Those who depart from this *magisterium,* even though they be the "'Pope' and the Bishops in union with him", are those who are guilty of rending the seamless garment of Christ.

The New Church is not only defective with regard to "unity", it is also clearly defective with regard to the quality of APOSTOLICITY. It has abandoned not only Apostolic doctrines, it has also abandoned the Apostolic "rites", and replaced them with rites of purely human origin. It has not replaced them with other and alternative Apostolic rites such as those of the Eastern Churches, but with rites that to all intents and purposes are a mixture of the Lutheran and the Anglican services. It has, in doing so, attacked all that is most sacred in the Church, and thus deprived itself of the quality of HOLINESS.[2] Finally, it can no longer claim the allegiance of traditional Catholics, and hence both in the material and in the spiritual sense, is deprived of the quality of CATHOLICITY. It is not the "ONE, HOLY CATHOLIC AND APOSTOLIC CHURCH", and any claim it makes to be so has no more validity than do similar claims on the part of the Anglicans and the Lutherans. The New and Post-conciliar Church is nothing but another in the long list of "ecclesiastical communities" that have abandoned the Church and the traditions established by Christ and His Apostles. It has lost both its creed and its credibility.

The results of this apostasy are all around us. Thousands upon thousands of priests have abandoned their sacerdotal function. Nuns have left the orders in unbelievable droves. The laity have become like sheep wandering in the desert.

---

2. Holiness in the Church is not only dependent upon her sacred "rites"; it is also characterized by the sacredness of her "Christ-given" doctrines, and by the "fruits" of her adherents as manifested in the sanctified lives of the faithful. After the Council of Trent we had a virtual plethora of saints, both canonized and uncanonized. After Vatican II — *res ipsa loquitur.*

The churches are desecrated, the altars stripped, the tabernacles removed and the perpetual Sacrifice abandoned. *The* Faith, once understood as giving assent to the doctrines taught by the Catholic Church, has been replaced by *a* faith, *any* faith, described in "experiential" terms as a "feeling" or "sublime aspiration". All that is required is that one be "sincere", and of "good will", and (perhaps) that one accept Christ as one's "personal Saviour". The Sacraments are no longer seen as vehicles of grace, but rather as expressions of Faith made by the community. The priest is no longer the performer of the Sacrifice, the intercessor between man and God; rather, he is the minister "presiding" over the "gifts", and the leader of the community. As it says in the *General Instruction on the Roman Missal:*

> "The mass is not an act of the priest with whom the people unite themselves, as it used to be explained. The Eucharist is, rather, an act of the people, whom the ministers serve by making the Saviour present sacra-mentally . . . This (former) formulation, which corresponded to the classical theology of recent centuries, was rejected because it placed what was relative and ministerial (the hierarchy) above the ontological and absolute (the People of God)."[3]

"Private Judgment" has been sanctioned by the Conciliar Church as a criterion for determining the Truth. No orthodox Catholic however should ever desire to "think for himself" in theological matters — be it doctrine or liturgy — but only to "think correctly". It is a modernist prejudice that spiritual matters are so vague and indefinite that, providing one is "good" (read "nice"), and "sincere" (read "convinced of one's own opinions"), nothing else matters. As soon as one places one's private judgment — usually a "private judgment" that reflects the current "mores" of the society in which one lives —

---

3. *The New Order of Mass,* Official Text of Instruction, English version and Commentary, translated by the Monks of Mount Angel Abbey, Liturgical Press: Collegeville, Minn., 1974.

To "think for oneself" is in fact a logical absurdity, for thought, if it is to have any value or basis in reality, must be "objective". Now the formulations of the traditional theologians provide one with this very "objectivity", that permits one to "reason" correctly.

on the same plane as divine Revelation one deprives oneself
of all access to traditional wisdom. To adhere to one's private
opinions in spiritual matters is nothing else than to glory in
that "self-love" which all spiritual writers castigate as inimical
to the life of prayer. To think one "knows better" than God
Himself — and it is Christ who speaks to us through the
Church of All Times — one is not only succumbing to, but
even more, embracing the "sin of pride". It matters not
whether this is done on an individual basis, or because one
goes along with the "communitarian" herd — the "collective"
apostasy of modern man is no less offensive to the Truth
because it has become, in effect, the statistical "norm". A
person who follows his own opinions in theological matters,
and especially if these "opinions" are a reflection of those of the
modern world, is not only misusing his intellect, he is, assuming
he is "sincere", misdirecting his will. Imagine Our Lord in the
Garden of Gethsemane carrying on a "dialogue" with the
Father, saying: "I really don't think your idea about the
Sacrifice is very good . . . perhaps we can figure out some
other way to achieve the same ends — a more 'lovable' and
'acceptable' way that won't be repugnant to the average person
(Perhaps we could have a public opinion poll!) I want to do it
my way — not yours!" This modernist exemplar for today's
man — and for the New Church — carries with it horrendous
spiritual implications. What results is that we live, not in
Christ, but "in ourselves". In reality it is to say, not God's
teaching, but our own; not God's authority, but our own; not
God's will, but our own. Ultimately, it can only lead to the
complete satanic "inversion" that places man in God's place
— "king of the world and prince of heaven!" — to quote
Montini. But then, "THE PEOPLE OF GOD ARE ONTO-
LOGICAL AND ABSOLUTE!"[4]

4. One is reminded of the "Constitutional Bishop" of Paris during the
French Revolution. Under the threat of death, Bishop Gobel stated that
"the will of the Sovereign People" had now become "his supreme law", and
since the Sovereign so willed it, there should be no other worship than that
of "liberty and holy equality". Accordingly he deposited his cross, ring and
other insignia upon the President's (Freemasonic leader's) desk, and put on
the red cap of liberty. Several of his vicars followed his example. As Nesta
Webster noted in her book *The French Revolution*, "this grotesque scene
gave the signal for the desecration of the churches throughout Paris and
the provinces". At Notre Dame, stripped of its crucifixes and images of the
saints, the Feast of Reason took place. The Freemasonic symbol (a pyramid

And yet, this is precisely what the New and Post-conciliar Church under the smoke-screen of "democratization", has brought about. One of the most drastic consequences resulting therefrom is that this "Church of the Latter-day Modernists" can no longer speak with authority. The traditional Church spoke with authority, and never as the Scribes and Pharisees. Her *Magisterium* came from Christ and the Apostles and functioned to preserve the "deposit of the faith" unadulterated. The New Church, having accommodated herself to the "separated brethren" and to the "world", can no longer do so. You do not speak with authority to those with whom you intend to treat on an "equal footing". What is extraordinary is that the Post-conciliar Church has destroyed its own authority by recognizing "officially" that "man is to be guided by his own judgment and to enjoy freedom" in religious matters. *(Decree on Religious Freedom)* However ambiguously this is worded, it places the "private judgment" of every human being on the same plane as Divine Revelation. It was of course essential that the New Church should do this if she were to seek "unity" with those who rejected the traditional teachings. But, if she recognized this "bastard" authority in those outside her fold, she had to concede the same privilege to those within. Thus, she has become an "open" Church, a Church that admits and accepts a "plurality" of differing opinions within her bosom. It follows then that her teachings no longer reflect the fullness of the Magisterium, of the "deposit of the faith", but rather, a variety of "private opinions". Unfortunately, the majority of those who hold to "private opinions" in religious matters are unable to agree on very much. Their "feelings" are easily influenced by the communications media, and by the "spirit of the times". Further, the Post-conciliar Church is, by its very nature, most careful not to step on the toes of other ecclesiastical and non-ecclesiastical "communities".[5] What

---

with a light) was raised in the aisle on the summit of a mountain, which become the center of adoration.

5. The failure of the Conciliar Church to take a strong stand on abortion until it was obvious that many of the Protestants felt the same way was scandalous and is clearly documented in Anne Roche's *The Gates of Hell*, McClelland: Toronto, 1974. Prior to Vatican II it would have been impossible for a law allowing for "abortion on demand" to have been passed in the United States. One word from the Church and the faithful would have voted in mass against it. Liberals of course would find such an

results then is that the "New Magisterium", the "Pope and the Bishops in union with him", is often little else than the "voice-box" of currently fashionable "public opinion". This Church speaks much of "peace" and "unity"; of the need for the "economic development of backward nations" (usually lands that have been "raped" and reduced to below-subsistence levels as a result of a modern and totally un-Christian, western economic and political imperialism); of "equality" and "progress"; of "human dignity" and "freedom", and of "defending the 'rights' of modern man" (usually the "right" to ignore prescriptions placed upon him by God — and what of the rights of traditional man?) None of these concepts requires a religious tradition, none offend the modern liberal ambiance — none even require a belief in God! This same Church speaks very little of sanctity, of the ascetical and spiritual life, of prayer and sacrifice. Even the most flagrant heretics and the wildest liturgical abuses are allowed without reprimand, for every person must now be allowed to "do his own thing". Only those who affirm and give witness to the totality of the Church's teachings and who insist upon retaining her traditional rites are "suspended" and threatened with "excommunication".

This absence of an audible "spiritual authority" will in the end lead to the most drastic enslaving of man that is possible. In an earlier (pre-Vatican II) age, when the Pope spoke out on an issue such as abortion, millions of the faithful would obey and even governments would fear to be toppled if they ignored his warnings. Today, when the "Pope" speaks, even his closest Bishops hasten to contradict him. His own followers decry his words before others have even had a chance to read them. If the Church can no longer be a force for Truth and Morality, then governments will become the means of legislating truth and morality.[6] Once this happens, those who cannot accept the "new morality" will become the "enemies

---

act offensive. But then, abortion is plain and simple murder, and whether modern man likes it or not, it is "a sin crying out to Heaven for vengeance".
6. To quote J. M. Cameron from a talk given at Yale University: "The conflict between the regal and the priestly power . . . no more exists. No one doubts that in the purely legal sense, the State is omnicompetent, and that if and when the command of the State is resisted on grounds of conscience or of interest, there is no body of recognized rules to which a cogent appeal can be made". Terry Lectures, 1966; Yale Univ. Press.

of the people". If euthanasia is proclaimed a government policy — and it was by the Nazis in Germany, a "Christian" country, and it will be again — then those who refuse to accept this "good" will have to be "re-educated". Our religious beliefs will be allowed only if we keep them "private", and do not teach them to our children. When we feel called upon to speak against the prevailing tide — to witness to the truth — when we refuse to accept the "rulings" of a numerical majority or reject the demands and directives of any power group that happens to control the government, then we will be "obstructing" the "will of the people", and will be declared "enemies of the State". And when this happens, where will the "visible" Church be? Who will speak for us? We shall have to stand alone and accept the consequences. As soon as the hierarchy abandons tradition, it abdicates its spiritual authority. The process has already begun and is well under way. There will be *"weeping and gnashing of teeth"*, if not in our day, then in the days of our children.

The New Church has done these things in greater part because she believes in "progress", and because she would unite herself with the "dynamic" and "evolutionary forces" that she believes will go to create a better world for all mankind — a sort of utopian "Kingdom of God on earth".[7] One

---

7. As an editorial of *L'Osservatore Romano* (Mar. 3, 1977) stated: "No one today any longer believes in tradition, but rather in rational progress. Tradition today appears as something that has been bypassed by history. Progress, on the other hand presents itself as an authentic promise inborn in the very soul of man — so much so that no one today can be at home with tradition which represents what has passed, but only in the future in an atmosphere of progress." Several further points should be made. Very few intelligent people still retain their "faith" in progress. As William Morris said, "I have no more faith than a grain of mustard seed in the future history of 'civilization', which I *know* is doomed to destruction: what a joy it is to think of!" Even a recent editorial in the *New York Times* stated: "It takes a touching faith in 'progress' — and a certain cultural arrogance — to believe that Western science and technology are bound to improve the lot of Third World peoples. It doesn't work out that way." The "Literature of indictment" is full of condemnations of this false "superstition". Why is it however such a powerful "opiate"? Why do those who have placed their faith in the present order of things place so much stress on this concept? The answer is simple. The present state of affairs, as is obvious to any thinking person, is so terrible, and so clearly fraught with danger on every plane, that it is necessary to provide some "hope" for future improvement. Progress has been touted as an aphrodisiac for the discontented masses ever since the Reformation. This along with a falsely

would like once more to make it clear that the traditional Church is not against "progress", if by this term we are referring to the advances of modern science.[8] The designing of "better mouse-traps" is clearly of advantage to society, providing of course that justice is not violated, and the true and proper ends of man are not hindered. She knows, however, that no progress and no tyranny will ever make an end of suffering.[9] As has been said by others, only the sanctification of all men

---

persuasive re-writing of history which presents mediaeval times as "horrible" — the "dark ages" — convinces modern man that things were far worse in the past and will be far better in the future. If he were convinced that the present situation was permanent, deprived of the consolations of Religion, he would openly revolt and destroy his present masters.

God spoke through Jeremiah: "You of this generation, take not of the word of the Lord: Have I been a desert to Israel, a land of darkness? Why do my people say 'we have moved on'?" (ii:12-17)

8. It is one of the falsest propositions of modern man to claim that the Church is against science. Some of the world's greatest scientists have been devout Catholics. Empirical science as a subject is restricted to the realm of measurable facts. Religion is not. It is only when modern science claims to encompass the whole of reality — to be, in effect, a religion — that the Church rightly protests.

9. Tied to the superstition of "progress" is the bland assumption that the scientific *theory* of evolution is a proven fact. This theory (and this is all that scientists have ever claimed it to be) is in fact based on the idea that what is greater can be produced by what is less — or, to put it differently, it violates the scientific law of the "conservation of matter". Neither man nor matter can create something out of nothing — it is to God alone that the ability to create *ex nihilo* belongs. The scientific evidence that Darwin hoped would be forthcoming to prove his theory has in fact never been found. What he called the missing link is in fact a whole series of missing links. Paleontological evidence demonstrates that every new form of life that has been found arose *de novo,* and that the intermediate forms such as evolution requires to prove its point have never been found. Furthermore, all attempts at "breeding", as with flies or cell cultures, have shown that there is no evidence forthcoming to prove the contention. Thus many scientists have abandoned "evolution" as a theory, not because of their religious beliefs, but because the evidence available is so strongly against it. Those interested in the subject are refered to Douglas Dewar, *The Transformist Illusion,* Dehoff Publications: Murfreesboro, Tenn. (U.S.A.) 1957, and Evan Shute, *Flaws in the Theory of Evolution,* Teamside Press: Phil. For a definitive refutation in principle of evolutionism the reader is referred back to footnote 12 on pp. 211-2.

It is interesting to note how far behind the times the *avant-garde* churchmen of post-conciliar persuasion are. Just as they are embracing Protestant theologies at a time when the Reformation sects are recognizing their own bankruptcy, so also they are embracing as scientific, theories that are all but discredited.

could bring this about. As to creating a perfect society on earth, a society that, as T.S. Eliot says, is "so perfect that no one will ever need to be good", she knows that this is an absurd dream. Even in the Garden of Eden a "snake" was to be found! Yet all this does not mean that man should not, in conformity with his nature and with simple good sense, attempt to overcome the evils he encounters in the course of life — for this however, he requires no injunctions, either divine or human. But to seek to establish a certain state of well-being with God in view is one thing, and to seek to institute a perfect state of happiness on earth apart from God, is quite another. In any event, the latter aim is foredoomed to failure, precisely because the lasting elimination of our miseries is dependent upon our conforming to the Divine Equilibrium, and upon our establishment of the "Kingdom of God" within our own souls. As long as men have not realized a sanctifying "inwardness", the abolition of earthly trials is not only impossible, it is not even desirable, because the sinner, "exteriorized" man, has need of suffering in order to expiate his faults and in order to tear himself away from sin; in order to escape from that very "outwardness" from which sin derives. From the spiritual point of view, which alone takes account of the true cause of our calamities, a society "perfect" in the worldly sense, a society with the maximum of comfort and so-called "justice", would, if the final ends of man were frustrated, be one of the most evil societies conceivable. Hence it is that the traditional Church teaches that to combat the calamities of this world without regard for the total truth and ultimate good, would be to create an incomparably greater calamity, starting off, in fact, with the denial of this truth and the elimination of this good. Those who dream of liberating man from his age-old "frustrations" are in fact the ones who are imposing on him the most radical and irreparable of all frustrations. The *Civitas Dei* and the worldly progression as envisaged by modern man and the Post-conciliar Church, cannot converge, and those who strive to accommodate the religious message to profane illusions and agitations are among those whom Christ would label as "scatterers". The idea that the world in which we live today is in any way "Christian" is totally absurd, and any attempt to adapt the Christian tradition to it can only result in a betrayal of Christ. The modern world, the "post-Christian world", dreams of abolishing evil by organizing sin. The dream of the New Church that "all may be one" with the kind of "unity" it has in mind, can only be achieved at the price of distorting Christ and the message he revealed beyond all recognition. It is a Teilhardian delusion that ignores the warnings of Scripture concerning the "last times", times that those who can recognize the "spirit of the times", the "spirit of Vatican II" (we agree with the modernist "periti" that these are one and the same), must admit are truly upon us. The faithful are bound to remain a "remnant" at war with the world — a world that increasingly has upon it "the mark of the beast" — for man, when he ignores his spiritual nature is nothing but a beast. To state all this is not to be "pessimistic", but rather to be "realistic". Discernment of the "real" is what Christianity is all about.

Those who insinuated themselves into high positions in the Church, and who wished to bring about the dominance of this new "liberal Christianity", had another problem to deal with. They knew that the world and our "separated brethren" would have no problem accepting it. But how could they change Catholicism without losing the loyalty of traditional believers? The answer was to pretend that "no changes of significance" had been intended, that nothing *de fide* had been changed, and that the eternal truths were only being expressed in "new ways".[10] On the other hand, our "separated brethren" are not total fools, and they had to be assured that the changes were real. This problem was resolved by the use of ambiguity — the use of phrases that could be understood in a variety of ways. When this was insufficient, the use of contradictory statement was resorted to. This is why Paul VI had to speak out of both sides of his mouth simultaneously.

For those who find difficulty in falling into line with the "new directions", the New Church has another tack. All must be "obedient". All must obey the "Pope" if they wish to be involved in what is called "the New Economy of the Gospel".

---

10. As has been noted in the body of this text, there was absolutely no need to express the "eternal truths" in "new ways". Anyone familiar with the "Penny Catechism" knows that the Catholic Church has always expressed these truths in clear and concise language. Both her adherents and her enemies never had any doubt as to what they were. "New ways", in the modernist "jargon" means ambiguous ways so that multiple interpretations are possible.

But this is of course a false obedience, for obedience to the New Church is disobedience to Christ and the tradition He established. As Savonarola said:

> "Neither the popes, nor their vicars have the right to teach anything contrary to the things instituted by God . . . I say this for those who pretend to find an excuse for their unworthy conduct in what they are pleased to call the broader view of life and doctrine . . . God's law is strict: 'strait is the gate and narrow is the way that leadeth unto life and few there be that find it . . .'"[11]

*   *   *

What then can the traditional Catholic do? Faced with the present situation, he must still be primarily concerned with the salvation of his own soul. No man can offer to his neighbour what he does not himself first possess, and no man can change the world without changing himself first. The kingdom of God, modernist opinion to the contrary, is still within us. Let us turn to St. Vincent of Lerins for advice in the present circumstance:

> "So what shall the Catholic Christian do if some part of the Church should come to detach itself from the communion, from the Universal Faith? What other side could he take than to prefer to the gangrenous and corrupted member, the body which is whole and healthy? And if some new contagion should seek to poison, not only a little part of the Church, but the whole Church at once, then his greatest care should once again be to adhere to antiquity, which obviously cannot be seduced by any deceitful novelty."

---

11. Some will question the appropriateness of quoting Savonarola as a traditional authority. Despite the attempts of the reformers to claim Savonarola as one of themselves, the facts are that this individual has never been accused of departing from orthodoxy. His textbooks were still used (up to Vatican II) for teaching in seminaries. He was considered as a saint and a martyr by many of the Beatified and Canonized saints of the Church, including Blessed Catharine of Raconigi, Blessed Sebastian Maggi, Blessed Osauna of Mantua, Blessed Columba of Rieti, St. Catherine of Ricci and St. Pius V. (c.f. *Jerome Savonarola*, Rev. J. L. O'Neil, O. P. Marlier Callanan: Boston 1898).

This has always been the attitude of the true Church. St. Athanasius was willing to stand alone against the bishops of the world — even to the point of having his excommunication confirmed by a Pope who allowed himself to be pressured by the "power structure" of the then existing "world". Yet, as Michael Davies points out, not only did Liberius retract and repent — even more, Athanasius is now a saint, and as for the other Bishops of that epoch, who can name one of them? Witness the words of St. Hilary of Poitiers who advised the Catholics of Milan to abandon their churches and assemble in the woods and caverns, rather than to remain under the Arian Bishop Auxentius: "Of one thing I bid you beware — of Antichrist. The love of walls ill possesses you; ill do you venerate the Church of God in roofs and edifices. Ill do you bear under these for the sake of peace. Safer to me are the mountains, the woods, lakes, prisons and deep caverns; for in these the prophets, either remaining or thrown, prophesy with the Spirit of God." Witness the words of St. Thomas More who said "I do not care if I have against me all the Bishops; I have with me the saints and all the doctors of the Church". As St. Athanasius said, when he was informed that all the bishops disagreed with him — "This only proves that they are all against the Church!"

In a certain sense, the faithful Catholic has no choice. He cannot ask with Pilate "what is Truth?" but must accept that "infallible Truth" that Christ revealed to His Church. It matters not whether the present evils derive from the Post-conciliar "Popes" directly, or only from those around them. It matters not whether the evidence I have presented can be controverted or absolutely proved. What matters is that the Catholic must adhere with all his heart, with all his mind, and with all his soul, to that same body of Truth which is the Truth of All Times. It is not just our "right", but rather, it is our "obligation" to do so.

It follows then that the Catholic must reject anything in the Second Vatican Council that in any way departs from the "deposit" of the Faith. He must also reject any ambiguous manner or equivocal way of stating the Truth. He must also reject anything in this manner that even slightly suggests "innovation". If the traditional "Canon" of the Mass is of "Apostolic" origin, there is no way in which he can accept an ersatz canon of purely "human" origin. All this is NOT a matter of his exercising his "personal freedom of conscience", it is a matter of an OBLIGATION in conscience — a well-formed conscience — a conscience molded by that traditional body of doctrine which has been "believed by all, believed always and believed everywhere" since the time of Christ. Any attempt by the New and Post-conciliar Church (whether deriving from the "Popes", from the hierarchy, or from the local ordinary) to hinder him in this is a direct attack on his soul.

> "It is lawful to resist him (the Pope) if he assaulted souls . . . It is lawful, I say, to resist him by not doing what he commands and hindering the execution of his will."
>
> Saint Cardinal Bellarmine

No one can hide behind the mask of ignorance. No one can claim that it is not his responsibility to know his faith. To do so is to liken oneself to those who were unable to come to the "marriage feast" because they had to care for their oxen. As St. Augustine said, "It will not be imputed to you as a fault that you are ignorant; but that you neglect to seek that of which you are ignorant." Indeed, it is only in the face of an overwhelming ignorance of the faith that the new theologians are heard at all. It is only in a society, the members of which are satisfied with television shows and picture magazines that the modernists can even be heard. The almost absolute lack of any internal consistency makes the sophisms of the New Church totally indefensible. It takes a prodigious lack of spiritual perception for anyone to take the contemporary theological thinking of such individuals as Karl Rahner, Bernard Haring, or the recent "Popes" as in any way being a "crystallization" of sacred (or even of worldly) wisdom. If one seeks any intellectual integrity in one's beliefs, if one wishes to have a faith that is more than a "feeling" and "a simple sublimating aspiration", one must return to the hallowed authors that have throughout history been given us as "exemplars" by the Church of All Times. In this regard it is worthy of note that, since the Council of Trent, only two Popes have been canonized; Pope Pius V who spoke out so clearly on liturgical issues, and Pope Pius X who did the same in the realm of doctrine. To reject what these remarkable men have said is tantamount to Apostasy!

No Catholic can evade the central issue raised by this book. (Every Post-conciliar Catholic who was brought up in the traditional Church knows in his heart that something is wrong.) He must either show that its contents are inconsistent with the teaching of the Church, or he must accept the logical consequences that its thesis demands. Be he "simple layman" or a priest, he has an obligation to believe, and he must therefore accept the responsibility of "discerning" what it is he should believe. To argue that such is not incumbent upon us is to claim that no one has an obligation even to be a Catholic, that all conversions are based on fortuitous or emotional circumstances, and that there is no sin in Apostasy.[12] While it is true that none of us can judge — as only God can — the soul of a Pope, or of any individual member of the hierarchy (or of a murderer), it is also true that we have the obligation to consider the actions of the Pope (and the hierarchy) when they depart from tradition and authority, just as we must judge the actions of a murderer when he departs from the natural law. One of the qualities man is endowed with is "Discernment". Discernment between what is real and unreal, between what is true and false, between what is traditional and what is anti-traditional, and between what is orthodox and what is heretical. And not only must we discern the truth in the intellectual realm, we must also adhere to it with all our will. Should we, as a result of such a "universal (Catholic)" outlook appear "dogmatic", or even "fanatical", this is only because the Absolute Truth has been relegated by modern man to the extreme fringe of the concepts and principles that he is willing to consider as "acceptable".

---

12. The fact that the person writing this book is a "layman" is irrelevant to its content. It is perfectly conceivable that a given layman may be more discerning that many priests indeed the times would seem to supply more than ample evidence of this contention. If the laity are not supposed to "think" and "speak" on such issues, then no one can blame the laity for not being able to discern what is heretical or for apostasizing from the Church. In point of fact, the laity have an obligation to know their catechism and to judge the innovations by it. It is tradition and orthodox doctrine that provide the laity with the means of making such judgments. By following these infallible guides they will neither be led astray, nor will they be guilty of presumption.

While we have by no means covered the entire scope of the Conciliar deviation, nor marshalled all the available evidence, it can honestly be stated that nothing in this book is either "new" or "original". All these things, as is obvious from the numerous quotations, have been said before. Just as the New Church has never answered the challenge of the Ottaviani Intervention — but only ignored it, so also she has refused to discuss or debate these issues when raised by innumerable other individuals. This is particularly true of Archbishop Lefebvre and those who like him adhere to the traditions. As Michael Davies states, this saintly prelate has been subjected to a great deal of inaccurate reporting in the secular press and to a campaign of systematic misrepresentation and denigration in some organs of the (so-called) Catholic press. His enemies consider that they have convicted him of a sin crying out to heaven for vengeance, simply by citing the fact that he has criticized Vatican II and the subsequent reforms and orientations purporting to implement this Council. At no time have his enemies ever dared to answer his criticisms, still less to allow the Catholic public to know what these criticisms are . . . No one is more competent to provide an objective criticism of the conciliar documents and reforms than Mgr. Lefebvre, and should his criticisms be accurate, then it is not he, but the rest of the world's bishops, who stand condemned for not taking their stand beside him. It is better to be alone and faithful to the truth than to abandon it to conform with the majority.[13]

Some would-be loyal Catholics have attempted to avoid these issues by taking a "conservative" stand. They accept Vatican II as a "legitimate" Council and stretch its statements to force them into an orthodox mold. They accept (admittedly with regret), the *Novus Ordo Missae* and seek out priests who will say it "properly", and especially in Latin. They stress certain orthodox statements of the "Post-conciliar Popes" and ignore or deny those that are clearly in conflict with tradition. Such is not the stance of traditional Catholics.

To admit that there is room within the New Church for conservative priests (and for a conservative laity) is to admit in one and the same breath that there is also room — and on an equally legitimate basis — for "liberal" priests, a liberal

13. Michael Davies, *Pope John's Council*, (Augustine Publ. House, Devon, England, 1977).

"mass" and a liberal . . . "theology". One must remember that if there are those who travel at great pains to attend a service that is recognizable as "Catholic", there are also those who attend a variety of bizarre "masses" who can claim and who are recognized as being just as "Catholic". It is perfectly clear that the New Church in no way favours a conservative ecclesiology over a liberal one. The post-conciliar laity are in fact encouraged to attend the kind of service that is most "relevant" and "pleasing" to them — the kind of service they "like". For a Catholic to take a "conservative stance", is for him to admit (and indeed to connive at) the fact that the New Church is in fact a "pluralistic" and "open" Church. He is, within this framework, simply "picking and choosing" what seems to him right. The conservative Catholic in fact is one who leans towards orthodoxy, but one who refuses to make the necessary commitment. As St. Jerome said many years ago:

"If you wander off the track a bit, it makes no difference if you veer to the right or to the left; the important thing is that you are not on the right road."

(Commentary on St. Matthew)

Another group of Catholics who admit that all that we have said is true, stay in the New Church because they hope they can reform it from "within" — they see themselves as "infiltrators" whose function it is to preserve the "true faith" among the innovators. The problem with such an attitude is that they give witness — however regretfully — to all that Vatican II teaches and all that the *Novus Ordo* implies. However much such individuals may abhor the "abuses" that prevail, as soon as they state that they do not accept *all* the teachings of Vatican II, or that they question the validity of the conciliar sacraments — especially the consecration in the New "mass", they are no longer *bona fide* members of the Conciliar Church. They, like their "conservative" counterparts, are also "picking and choosing" what they will accept, and as such are also acting the part of the Protestant. Such individuals do a great deal of harm, for being "conservative", they lend an aura of respectability to what they claim to abhor.

There are two fundamental errors that such individuals make. First, they are seemingly (if not in fact), denying the true Catholic faith, which no Catholic can do. What saint of the Church has ever infiltrated the Lutheran or Anglican bodies to bring them back to orthodoxy? What martyr ever became a follower of the Roman gods to convert Caesar? The second error is to suppose that it is possible for Truth to infiltrate error. The very act involves a dissimulation and a lie. It is a "freedom" given to satan that he can act in this manner, for he is not bound by morality. The modernists, the Albigensians, the communists and the Freemasons can do such things. The Catholic must declare his faith — and if he is not obliged to do so under every circumstance, he can never deny it, and he certainly cannot act in such a manner as would seem to give support to the enemies of the Church — or the enemies of Christ, which is the same thing.

A Catholic who accepts the position which this book espouses is in no way turning his back on the "existing" Church. On the contrary, in opposing the New "mass" and the doctrinal changes introduced by Vatican II, he is only remaining faithful to what the Church has always taught. There is no such thing as the "existing" Church in opposition to the "Church of the past". There is only one Church, and those of "Conciliar" persuasion have apostasized from it. This is something we dare not do. As Yves Dupont has said, "This ship (the bark of Peter) was entrusted to us also; we have no right to desert it. We may be bullied by the crew, the skipper himself may exude symptoms of disorientation, yet we must stay aboard. And, if we are to die, we shall die on the ship, not in the muddy waters of an unglorious desertion." We are not "rebels" because we are faithful to the "owner" of the ship and refuse to join with those who would "mutiny" and steer the ship into unknown and dangerous ports. The accusation that traditional Catholics are "rebels" is as absurd as to label Thomas More and John Fisher as rebellious to God because they refused to obey the legitimately crowned king, Henvy VIII of England. Was Christ a "rebel" for refusing to bow down to satan?

Many of the former faithful are confused and simply cannot believe that what is happening is in fact happening. "How can it be", they ask, "that so many people are wrong?" "God would never allow such a thing to happen", and Christ promised us that "the Gates of hell shall not prevail against" the Church. Yet, we have been adequately warned of these things by Christ Himself, by Holy Scripture, by the saints, and in recent times, by the Blessed Mother herself. Listen to her words:

"Even in the highest places, it will be satan who rules and decides the march of events. He will even insinuate himself into the highest summits of the Church. It will become a time of difficult trials for the Church. Cardinals will be opposed to Cardinals, Bishops against Bishops . . . Satan will be entrenched among their ranks . . . The Church will be hidden and the world plunged into disorder."

Our Lady of Fátima

"Rome will become the seat of Anti-Christ."

Our Lady of La Sallette

As St. Cyril said in his Catechismal instructions, "Let no one at that day say in his heart . . . 'unless God willed it, He would not have permitted it'. No: the Apostle forewarns you, saying beforehand, 'God shall send them a strong delusion', not that they may be excused, but condemned . . ." Search the Scriptures. Paul warns us of the "Great Apostasy" that shall prevail in the final days. Cardinal Newman sums up the pertinent facts available from Holy Scripture:

"The coming of Christ will be immediately preceeded by a very awful and unparalleled outbreak of evil, called by St. Paul an Apostasy, a falling away, in the midst of which a certain terrible Man of sin and child of perdition, the special and singular enemy of Christ, or Antichrist, will appear: that this will be when revolutions prevail, and the present framework of society breaks to pieces; and that at present, the spirit which he will embody and represent is kept under 'the powers that be', but that on their dissolution, he will rise out of their bosom and knit them together again in his own evil way, under his own rule, to the exclusion of the Church."

The argument that "it simply isn't possible", is absurd. Let me ask those who pose this objection why it is that so many "sincere" and "well intentioned" Protestants have throughout history refused to re-enter the Church. How was it possible for the entire English nation (with a few notable exceptions) to apostasize?[14] Why did the people of Israel refuse Christ when He presented Himself, as it were, "in person"? It has all happened before as those who read the Books of Daniel and Macabees can learn.[15] The fact remains that it has happened and is, happening. We were told that it would happen, and that at the end of time only a "remnant" would remain faithful to tradition.

The promise of Christ that "the gates of hell will not prevail" has always been fulfilled. This promise was never given to the Post-conciliar Church, but to the Universal Church, the Church of All Times, the Church that Christ established — to the "remnant" that the still traditional Church represents. As Leo XIII said:

"All the world knows that this Divine promise ought to be understood to apply to the Universal Church, and not to any part of the Church taken in isolation, for individual segments may, and indeed have, been overcome by the forces of evil."

Satis Cognitum

To conceive of the Catholic Church as only existing in the present time is to view her with myopic eyes. The Universal Church will exist throughout time — *in saecula saeculorum* — throughout the ages, to use a phrase taken from the traditional liturgy and dropped by the New Church. To quote Leo XIII again, "The Church must, by the will of its Founder, be of necessity one in all lands and *throughout all time . . .*" In the light of the millions of Catholics that have lived by and died in or for the true Faith, the number of Conciliar Catholics alive today is but "a drop in a bucket". And even if such were not the case, the facts of the situation remain patently

---

14. Those interested in the methods used to bring about the apostasy of England are referred to *The Church under Queen Elizabeth* by Frederick George Lee, Thomas Baker: London, 1896, and *The Protestant Reformation* by W. Cobbett, Burns Oates, London: 1929.
15. A discussion of the Scriptural prophecies by the present author is to be found in *The Roman Catholic* (Vol. 1, No. 1, 1978) under the title "Have These Things Been Foretold?".

clear. The truth is never a matter of conforming to some statistical "norm", — it is a matter of conforming to tradition — that is to say, for us, to the Catholic tradition established for all time by Christ and the Apostles. Even if there were only one orthodox Catholic alive in the entire world, it would be with him that "unity" would be found.

We are not tried beyond our strength. There is nothing that has ever prevented us from being Catholic but our own cowardice. Despite all that the New Church has achieved in destroying the Christian tradition, throughout the world, in almost every major city, traditional Catholics gather and participate in the true Mass. As in the days of St. Athanasius, "they may not have the Church buildings, but they have the true faith". Many traditional priests are still available.[16] What greater proof of the validity of the promise is there than the heroic stand of Archbishop Lefebvre? Priests are being trained at Econe and other seminaries of the Society of Pius X, and, at great personal sacrifice, are travelling throughout the world distributing valid sacraments and saying the Mass of All Times.[17] Given the present circumstances, it is not necessary, because it is not possible, for Catholics to receive the sacraments as regularly as in former days. God does not ask the impossible. It is however, essential that they live their faith to the fullest, and that they refuse to participate in false forms of worship and to support those who have usurped the outer trappings of the Catholic Church. No Catholic can attend the *Novus Ordo Missae* in good conscience (that is to say, with a "Catholic" conscience), no matter how "reverentially" it is said. No Catholic can teach his children from the New "official" Catechisms of the Post-conciliar Church. No Catholic owes blind assent to the errors of Vatican II or obedience to the sinful commands of anyone, no matter what his ecclesiastical rank. No Catholic can expect to keep

---

16. It is estimated that in Paris each Sunday, 14 traditional Masses are said; throughout France, some 400.

17. No implication that only the Society of Pius X provides valid sacraments is meant. The Orthodox Roman Catholic Movement (O.R.C.M.) and many individual priests that have no connection with this Society, exist for the same purpose. Those who are interested in finding a traditional Mass in North America can write for information to The Society of Piux X, 8 Pond Place, Oyster Bay Cove, N.Y. 11771. In the United Kingdom they should contact the Society in London.

his faith without considerable sacrifice and suffering. Christ never promised us an "open", and "accommodating" Church, "free of mediaeval rigorism". Indeed, he forewarned us of a time of *"great tribulation, such as hath not been from the beginning of the world . . ."* (Matt. xxiv:21). It would seem that such times are approaching, if they are not upon us already. And modern man, confused and bewildered, can he turn to the social philosophers of our day for solutions? Can he be satisfied with the ephemeral promises of a future "progress" that is dangled before him like the carrot before the proverbial donkey? Can the increasingly tyrannical forms of economic and governmental power provide for him any food for his soul? I for one am strongly inclined to doubt it. But can he look to the Post-conciliar Church as a guide? There he will only find an organization that has embraced the modern world and all its dubious values. Where then is he to turn? Ancient man could always look forward to the coming of the Messiah, but modern man cannot have such a hope. He can only look forward to the "end of time" and the "final coming". And while he awaits both his own and the world's ultimate end, where else can he turn for the truth, but to the true Church and tradition. And thus it is that Christ taught us *"He that shall be ashamed of Me and of My words"* would find that Christ would, at the final reckoning, be ashamed of him (*Luke* ix:26). Finally, he promised us that *"He that shall presevere to the end, he shall be saved"* (Matt. xxiv: 13). Let us pray that we may be among *"the remnant"* in whom the Christian tradition is preserved.

> "Whosoever you be who assert new dogmas, I beg you to spare Roman ears, spare that faith which was praised by the mouth of the Apostle. Why, after four hundred years do you try to teach us what we knew till now? Why do you produce doctrines which Peter and Paul did not think fit to proclaim? Up to this day the world has been Christian without your doctrine. I will hold to that faith in my old age in which I was regenerated as a boy".
>
> *St. Jerome*

APPENDICES

THE OTTAVIANI INTERVENTION

(Reprinted from *The Maryfaithful Supplement*,
July-August 1976)

*On September 25, 1969, Alfredo Cardinal Ottaviani,
prefect-emeritus of the Sacred Congregation for the
Faith, sent a letter to Pope Paul VI. Accompanying the
letter was a theological Study of the New Order of the
Mass* (Novus Ordo Missae), *written by a group of Roman
theologians. Cardinal Ottaviani's letter was a plea to His
Holiness "not to deprive us of the possibility of continuing
to have recourse to the fruitful integrity of that* Missale
Romanum *of St. Pius V, so highly praised by Your
Holiness and so deeply loved and venerated by the whole
Catholic world". It was apparently in response to the
Ottaviani intervention that Pope Paul subsequently
ordered a delay of two years in the deadline for manda-
tory implementation of the new* Ordo. *On the following
pages we reprint, in English translation,[1] the Ottaviani
letter and the Study of the Roman theologians.*

Letter from Cardinal Ottaviani
to His Holiness Pope Paul VI

Rome, September 25, 1969

Most Holy Father,
   Having carefully examined, and presented for the scrutiny
of others, the *Novus Ordo Missae* prepared by the experts of
the *Consilium ad exequendam Constitutionem de Sacra
Liturgia,* and after lengthy prayer and reflection, we feel it to
be our bounden duty in the sight of God and towards Your
Holiness, to put before you the following considerations:

---

1. Translated from the Italian by Miss Mary Ambrose, Department of
Spanish, University of Durham, England.

1. The accompanying critical study of the *Novus Ordo Missae,* the work of a group of theologians, liturgists and pastors of souls, shows quite clearly in spite of its brevity that if we consider the innovations implied or taken for granted, which may of course be evaluated in different ways, the *Novus Ordo* represents, both as a whole and in its details, a striking departure from the Catholic theology of the Mass as it was formulated in Session XXII of the Council of Trent. The "canons" of the rite definitively fixed at that time provided an insurmountable barrier to any heresy directed against the integrity of the Mystery.

2. The pastoral reasons adduced to support such a grave break with tradition, even if such reasons could be regarded as holding good in the face of doctrinal considerations, do not seem to us sufficient. The innovations in the *Novus Ordo* and the fact that all that is of perennial value finds only a minor place, if it subsists at all, could well turn into a certainty the suspicion, already prevalent, alas, in many circles, that truths which have always been believed by the Christian people, can be changed or ignored without infidelity to that sacred deposit of doctrine to which the Catholic faith is bound for ever. Recent reforms have amply demonstrated that fresh changes in the liturgy could lead to nothing but complete bewilderment on the part of the faithful who are already showing signs of restiveness and of an indubitable lessening of faith. Amongst the best of the clergy the practical result is an agonizing crisis of conscience of which innumerable instances come to our notice daily.

3. We are certain that these considerations, which can only reach Your Holiness by the living voice of both shepherds and flock, cannot but find an echo in Your paternal heart, always so profoundly solicitous for the spiritual needs of the children of the Church. It has always been the case that when a law meant for the good of subjects proves to be on the contrary harmful, those subjects have the right, nay the duty of asking with filial trust for the abrogation of that law.

Therefore we most earnestly beseech Your Holiness, at a time of such painful divisions and ever-increasing perils for the purity of the Faith and the unity of the Church, lamented by You our common Father, not to deprive us of the possibility of continuing to have recourse to the fruitful integrity of that

Missale Romanum of St. Pius V, so highly praised by Your Holiness and so deeply loved and venerated by the whole Catholic World.

/s/ A. Card. Ottaviani

/s/ A. Card. Bacci
Feast of St. Pius X

SUMMARY

The document which Cardinal Ottaviani submitted to the Holy Father, which has been submitted also to the Bishops of Italy, is printed in the following pages. It is the work of a group of theologians and liturgists in Rome, of different nationalities and differing tendencies.

Because the document was submitted as evidence in support of points made in the Cardinal's letter, the Italian original has been faithfully translated, which explains why it is not entirely suited to the English language. It does however raise so many questions of such profound importance, some of considerable complexity, that it would be wrong to depart from the Italian text.

The evidence is cumulative and does not stand or fall on any single part. A brief summary is however provided to direct the attention of the reader to what may be of particular interest to him. — Lumen Gentium Foundation.

NOTES

I: History of the change.
      The new form of Mass was substantially rejected by the Episcopal Synod, was never submitted to the collegial judgment of the Episcopal Conferences and was never asked for by the people. It has every possibility of satisfying the most modernist of Protestants.

II: Definition of the Mass.
      By a series of equivocations the emphasis is obsessively placed upon the "supper" and the "memorial" instead of on the unbloody renewal of the Sacrifice of Calvary.

III: Presentation of the ends.
      The three ends of the Mass are altered; no distinction is allowed to remain between Divine and human sacrifice; bread and wine are only "spiritually" (not substantially) changed.

IV: Presentation of the essence.
      The Real Presence of Christ is never alluded to and belief in it is implicitly repudiated.

V: Presentation of the four elements of the Sacrifice.
      The position of both priest and people is falsified and the Celebrant appears as nothing more than a Protestant minister, while the true nature of the Church is intolerably misrepresented.

VI: The destruction of unity.
      The abandonment of Latin sweeps away for good and all unity of worship. This may have its effect on unity of belief and the New Order has no intention of standing for the Faith as taught by the Council of Trent to which the Catholic conscience is bound.

VII: The alienation of the Orthodox.

While pleasing various dissenting groups, the New Order will alienate the East.

VIII The abandonment of defenses.

The New Order teems with insinuations or manifest errors against the purity of the Catholic religion and dismantles all defenses of the deposit of Faith.

A CRITICAL STUDY OF
THE "NOVUS ORDO MISSAE"

By a group of Roman Theologians

I

In October 1967, the Episcopal Synod called in Rome was requested to pass a judgment on the experimental celebration of a so-called "normative Mass", devised by the Consilium for implementing the Constitution on the Sacred Liturgy. This Mass aroused the most serious misgivings. The voting showed considerable opposition (43 *non placet*), very many substantial reservations (62 *juxta modum*), and 4 abstentions out of 187 voters. The international press spoke of a "refusal" of the proposed "normative Mass" on the part of the Synod. Progressively-inclined papers made no mention of this.

In the *Novus Ordo Missae* lately promulgated by the Apostolic Constitution *Missale Romanum*, we once again find this "normative Mass", identical in substance, nor does it appear that in the intervening period the Episcopal Conferences, at least as such, were ever asked to give their views about it.

In the Apostolic Constitution, it is stated that the ancient Missal promulgated by St. Pius V, 13th July 1570, but going back in great part to St. Gregory the Great and to still remoter antiquity,[1] was for four centuries the norm for the celebration

---

1. "The prayers of our Canon are found in the treatise *De Sacramentis* (4th-5th centuries) . . . Our Mass goes back, without essential changes, to the epoch in which it developed for the first time from the most ancient common liturgy. It still preserves the fragrance of that primitive liturgy, in times when Caesar governed the world and hoped to extinguish the Christian faith: times when our forefathers would gather together before dawn to sing a hymn to Christ as to their God . . . (cf. Pl. jr., Ep. 96) . . . *There is not, in all Christendom, a rite so venerable as that of the Roman Missal.*" (A. Fortescue).

"The Roman Canon, such as it is today, goes back to St. Gregory the Great. Neither in East nor West is there any Eucharistic prayer remaining

of the Holy Sacrifice for priests of the Latin rite, and that, taken to every part of the world, "it has moreover been an abundant source of spiritual nourishment to many holy people in their devotion to God". Yet, the present reform, putting it definitively out of use, was claimed to be necessary since "from that time the study of the Sacred Liturgy has become more widespread and intensive amongst Christians".

This assertion seems to us to embody a serious equivocation. For the desire of the people was expressed, if at all, when — thanks to St. Pius X — they began to discover the true and everlasting treasures of the liturgy. The people never on any account asked for the liturgy to be changed or mutilated so as to understand it better. They asked for a better understanding of a changeless liturgy, and one which they would never have wanted changed.

The Roman Missal of St. Pius V was religiously venerated and most dear to Catholics, both priests and laity. One fails to see how its use, together with suitable catechesis, could have hindered a fuller participation in, and greater knowledge of, the Sacred Liturgy, nor why, when its many outstanding virtues are recognized, this should not have been considered worthy to continue to foster the liturgical piety of Christians.

Since the "normative Mass", now reintroduced and imposed as the *Novus Ordo Missae,* was in substance rejected by the Synod of Bishops, was never submitted to the collegial judgment of the Episcopal Conferences, and since the people — least of all in mission lands — have never asked for any reform of Holy Mass whatsoever, one fails to comprehend the motives behind the new legislation which overthrows a tradition unchanged in the Church since the fourth and fifth centuries, as the Apostolic Constitution itself acknowledges. As no popular demand exists to support this reform, it appears devoid of any logical grounds to justify it and make it acceptable to the Catholic people.

The Vatican Council did indeed express a desire (para. 50 Constitution *Sacrosanctum Concilium*) "that the various parts of each single part and its relationship to the other part might

---

in use today that can boast such antiquity. For the Roman Church to throw it overboard would be tantamount, in the eyes not only of the Orthodox, but also of Anglicans and even Protestants having still to some extent a sense of tradition, to a denial of all claim any more to be the true Catholic Church." (Fr. Louis Bouyer).

appear more clearly". We shall now see how the *Ordo* recently promulgated corresponds with this original intention.

An attentive examination of the *Novus Ordo* reveals changes of such magnitude as to justify in themselves the judgment already made with regard to the "normative Mass". Both have in many points every possibility of satisfying the most modernistic of Protestants.

II

Let us begin with the definition of the Mass given in No. 7 of the *Institutio Generalis* at the beginning of the second chapter of the *Novus Ordo: "De structura Missae"*:

"The Lord's Supper or Mass is *a sacred meeting or assembly of the People of God*, met together *under the presidency of the priest*, to celebrate *the memorial of the Lord.*[2] Thus the promise of Christ, 'where two or three are gathered together in my name, there am I in the midst of them', is eminently true of the local community in the Church (Mt. XVIII, 20)".

The definition of the Mass is thus limited to that of a

---

2. For such a definition, the *Novus Ordo* refers one in a note to two texts of Vatican II. But rereading these texts *one finds nothing to justify the definition.*

The first text referred to (Decree *Presbyterorum Ordinis*, no. 5) runs as follows:". . . through the ministry of the Bishop, God consecrates priests so that they can share by a special title in the priesthood of Christ. Thus, in performing sacred functions they can act as the ministers of Him who in the liturgy continually exercises His priestly office on our behalf by the action of His Spirit . . . And especially by the celebration of Mass, men offer sacramentally the sacrifice of Christ." (Documents of Vatican II, Ed. Walter M. Abbott, S.J.).

The second text runs thus, and is from the Constitution *Sacrosanctum Concilium*, no. 33: ". . . in the liturgy God speaks to His people and Christ is still proclaiming His Gospel. And the people reply to God both by song and by prayer.

"Moreover, the prayers addressed to God *by the priest* presiding over the assembly *in the person of Christ* are said in the name of the entire holy people as well as of all present." (Ibid. — our italics)

One is at a loss to explain how, from such texts as these, the above definition could have been drawn.

We note, too, the radical alteration, in this definition of the Mass, of that laid down by Vatican II (*Presbyterorum Ordinis*, 1254): "The Eucharist is therefore *the very heart of the Christian Community*". The *centrum* having been spirited away, in the *Novus Ordo* the *congregatio* itself has usurped its place.

"supper", and this term is found constantly repeated (nos. 8, 48, 55d, 56). This "supper" is further characterized as an assembly presided over by the priest and held as a memorial of the Lord, recalling what He did on the first Maundy Thursday. None of this in the very least implies either the *Real Presence,* or *the reality of the sacrifice,* or the *Sacramental function* of the consecrating priest or the *intrinsic value* of the Eucharistic Sacrifice independently of the people's presence.[3] It does not, in a word, imply *any* of the essential dogmatic values of the Mass which together provide its true definition. Here, the deliberate omission of these dogmatic values amounts to their having been superseded and therefore, at least in practice, to their denial.[4]

In the second part of this para. 7 it is asserted, aggravating the already serious equivocation, that there holds good, *"eminenter",* for this assembly Christ's promise that *"Ubi sunt duo vel tres congregati in nomine meo; ibi sum in medio eorum"* (Mt. XVIII, 20). This promise, which refers only to the *spiritual presence* of Christ with His grace, is thus put on the same qualitative plane, save for the greater intensity, as the *substantial* and *physical* reality of the *Sacramental Eucharistic Presence.*

In no. 8 a subdivision of the Mass into "liturgy of the word" and "Eucharistic" liturgy immediately follows, with the affirmation that in the Mass is made ready *"the table of God's word"* as of *"the Body of Christ",* so that the faithful "may be built up and refreshed" — an altogether improper assimilation of the two parts of the liturgy, as though between two points of equal symbolic value. More will be said about this later.

The Mass is designated by a great many different expressions, all acceptable relatively, all unacceptable if employed,

---

3. The Council of Trent reaffirms the Real Presence in the following words: "Principio docet Sancta Synodus et aperte et simpliciter profitetur in almo Sanctae Eucharistiae sacramento post panis et vini, consacrationem Dominum nostrum Jesum Christum *verum Deum atque hominem vere, realiter ac substantialiter* (can. I) sub specie illarum rerum sensibilium contineri". (DB. no. 874) In session XXII, which interests us directly *(De sanctissimo Missae Sacrificio),* the approved doctrine (DB. nos. 937a-956) is clearly synthesized in *nine* canons.

4. It is superfluous to assert that, if a single defined dogma were denied, all dogma would *ipso facto* fall, insofar as the very principle of the infallibility of the supreme hierarchial Magisterium, whether papal or consiliar, would thereby be destroyed.

as they are, separately and in an absolute sense. We cite a few: the Action of Christ and of the People of God; the Lord's Supper or Mass; the Paschal Banquet; the Common participation in the Lord's Table; the memorial of the Lord; the Eucharistic Prayer; the Liturgy of the Word and the Eucharistic Liturgy; etc.

As is only too evident, the emphasis is obsessively placed upon the supper and the memorial instead of upon the unbloody renewal of the Sacrifice of Calvary. The formula "the Memorial of the Passion *and* Resurrection of the Lord" is, besides, inexact, the Mass being the memorial of the Sacrifice alone in itself redemptive, whilst the Resurrection is the consequent fruit of it.[5]

We shall later see how, in the same consecratory formula, and throughout the *Novus Ordo,* such equivocations are renewed and reiterated.

III

We come now to the ends of the Mass.

1. **Ultimate end.** This is that of the Sacrifice of praise to the Most Holy Trinity according to the explicit declaration of Christ in the primary purpose of His very Incarnation: "Coming into the world he saith: sacrifice and oblation thou wouldst not but a body thou has fitted me" (Ps. XXXIX, 7-9 in Heb. X, 5).

This end *has disappeared:* from the Offertory, with the disappearance of the prayer *"Suscipe, Sancta Trinitas";* from the end of the Mass with the omission of the *"Placet tibi Sancta Trinitas";* and from the Preface which on Sunday will no longer be that of the Most Holy Trinity, as this Preface will be reserved only to the Feast of the Trinity, and so in future will be heard but once a year.

2. **Ordinary end.** This is the propitiatory Sacrifice. It too has been deviated from; for instead of putting the stress on *the remission of sins* of the living and the dead it lays emphasis on the nourishment and sanctification of those present (no. 54). Christ certainly instituted the Sacrament of the Last

---

5. The Ascension should be added if one wished to recall the *"Unde et memores"* which furthermore does not associate but clearly and finely distinguishes: ". . . tam beatae Passioni, *nec non* ab inferis Resurrectionis, sed et in caelum gloriosae Ascensionis."

Supper putting Himself in the state of Victim in order that we might be united to Him in this state but his self-immolation precedes the eating of the Victim, and has an antecedent and full redemptive value (the application of the bloody immolation). This is borne out by the fact that the faithful present are not bound to communicate, sacramentally.[6]

3. **Immanent end.** Whatever the nature of the Sacrifice, it is absolutely necessary that it be pleasing and acceptable to God. After the Fall no sacrifice can claim to be acceptable in its own right other than the Sacrifice of Christ. The *Novus Ordo* changes the nature of the offering, turning it into a sort of exchange of gifts between man and God: man brings the bread, and God turns it into the "bread of life"; man brings the wine, and God turns it into a "spiritual drink".

"Thou art blessed Lord God of the Universe, because from thy generosity we have received the bread (or "wine") which we offer thee, the fruit of the earth (or "vine") and of man's labour. May it become for us the bread of life (or "spiritual drink").[7]

There is no need to comment on the utter indeterminateness of the formulae *"panis vitae"* and *"potus spiritualis"*, which might mean anything. The same capital equivocation is repeated here, as in the definition of the Mass: there, Christ is present only spiritually among His own: here, bread and wine are only "spiritually" (not substantially) changed.[8]

---

6. This shift of emphasis is met with also in the surprising elimination, in the new Canons, of the *Memento* of the dead and of any mention of the sufferings of the souls in Purgatory, to whom the propitiatory Sacrifice was applied.

7. Cf. *Mysterium Fidei* in which Paul VI condemns the errors of symbolism together with the new theories of "transignification" and "transfinalization": ". . . Nor is it right to be so preoccupied with considering the nature of the sacramental sign that the impression is repeated that the symbolism — and no one denies its existence in the most Holy Eucharist — expresses and exhausts the whole meaning of Christ's presence in this sacrament. Nor is it right to treat of the mystery of transubstantiation without mentioning the marvellous change of the whole of the bread's substance into Christ's body, and the whole of the wine's substance into His blood, of which the Council of Trent speaks, and thereby make these changes consist of nothing but a 'transignification' or a 'transfinalization', to use these terms." (C.T.S. trans. *Mysterium Fidei,* art. II).

8. The introduction of new formulae, or expressions, which, though occurring in texts of the Fathers and Councils, and of the Church's magisterium, are used in a univocal sense not subordinated to the

In the preparation of the offering, a similar equivocation results from the suppression of two great prayers. The *"Deus qui humanae substantiae dignitatem mirabiliter condidisti et mirabilius reformasti"* was a reference to man's former condition of innocence and to his present one of being ransomed by the Blood of Christ: a recapitulation of the whole economy of the Sacrifice, from Adam to the present moment. The final propitiatory offering of the chalice, that it might ascend *"cum odore suavitatis"*, into the presence of the divine majesty, whose clemency was implored, admirably reaffirmed this plan. By suppressing the continual reference to God in the Eucharistic prayers, there is no longer any clear distinction *between divine and human sacrifice.*

Having removed the keystone, the reformers have had to put up scaffolding; suppressing real ends, they have had to substitute fictitious ends of their own; leading to gestures intended to stress the union of priest and faithful, and of the faithful among themselves; *offerings for the poor and for the church* superimposed upon the Offering of the *Host to be immolated.* There is a danger that the uniqueness of this offering will become blurred, so that participation in the immolation of the Victim comes to resemble a philanthropical meeting, or a charity banquet.

IV

We now pass on to the essence of the Sacrifice.

---

substance of doctrine with which they form an inseparable whole (e.g. "spiritualis alimonia", "cibus spiritualis", "potus spiritualis", etc.) is amply denounced and condemned in *Mysterium Fidei*. Paul VI states that: "When the integrity of faith has been preserved, a suitable manner of expression has to be preserved as well. Otherwise our use of careless language may, though it is to be hoped that it will not, give rise to false opinions on belief in very deep matters", and quotes St. Augustine: "There is a claim on us to speak according to a fixed rule so that unchecked words do not speak also to an impious view of the matters which we express". He continues: "This rule of speech has been introduced by the Church in the long work of centuries with the protection of the Holy Spirit. She has confirmed it with the authority of the Councils. It has become more than once the token and standard of orthodox faith. It must be observed religiously. No one may presume to alter it at will, or on the pretext of new knowledge . . . It is equally intolerable that anyone on his own initiative should want to modify the formulae with which the Council of Trent has proposed the eucharistic doctrine of belief." (*Idem*, Art. 23).

The mystery of the Cross is no longer explicitly expressed. It is only there obscurely, veiled, imperceptible for the people.[9] And for these reasons:

1. The sense given in the *Novus Ordo* to the so-called *"prex eucharistica"* is: "that the whole congregation of the faithful may be united to Christ in proclaiming the great wonders of God and in offering sacrifice" (no. 54, the end).

Which sacrifice is referred to? Who is the offerer? No answer is given to either of these questions. The initial definition of the *"prex eucharistica"* is as follows: "The center and culminating point of the whole celebration now has a beginning, namely the Eucharistic Prayer, a prayer of thanksgiving and of sanctification" (no 54, pr.). The effects thus replace the causes, of which *not one single word* is said. The explicit mention of the object of the offering, which was found in the *"suscipe"*, has not been replaced by *anything*. The change in formulation reveals the change in doctrine.

2. The reason for this non-explicitness concerning the Sacrifice is quite simple, namely that the Real Presence has been removed from the central position which it occupied so resplendently in the former Eucharistic liturgy. There is but a single reference to the Real Presence (a quotation — in a footnote — from the Council of Trent), and again the context is that of *"nourishment"* (no. 241, note 63).

The Real and permanent Presence of Christ, Body, Blood, Soul and Divinity, in the transubstantiated Species is never alluded to. The very word transubstantiation is *totally ignored*.

The suppression of the invocation to the Third Person of the Most Holy Trinity *("Veni Sanctificator")* that He may descend upon the oblations, as once before into the womb of the Most Blessed Virgin to accomplish the miracle of the divine Presence, is yet one more instance of the systematic and tacit negation of the Real Presence.

Note, too the eliminations:

of the genuflections (no more than three remain to the priest, and one, with certain exceptions, to the people, at the Consecration);

of the purification of the priest's fingers in the chalice;

of the preservation from all profane contact of the priest's fingers after the Consecration;

---

9. Contradicting what is prescribed by Vatican II. *(Sacros. Conc.* no. 48).

of the purification of the vessels, which need not be immediate, nor made on the corporal;

of the pall protecting the chalice;

of the internal gilding of sacred vessels;

of the consecration of movable altars;

of the sacred stone and relics in the movable altar or upon the *"mensa"* — "when celebration does not occur in sacred precincts" (this distinction leads straight to "eucharistic suppers" in private houses);

of the three altar-cloths, reduced to one only;

of thanksgiving kneeling (replaced by a thanksgiving, *seated,* on the part of priest and people, a logical enough complement to Communion standing);

of all the ancient prescriptions in the case of the consecrated Host falling, which are now reduced to a single, casual direction: *"reverenter accipiatur"* (no 239);

all these things only serve to emphasize how outrageously faith in the dogma of the Real Presence is implicitly repudiated.

3. *The function assigned to the altar* (no. 262). The altar is almost always called *mensa.*[10] *The altar or table* of the Lord, which is the center of the whole Eucharistic liturgy" (no. 49, Cf. 262). It is laid down that the altar must be detached from the walls so that it is possible to walk round it and celebration may be facing the people (no. 262); also that the altar must be the center of the assembly of the faithful so that their attention is drawn spontaneously toward it (ibid). But a comparison of nos. 262 and 276 would seem to suggest that the reservation of the Blessed Sacrament on this altar is excluded. This will mark an irreparable dichotomy between the presence, in the celebrant, of the eternal High Priest and that same Presence brought about sacramentally. Before, they were *one and the same presence.*[11]

Now it is recommended that the Blessed Sacrament be kept in a place apart for the private devotion of the people (almost

---

10. The altar's primary function is recognized once (no. 259): "the altar on which the sacrifice of the Cross is renewed under the sacramental signs." This single reference does not seem to remove to any extent the equivocations of the other repeated designation.

11. "To separate the Tabernacle from the altar is tantamount to separating two things which, of their very nature, must remain together." (Pius XII, Allocution to the International Liturgy Congress, Assisi-Rome, Sept. 18-23, 1956) Cf. also *Mediator Dei,* 1, 5, note 28.

as though it were a question of devotion to a relic of some kind) so that, on going into a church, attention will no longer be focused upon the Tabernacle but upon a stripped bare table. Once again the contrast is made between *private* piety and *liturgical* piety: altar is set up against altar.

In the insistent recommendation to distribute in Communion the Species consecrated during the same Mass, indeed to consecrate a loaf[12] for the priest to distribute to at least some of the faithful, we find reasserted a disparaging attitude toward the Tabernacle, as toward every form of Eucharistic piety outside of the Mass. This constitutes yet another violent blow to faith in the Real Presence as long as the consecrated Species remain.[13]

4. *The formulae of consecration.* The ancient formula of consecration was properly a *sacramental* not a narrative one. This was shown above all by three things:

a) The Scriptural text not taken up word for word: the Pauline insertion *"mysterium fidei"* was an immediate confession of the priest's faith in the mystery realized by the Church through the hierarchical priesthood.

b) The punctuation and typographical lettering: the full stop and new paragraph marking the passage from the narrative mode to the *sacramental and affirmative* one, the sacramental words in larger characters at the center of the page and often in a different color, clearly detached from the historical context. All combined to give the formula *a proper and autonomous value.*

---

12. Rarely in the *Novus Ordo* is the word *"hostia"* used, a traditional one in liturgical books with its precise significance of "victim". This needless to say is part of the reformers' plan to emphasize only the aspects "supper", "food".

13. In accordance with the customary habit of the reformers of substituting and exchanging one thing for another, the Real Presence is made equivalent to the Presence *in the word* (no. 7, 54). But this latter presence is really of quite another nature, having no reality except *in usu;* whilst the former *is,* in a stable manner, objective and independent of the communication that is made of it in the Sacrament. The formulae "God speaks to His people . . . By His word Christ is present in the midst of the faithful" (no. 33, Cf. *Sacros, Conc.* no. 33 and 7), are typically Protestant ones, which strictly speaking, have no meaning, as the presence of God in the word is mediated, bound to an act of the spirit, to the spiritual condition of the individual and limited in time. This error has the most serious consequences; the affirmation (or insinuation) that the Real Presence is bound to the *usus,* and ends together with it.

c) The anamnesis *("Haec quotiescumque feceritis in mei memoriam facietis"),* which in Greek is "eis tén emòu anàmnesin" *(directed to my memory).* This referred to Christ operating and not to the mere memory of Him, or of the event: an invitation to recall *what* He did *("haec . . . in mei memoriam facietis") in the way* He did it, not only His Person, or the Supper. The Pauline formula *("Hoc facite in meam commemorationem")* which will now take the place of the old — proclaimed as it will be daily in vernacular languages — will irremediably cause the hearers to concentrate on the *memory* of Christ as the *end* of the Eucharistic action, whilst it is really the *beginning.* The concluding idea of *commemoration* will certainly once again take the place of the idea of sacramental action.[14]

The narrative mode is now emphasized by the formula "narratio institutionis" (no. 55d) and repeated by the definition of the anamnesis, in which it is said that "The Church recalls *the memory* of Christ Himself" (no. 556).

In short: the theory put forward by the epiclesis, the modification of the words of Consecration and of the anamnesis, have the effect of modifying the *modus significandi* of the words of Consecration. The consecratory formulae are here pronounced by the priest as the constituents of a historical narrative and no longer *enunciated as expressing the categorical and affirmative judgment uttered by Him in whose Person the priest acts: "Hoc est Corpus Meum"* (not, *"Hoc est Corpus Christi").*[15]

Furthermore the acclamation assigned to the people immediately after the Consecration: ("we announce thy death,

---

14. The sacramental action of the institution is emphasized as having come about in Our Lord's giving the Apostles His Body and Blood "to eat" under the species of bread and wine, not in the *act* of consecration and in the mystical *separation* therein accomplished *of the Body from the Blood,* essence of the Eucharistic Sacrifice. (Cf. the whole of chapter I, part. II — "The cult of the Eucharist" — *Mediator Dei)*

15. The words of Consecration as inserted in the context of the *Novus Ordo* can be valid by virtue of the minister's intention. They could also not be valid because they are no longer so *ex vi verborum,* or, more precisely, by virtue of the *modus significandi* they had in the Mass up to the present time.

Will priests of the near future who have not received the traditional formation, and who rely on the *Novus Ordo* with the intention of "doing what the Church does", consecrate validly? One may be allowed to doubt it.

O Lord, *until Thou comest"*) introduces yet again, under cover of eschatology, *the same ambiguity concerning the Real Presence*. Without interval or distinction, the expectation of Christ's Second Coming at the end of time is proclaimed just as the moment when He is *substantially present* on the altar, almost as though the former, and not the latter, were the true Coming.

This is brought out even more strongly in the formula of optional acclamation no. 2 (Appendix): "As often as we eat of this bread and drink of this chalice we announce thy death, O Lord, until thou comest", where the juxtaposition of the different realities of immolation and eating, of the Real Presence and of Christ's Second Coming, reaches the height of ambiguity.[16]

We now come to the realization of the Sacrifice, the four elements of which were: 1) Christ, 2) the priest, 3) the Church, 4) the faithful present.

In the *Novus Ordo,* the position attributed to the faithful is autonomous *(absoluta),* hence totally false from the opening definition — *"Missa est sacra synaxis seu congregatio populi"* — to the priest's salutation to the people which is meant to convey to the assembled community the "presence" of the Lord (no. 28). *"Qua salutatione et populi responsione manifestatur ecclesiae congregatae mysterium".*

A true presence, certainly, of Christ but only spiritual, and a mystery of the Church, but solely as assembly manifesting and soliciting such a presence.

This interpretation is constantly underlined: by the obsessive references to the communal character of the Mass (nos. 74-152); by the unheard of distinction between "missa cum populo" and *"misa sine populo"* (nos. 203-231); by the definition of the *"oratio universalis seu fidelium"* (no. 45), where once more we find stressed the "sacerdotal office" of the people *("populus sui sacerdotii munus excercens")* presented in an equivocal way because its subordination to that of the priest is not mentioned, and all the more since the priest, as consecrated mediator, makes himself the interpreter

---

16. Let it not be said, according to the well-known Protestant critical procedure, that these phrases belong to the same scriptural context. The Church has always avoided their juxtaposition and super-imposition precisely in order to avoid any confusion of the *different realities* here expressed.

of all the intentions of the people in the *Te igitur* and the two *Memento*.

In *"Prex eucharistica III"* (*Vere sanctus"*, p. 123) the following words are addressed to the Lord: "from age to age you gather a people to yourself, in order that from east to west a perfect offering may be made to the glory of your name", the *in order that* making it appear that the people, rather than the priest,[17] are the *indispensable* element in the celebration; and since not even here is it made clear *who* the offerer is, the people themselves appear to be invested with *autonomous priestly powers.* From this step it would not be surprising if, before long, the people were authorized to join the priest in pronouncing the consecrating formulae (which actually seems here and there to have already occurred).

The priest's position is minimized, changed and falsified. Firstly in relation to the people for whom he is, for the most part, a mere *president,* or *brother,* instead of the consecrated minister celebrating *in persona Christi.* Secondly in relation to the Church, as a *"quidam de populo".* In the definition of the epiclesis (no. 55), the invocations are attributed anonymously to the Church: the part of the priest has vanished.

In the *Confiteor* which has now become collective, he is no longer judge, witness and intercessor with God; so it is logical that he is no longer empowered to give the absolution, which has been suppressed. He is integrated with the *fratres.* Even the server addresses him as such in the *Confiteor* of the *"Missa sine populo".*

Already, prior to this latest reform, the significant distinction between the Communion of the priest — the moment in which the Eternal High Priest and the one acting *in His Person* were brought together in closest union — and the Communion of the faithful had been suppressed.

Not a word do we now find as to the priest's *power to sacrifice, or about his act of consecration,* the bringing about through him of the *Eucharistic Presence.* He now appears as nothing more than a Protestant minister.

---

17. As against the Lutherans who affirmed that all Christians are priests and hence offerers of the Supper, see A. Tanquerey: *"Synopsis theologiae dogmaticae"*, vol. III, Desclee, 1930: "Each and every priest is, strictly speaking, a secondary minister of the sacrifice of the mass. Christ Himself is the principal minister. *The faithful offer through the intermediary of the priest but not in the strict sense".* (Cf. Conc. Trid XXII Can. 2).

The disappearance, or optional use, of many sacred vestments (in certain cases the alb and stole are sufficient — n. 298) obliterates even more the original conformity with Christ: the priest is no more clothed with all His virtues, becoming merely a "graduate" whom one or two signs may distinguish from the mass of people:[18] "a little more a man than the rest", to quote the involuntarily humorous definition by a Dominican preacher.[19] Again, as with the "table" and the Altar, there is separated what God has united: the sole Priesthood of the Word of God.

Finally, there is the Church's position in relation to Christ. In one case, namely the *"missa sine populo"*, is the Mass acknowledged to be *"Actio Christi et Ecclesiae"* (no. 4, cf. Presb. Ord. no. 13), whereas in the case of the *"missa cum populo"* this is not referred to except for the purpose of "remembering Christ" and sanctifying those present. The words used are: "In offering the sacrifice *through Christ in the Holy Ghost* to God the Father, the priest associates the people with himself" (no. 60), instead of words which would associate the people *with Christ* Who offers *Himself "per Spiritum Sanctum Deo Patri"*.

In this context the following are to be noted: 1) the very serious omission of the phrase *"Per Christum Dominum Nostrum"*, the guarantee of being heard given to the Church in every age (John XIV, 13-14; 15; 16; 23; 24;); 2) the all-pervading "paschalism", almost as though there were no other, quite different and equally important, aspects of the communication of grace; 3) the very strange and dubious eschatologism whereby the communication of supernatural grace, a reality which is permanent and eternal, is brought down to the dimensions of time: we hear of a people on the march, a pilgrim Church — no longer *militant* against the *Potestas tenebrarum* — looking toward a future which having lost its link with eternity is conceived in purely temporal terms.

The Church — One, Holy, Catholic, Apostolic — is

---

18. We note in passing an incredible innovation which is sure to have the most serious psychological effects: the Good Friday liturgy in red vestments instead of black (no. 308b) — the commemoration, that is, of any martyr instead of the mourning of the whole Church for her Founder. (Cf. *Mediator Dei*, I, 5, note 28).

19. Fr. Roquet, O.P., to the Dominicans of Bethany, at Plesschenet.

diminished as such in the formula that, in the *"Prex Eucharistica IV"*, has taken the place of the prayer of the Roman Canon "on behalf of all orthodox believers of the Catholic and apostolic faith". Now they are no more nor less than: "all who seek you with a sincere heart".

Again, in the *Memento* of the dead, these have no longer passed on "with the sign of faith and sleep the sleep of peace" but only "who have died in the peace of thy Christ", and to them are added, with further obvious detriment to the concept of visible unity, the host of all the dead "whose faith is known to you alone".

Furthermore, in none of the three new Eucharistic Prayers is there any reference, as has already been said, to the state of suffering of those who have died, in none the possibility of a particular *Memento:* all of this, again, must *undermine faith in the propitiatory and redemptive nature of the Sacrifice.*[20]

Desacralizing omissions everywhere debase the mystery of the Church. She is not presented above all as a sacred hierarchy: Angels and Saints are reduced to anonymity in the second part of the collective *Confiteor:* they have disappeared, as witnesses and judges, in the person of St. Michael, from the first.[21] The various hierarchies of angels have also disappeared (and this is without precedent) from the new Preface of "Prex II". In the *Communicantes* the reminder of the Pontiffs and holy martyrs on whom the Church of Rome is founded and who were, without doubt, the transmitters of the apostolic traditions, destined to be completed in what became, with St. Gregory, the Roman Mass, has been suppressed. In the *Libera nos* the Blessed Virgin, the Apostles and all the Saints are no longer mentioned: her and their intercession is thus no longer asked, even in time of peril.

The unity of the Church is gravely compromised by the wholly intolerable omission from the entire Ordo, including the three new Eucharistic Prayers, of the names of the Apostles Peter and Paul, Founders of the Church of Rome, and the

---

20. In some translations of the Roman Canon, the "locus refrigerii, lucis et pacis" was rendered as a simple state ("blessedness, light, peace"). What is to be said, then, of the disappearance of every explicit reference to the Church suffering?

21. In all this welter of curtailment a single enrichment only: the mention of *omission* in the accusation of sins at the Confiteor . . .

names of the other Apostles, foundation and mark of the one and universal Church, the only remaining mention being in the *Communicantes* of the Roman Canon.

A clear attack upon the dogma of the Communication of Saints is the omission, when the priest is celebrating without a server, of all the salutations and the final Blessing, not to speak of the *Ite Missa est*[22] now not even said in Masses celebrated with a server.

The double *Confiteor* showed how the priest — in his capacity of Christ's Minister, bowing down deeply and acknowledging himself unworthy of his sublime mission, of the "tremendous mysterium" about to be accomplished by him and of even (in the *Aufer a nobis*) entering into the Holy of Holies — invoked the intercession (in the *Oramus te, Domine*) of the merits of the martyrs whose relics were sealed in the altar. Both these prayers have been suppressed; what has been said previously in respect of the double *Confiteor* and the double Communion is equally relevant here.

The outward setting of the Sacrifice, evidence of its sacred character, has been profaned. See, for example, what is laid down for celebration outside sacred precincts, in which the altar may be replaced by a simple *"mensa" without consecrated stone or relics,* and with a single cloth (nos. 260, 265). Here too all that has been previously said with regard to the Real Presence applies, the disassociation of the *"convivium"* and of the sacrifice of the supper from the Real Presence Itself.

The process of desacralization is completed thanks to the new procedures for the offering: the reference to ordinary not unleavened bread; altar-servers (and lay people at Communion *sub utraque specie*) being allowed to handle sacred vessels (no. 244d); the distracting atmosphere created by the ceaseless coming and going of priest, deacon, subdeacon, psalmist, commentator (the priest becomes a commentator himself from his constantly being required to "explain" what he is about to accomplish) — of readers (men and women), of servers or laymen welcoming people at the door and escorting them to their places whilst others carry and sort offerings.

---

22. At the press conference introducing the Ordo, Fr. Lecuyer, in what appears to be, objectively speaking, a profession of purely rationalistic faith, spoke of converting the *salutationes* in the "Missa sine populo" into: "Dominus tecum", "Ora, frater", etc., "so that there should be nothing which does not correspond with the truth".

And in the midst of all this prescribed activity, the *"mulier idonea"* (anti-scriptural and anti-Pauline) who for the first time in the tradition of the Church will be authorized to read the lessons and also perform other *"ministeria quae extra presbyterium peraguntur"* (no. 70). Finally, there is the concelebration mania, which will end by destroying Eucharistic piety in the priest, by overshadowing the central figure of Christ, sole Priest and Victim, in a collective presence of concelebrants.[23]

VI

We have limited ourselves to a summary evaluation of the new *Ordo* where it deviates most seriously from the Theology of the Catholic Mass and our observations touch only those deviations that are typical. A complete evaluation of all the pitfalls, the dangers, the *spiritually and psychologically destructive elements* contained in the document — whether in text, rubrics or instructions — would be a vast undertaking.

No more than a passing glance has been taken at the three new Canons, since these have already come in for repeated and authoritative criticism, both as to form and substance. The second of them[24] gave immediate scandal to the faithful on account of its brevity. Of Canon II it has been well said, amongst other things, that it could be recited with perfect tranquility of conscience by a priest who no longer believes either in Transubstantiation or in the sacrificial character of the Mass — hence even by a Protestant minister.

The new Missal was introduced in Rome as "a text of ample pastoral matter", and "more pastoral than juridical", which the Episcopal Conferences would be able to utilize according to the varying circumstances and genius of different peoples. In this same Apostolic Constitution we read: "we have introduced into the new missal *legitimate variations and adaptations*". Besides, Section I of the new Congregation for Divine Worship will be responsible "for the publication and *constant revision* of the liturgical books". The last official

---

23. We note in this connection that it seems lawful for priests obliged to celebrate alone either before or after concelebration to communicate again *sub utraque specie* during concelebration.

24. It has been presented as "The Canon of Hippolytus" but in fact nothing remains of this but a few remembered words.

bulletin of the Liturgical Institutes of Germany, Switzerland and Austria[25] says: "The Latin texts will now have to be translated into the languages of the various peoples; the 'Roman' style will have to be adapted to the individuality of the local Churches: that which was conceived beyond time must be transposed into the changing context of concrete situations in the constant flux of the Universal Church and of its myriad congregations."

The Apostolic Constitution itself gives the *coup de grace* to the Church's universal language (contrary to the express will of Vatican Council II) with the bland affirmation that *"in such a variety of tongues* one (?) and the same prayer of all . . . may ascend more fragrant than any incense".

The demise of Latin may therefore be taken for granted; that of Gregorian chant — which even the Council recognized as *"liturgiae romanae proprium"* (Sacros. Conc. no. 116), ordering that *"principem locum obtineat"* (ibid.) — will logically follow, with the freedom of choice, amongst other things, of the texts of *Introit* and *Gradual*.

From the outset therefore the new rite is launched as *pluralistic and experimental,* bound to time and place. *Unity of worship* being thus swept away for good and all, what will now become of the unity of faith that went with it, and which, we were always told, was to be defended without compromise!

It is evident that the *Novus Ordo has no intention of presenting the Faith as taught by the Council of Trent, to which, nonetheless, the Catholic conscience is bound forever.* With the promulgation of the *Novus Ordo,* the loyal Catholic is thus faced with a most tragic alternative.

VII

The Apostolic Constitution makes explicit reference to a wealth of piety and teaching in the *Novus Ordo* borrowed from the Eastern Churches. The result — utterly remote from and even opposed to the inspiration of the oriental Liturgies — can only repel the faithful of the Eastern Rites. What, in truth, do these ecumenical options amount to? Basically to the *multiplicity* of anaphora (but nothing approaching their beauty and complexity), to the presence of the deacons, to Communion *sub utraque specie.* Against this

---

25. *"Gottesdienst"*. no. 9, May 14th 1969.

the *Ordo* would appear to have been deliberately shorn of everything which in the Liturgy of Rome came close to those of the East.[26] Moreover, in abandoning its unmistakable and immemorial Roman character, the *Ordo* lost what was spiritually precious of its own. Its place has been taken by elements which bring it closer only to certain other reformed liturgies (not even to those closest to Catholicism) and which debase it at the same time. The East will be ever more alienated, as it already has been by the preceding liturgical reforms.

By way of compensation the new Liturgy will be the delight of the various groups who, hovering on the verge of apostasy, are wreaking havoc in the Church of God, poisoning her organism and undermining her unity of doctrine, worship, morals and discipline in a spiritual crisis without precedent.

VIII

St. Pius V had the Roman Missal drawn up (as the present Apostolic Constitution itself recalls) so that it might be an instrument of unity among Catholics. In conformity with the injunctions of the Council of Trent it was to exclude all danger, in liturgical worship, of errors against the Faith, then threatened by the Protestant Reformation. The gravity of the situation fully justified, and even rendered prophetic, the

---

26. One has only to think of the Byzantine liturgy, for example, with its reiterated and lengthy penitential prayers; the solemn rites of vesting of the celebrant and deacon: the preparation of the offerings at the *proscomidia*, a complete rite in itself; the continual presence in the prayers, even those of the offerings, of the Blessed Virgin, the Saints and Choirs of Angels (who are actually invoked, at the entrance with Gospel, as "invisibly concelebrating", the choir *identifying itself with them* in the Cherubicon): the *iconostasis* which *divides the sanctuary from the rest of the church, the clergy from the people;* the hidden Consecration, symbolizing the divine mystery to which the entire liturgy alludes; the celebrant's position *versus ad Deum,* never *versus ad populum;* Communion given always and only by the celebrant: the continual marks of profound adoration shown to the Sacred Species; the essentially contemplative attitude of the people. The fact that these liturgies, even in their less solemn forms, last for over an hour, and are constantly defined as "tremendous and unutterable . . . celestial, life-giving mysteries . . ." need no elaborating. It is finally worth noting how, in the Divine Liturgy of St. John Chrysostom, and in that of St. Basil, the concept of "supper" or "banquet" appears clearly subordinate to that of sacrifice, as it did in the Roman Mass.

saintly Pontiff's solemn warning given at the end of the Bull promulgating his Missal: "Should anyone presume to tamper with this, let him know that he shall incur the wrath of God Almighty and of his Blessed Apostles, Peter and Paul" (*Quo Primum*, July 13, 1570).[27]

When the *Novus Ordo* was presented at the Vatican Press Office, it was asserted with great audacity that the reasons which prompted the Tridentine decrees are no longer valid. Not only do they still apply, but there also exist, as we do not hesitate to affirm, *very much more serious one's today*. It was precisely in order to ward off the dangers which in every century threaten the purity of the deposit of faith (*"depositum custodi, devitans profanas vocum novitates"*. — I Tim. VI, 20) that the Church has had to erect under the inspiration of the Holy Ghost the defenses of her dogmatic definitions and doctrinal pronouncements. These were immediately reflected in her worship, which became the most complete monument of her faith. To try and bring the Church's worship back at all cost to the ancient practice by refashioning, artificially and with that "unhealthy archeologism" so roundly condemned by Pius XII,[28] what in earlier times had the grace of original spontaneity means — as we see today only too clearly — to dismantle all the theological ramparts erected

---

27. In Session XXIII (decree on the Most Holy Eucharist), the Council of Trent manifested its intention "ut stirpitus convelleret *zizania execrabilum errorum et schismatum,* quae inimicus homo . . . in doctrina fidei *usu et cultu* Sacrosanctae Eucharistiae superseminavit — Mt. 13, 25 et seq. — quam alioqui Salvator noster in Ecclesia sua tamquam symbolum reliquit eius unitatis et caritatis, qua Christianos omnes inter se coniunctos et copulatos, esse voluit". (DB. 873).

28. "To go back in mind and heart to the sources of the sacred liturgy is wise and praiseworthy. The study of liturgical origins enables us to understand better the significance of festivals and the meanings of liturgical formulas and ceremonies. *But the desire to restore everything indiscriminately to its ancient condition is neither wise nor praiseworthy. It would be wrong,* for example, *to want the altar restored to its ancient form of table, to want black eliminated from liturgical colors, and pictures and statues excluded from our churches, to require crucifixes that do not represent the bitter sufferings of the Divine Redeemer . . .* This attitude is to attempt to revive the 'archeologism, to which the pseudo-synod of Pistoia gave rise; it seeks also to reintroduce the many pernicious errors which led to that synod and resulted from it and which the Church in her capacity of watchful guardian of the 'deposit of faith' entrusted to her by her Divine Founder, has rightly condemned." (*Mediator Dei,* C.T.S. trans. Art. 66 and 68).

for the protection of the Rite and to take away all the beauty by which it was enriched over the centuries.

And all this at one of the most critical moments — if not *the* most critical moment — of the Church's history! Today, division and schism are officially acknowledged to exist not only outside of but within the Church.[29] Her unity is not only threatened *but already tragically compromised.*[30] Errors against the Faith are not merely insinuated but positively imposed by means of liturgical abuses and aberrations which have been equally acknowledged.[31] To abandon a liturgical tradition which for four centuries was both the sign and the pledge of unity of worship[32] (and to replace it with another which cannot but be a sign of division by virtue of the countless liberties implicitly authorized, and which teems with insinuations or manifest errors against the integrity of the Catholic religion) is, we feel in conscience bound to proclaim, an incalculable error.

---

29. "A practically schismatic ferment divides, subdivides, splits the Church . . ." (Paul VI, Homily *in Coena Domini* 1969).

30. "There are also amongst us those 'schismata', those 'scissurae' which St. Paul in I Corinthians sadly denounces . . ." (Cf. Paul VI, ibid.).

31. It is well-known how Vatican II is today being "contested" by the very men who gloried in being its leaders, those who — whilst the Pope in closing the Council declared that it had changed nothing — came away determined to "explode" the content in the process of actual application. Alas that the Holy See, with a haste that is really unexplainable, should appear to have given approval and even encouragement, through the *Consilium ad exequendam Constitutionem de Sacra Liturgia,* to an ever increasing infidelity to the Council, from such apparently formal aspects as Latin, Gregorian, the suppression of venerable rites and ritual, to the substantial ones now sanctioned by the *Novus Ordo.* To the disastrous consequences, which we have endeavoured to set out, must be added those which, with psychologically even greater effect, will make themselves felt in the fields of discipline and of the Church's teaching authority, by undermining, with the standing of the Holy See, the docility due to its rulings.

32. ". . . Do not let us deceive ourselves with the suggestion that the Church, which has become great and majestic for the glory of God, as a magnificent temple of His, must be brought back to its original and smallest proportions, as though they were the only true ones, the only good ones . . ." (Paul VI, *Ecclesiam suam).*